A GUIDE TO TRAVELLING ON A SHOESTRING

BUDGET TRAVEL

EXPLORE THE WORLD

A Discount Overseas Adventure Trip: Gap Year, Backpacking, Volunteer-Vacation & Overlander

MATHEW BACKHOLER

Budget Travel, a Guide to Travelling on a Shoestring
Explore the World, a Discount Overseas Adventure Trip
Gap Year, Backpacking, Volunteer-Vacation & Overlander

Copyright © Mathew Backholer 2017 - ByFaith Media
www.ByFaith.org - All Rights Reserved.

Paperback 978-1-907066-54-2
Also available as an eBook on many platforms

British Library Cataloguing In Publication Data
A Record of this Publication is available from the British Library

First Published in February 2017 by ByFaith Media

In Kathmandu, Nepal, we woke up one day to find a snake charmer outside our hotel. Whilst the cobra had probably been defanged, we were not going to hang around to find out.

In one city in Vietnam, it was cheaper to rent a bicycle for a day than to buy a 2L bottle of water.

One man flew to Delhi, India, with his bicycle and rode all the way to Nepal. His biggest souvenir which he intends on keeping for life – is his Nepalese wife.

Contents

Section 1. Where to Travel, with Whom and Preparation

Section 2. Safety, Medical, Health, Survival and Extreme

Section 3. Budgeting, Money, What to Buy and Pack

Section 4. Plane Ticket, Visa, Airport and Accommodation

Section 5. Hygiene, Scams, Settling in, Language and Law

Contents

Contents

Section
1. Chapters 1-5: Where to Travel, with Whom and Preparation.
2. Chapters 6-10: Safety, Medical, Health, Survival and Extreme.
3. Chapters 11-16: Budgeting, Money, What to Buy and Pack.
4. Chapters 17-21: Plane Ticket, Visa, Airport, Reservations, and Accommodation.
5. Chapters 22-26: Hygiene, Scams, Settling in, Language and Law.
6. Chapters 27-32: Food, Writing a Journal, Culture, Oppression, Exploitation and Photography.
7. Chapters 33-36: Public Transport, your own Vehicle, Renting, Overland Bus and Researching an Organization.
8. Chapters 37-42: Aid Work, Volunteer-Vacation, Advice for Leaders, A Working Team, Can you Help Me (Money) and Returning Home.

Quick Reference Guide for Item to Take

Chapter
8. For health related items.
10. For survival items in case of extreme travel.
15. What to buy and to consider buying.
16. What to take, including a kit list.

Preface

I have been able to go on more than thirty trips in over forty countries of the world, though I have actually passed through nearly fifty nations. These travels have included the entire length of Africa on public transport, the length of South-East Asia, the Trans-Siberian Railway, China, around Britain, across Europe and into North Africa and America. *Budget Travel A Guide to Travelling on a Shoestring* has been written from first-hand experience and incorporates the travel testimonies from people across the globe.

I was seventeen when I first went abroad. My friend worked as a travel agent and had accrued enough commission so that we could visit Holland in the Netherlands for the weekend. It was a great budget travel trip as we only had to pay for our food, everything else was free. Before then, I had travelled around Britain, staying in B&Bs, sleeping on a friend's floor or in a caravan, pitching a tent or sleeping in the car. It was all an adventure and still is. Special times with special memories.

My adventures have taken me on a walking tour of the Pyrenees Mountains with a group of friends, a whistle-stop tour of the Holy Land for a third of the cost; with Korean friends we drove around eastern Europe. I have used budget airlines to get to a number of countries, travelled 22,000km overland from Cairo in Egypt to the Cape in South Africa, across South-East Asia from India to Vietnam and from Nepal to Russia, which included Hong Kong, Macau, China and a 5-day stint on the Trans-Siberian Railway from Ulaanbaatar, Mongolia, to Moscow, Russia. Over the decades I have visited many countries by plane, train, car, ferry, coach and on foot.[1]

This book will aid you in your budget travels, whether you are an individual exploring the options, or travelling with a group of friends. You may have two weeks free, a three months semester or be taking a gap year. You may want to visit a particular people group, country, or continent. You may be looking to do humanitarian work with a charity or non-governmental organization (NGO). You may be looking for the perfect overland tour company, considering buying a 4x4 (4 wheel drive vehicle/4WD) to explore the world or hit the railway and let the train take the strain across a country. This book will assist you in these areas, give you firm foundations for budget travel and will guide you through the process, before and during your trip. This book will aid you on your journey and will assist you in areas of need, with many options and ideas: where to go, what to do, who to go with, how to finance it, what to pack, how to plan your budget travels, your expedition, what to see. It also includes: getting the best deals, buying your plane ticket, airport etiquette, medical issues, what to buy, kit list, visa issues, accommodation, transportation, scams and warnings, local cuisine, working with the locals, cultural and language issues, plus much more, and will guide you through the entire travelling process from start to finish.

Budget Travels is full of anecdotes and advice with informative stories, and insights, to help you engage in cross-cultural travel with viable solutions to common issues to make your trip of a lifetime more effective, exciting and enjoyable, whilst keeping your stress levels low and your money under control. The application of the truths within this book, learnt and experienced over many decades will greatly help you on your journey of discovery and exploration into new lands and cultures on your budget travels.

In some chapters, the author refers to 'we,' this is himself and any other person or group whom he was travelling with. The boxed testimonies are all real events, though some of the names have been changed. Throughout the book, prices of items are stated in American dollars ($) and British pound sterling (£), at the exchange rate of $1.6 to £1.00. Some prices are rounded to the nearest whole figure.[2]

Mathew Backholer
Co-founder of ByFaith Media

Introduction

Dream Travel on a Budget

You have a dream of travelling the world, a country or continent, yet you have limited finances. It is possible to do, but you must first accept reality. You cannot fly business class or stay in 5-star hotels in the major cities of New York, London or Sydney. Budget travel means economy, but it does not mean dirty hovels or locked in the hold of a cargo ship. If you want to spend two month's travel money on a week of luxury accommodation, you can, but you don't have to; when you travel on a shoestring you have to make cutbacks and intelligent decisions, but you do not need to go without. You can easily blow your budget within a week on a luxury safari, staying in a private lodge in Botswana or Tanzania, but instead, you could do a budget safari in Malawi, see most of the big game and travel the length of Africa or other continents for the same amount of money, the choice is yours. You have to do your research and make educated and informed decisions.

Budget travel means sacrificing some luxuries for one great adventure. It can be done. I've spent months in South-East Asia on a daily budget of £10 ($16) and £20 ($38) a day, and in Africa on £18 ($29) a day. Staying in cheap and austere accommodation, though some had TV and Air Conditioning (AC), travelling on local buses, coaches and trains, whilst eating at food-stalls, cafes and restaurants and having a great time, seeing the sights, meeting the locals, broadening one's horizons and soaking up the atmosphere. There have been splurges on petrol go-karts, a helicopter flight over Victoria Falls, guided tours, private taxis, hotel swimming pools and many historical sites etc., but you offset one against the others and balance the budget from one week to one month to the next.

Travelling on a shoestring involves planning ahead, and not taking the first option that comes along, but to shop around, investigate and inquire after the best deals. I have saved thousands by using local transport, sleeping in basic to good accommodation and discovered hidden gems off the standard traveller's trail. Why spend $200 (£125) to fly into the next country when you can take the coach to the border for $20 (£12.50)! Why spend $2,000 (£1,250) for a week in Japan, plus airfare, when you could spent three months in Cambodia, Thailand, Vietnam and Malaysia for the same amount. You can travel Japan on a budget, but some countries are more expensive than others. If staying in Japan is more expensive than

Korea and you only have two months away, you need to decide whether you will spend one month in each country, or a week or two less in the more expensive country, so as to be able to balance your budget. If you are travelling across a continent, some countries or cities you may wish to skip through due to the exorbitant cost of living. This means a higher cost of accommodation, travel and food.

When you travel on a budget, you experience the real country you are in and not the five star Western imitation, branded hotel chains. You can spend $200 a night for a hotel in Khartoum, Sudan, or in Addis Ababa, Ethiopia, or one for $20. I know what I would choose, when the money comes out of my pocket and I am on the road for 3-6 months. Most budget travellers do not want the Western sanitized view of the country they are visiting, but wish to be more like the locals and experience their way of life, with a few luxuries thrown in along the way and some Western food treats. Upmarket restaurants are wildly overpriced, yet you can still eat crab in a beach-shack in Cambodia for $6 (£4) or lobster for more, but at a greatly reduced price compared to the upmarket restaurant where, many holidaying clientele dress-up to go out. There are many vegetarian options abroad and in most developing countries, the fruit and vegetables are really fresh.

You can go on a snorkelling day-trip for $20 (£13) per person, or speak to a local who can buy/rent a snorkel and mask (or goggles) and hire a small boat with a motor for just $8 (£5) for two guests.

Budget travel means making every pound, dollar and euro count. You cannot buy a souvenir in every village, town and city you pass through, though you can take photographs, film, write a journal, do some sketches and meet the locals and their sights to help you remember where you have been. Budget travel is best accomplished when you travel light and your journey can be a delight. Items and knickknacks can become cumbersome, though items of clothing and things that need to be repaired can easily be bought and paid for on the go.

Perhaps you are thinking of buying a round-the-world plane ticket, but you may be able to save money by using local budget airlines to get you to your start or end destination. Do you like sharing? Budget travel means sharing the bus or coach with other passengers, or on the top of a truck in Africa, a pick-up in Papua New Guinea or sharing the aisle with chickens on a bus in South America. In many food establishments, the table is not exclusively yours, but for any guest to use. You can take a night train in India or Europe, or the Trans-Siberian Railway from Moscow, Russia, through Mongolia to Beijing, China, or a ferry on the Amazon River, but if you want your money to stretch you cannot have a private booth or compartment, but may have a foldout bed or a place to hang your hammock.

Budget travel can on occasions be hard, your last meal may not have agreed with you, the other guests in the hostel are a bit too noisy and inconsiderate, the bus seat is uncomfortable, you may be hungry or pine for your favourite food back at home. You can treat yourself, move accommodation or take time-out and rest. Western comforts will return when you go home, but in the present you are having an experience of a lifetime and stories that can be shared and retold on different occasions. Today is a day for living and a sleepless night on a bus in China or a cramped train in India will be an experience that can live on forever. I have had many firsts, and a number of them I would not wish to be repeated due to the inconveniences or the discomfort endured, but if it were possible, I would not go back with the use of a time-machine and alter the sequence of events that led to the instances and experiences. Life is a learning curve and part of the college of life can be experienced when you are out and about, outside of familiar surroundings and your usual comfort zone.

In all the countries and continents I have travelled, South-East Asia has been the cheapest, whilst Central East Africa was a bit more expensive. Renting/hiring a vehicle with friends and staying in youth hostels across Eastern and Western Europe dramatically lowered the cost of travelling. China can be travelled on a budget but it is getting more expensive in the Orient, whilst the Middle East has become increasing unstable in recent years and is not as safe as it once was. South America is relatively cheap, but for English only speakers, can be a problem, go learn some Spanish!

When planning your trip, you can have comfortable and cosy for a short while, or adventure and some discomfort for the long journey. Life is a gift from God, enjoy it and discover the world and see how other people live on your discount overseas adventure trip and discover yourself and new realms.

Chapter 1

Why Travel

Travelling is part of the college of life. It can be an adventure or time-out between studies or a job. People that go often use their holiday/vacation time, take a gap year or go outside of term time when schools, colleges and universities have finished for the term/semester. If you are overweight, you may also lose a few pounds or kilograms; so that cannot be bad! It has been good for me!

Going on travels can help build character and are potential life-changing experiences. It can broaden one's horizons, it can open our eyes to see how the other half live and how well-off we really are. Travel can challenge us to the lives and views of others, and can make it personal, rather than distant. The world is a large place with much to see, do and explore. But you have to get off your sofa and go.

There are many reasons why people like to travel:
- To see the world and explore. An experience of a lifetime.
- Gap year – often between college, university or work.
- Frustrations at college, university or work. Throw in the towel, or take a gap year and travel to clear their head.
- Adventure – to see new places and time-out from the routine. Some people have itchy feet and have to keep on the go.
- They have disposable income and holiday/vacation time and desire to see new sights.
- Concerned for the eco system and environment, what is it like and what can be done about it.
- To see famous sights off-the-beaten-track and indigenous tribes before their way of life disappears.
- Escaping from problems or heartache at home. Time of trauma, heartbreak or tragedy and need to get away from familiar surroundings or bad memories. A good opportunity to help them start again.
- To make a person feel better when doing humanitarian work, a sense of worth and achievement.
- To enhance a skill set, learn a new hobby, trade or language by immersing themselves in it.
- Extended travels can make you wiser and make you see different things from different perspectives.

- It can look good on a C.V./résumé. It shows initiative.
- To delay further education, to put off the inevitable of getting a job.
- The advice of a teacher, employer or someone trusted.
- To help others with the talents and skills that they have acquired and wish to pass on to others.
- Part of the job, travel writer or photographer.
- Asked to join a team for the exposure to travels abroad or because of their skills and talents.
- Because my friend is going and I want to join her/him.
- Someone has offered to pay for them to take time-out and travel. The joy of generous grandparents or wealthy parents.

Volunteer Work

You may wish to go abroad and see different cultures by joining a non-governmental organization (NGO), help out with a charity (e.g. helping the poor or sport related deeds), a religious group (e.g. a short-term mission[1]), different forms of humanitarian work (e.g. building work, drilling bore wells, maintenance, agricultural assistance), or as an English teacher, nurse, dentist or surgeon etc. It could be pure travel then voluntary work, a combination of travel and work or all work. You could describe your time away as a working holiday, volunteer-vacation, gap year or just time-out. You may consider getting casual jobs and work around the world. Some countries offer 'working holiday visas' like Australia, New Zealand and Canada. There are also Kibbutzim (plural of Kibbutz) in Israel and many European countries need labourers to pick the crops in season, winter, spring, summer and autumn/fall. You could work with an orphanage in a developing country, many are run by religious groups or charities. If you are an American, you could join the Peace Corps for voluntary work abroad.

Not the Romantic Ideal

Travel is not always the romantic ideal that it is made up to be, budget travel may lead you to accommodation that you are not used to, eating a diet which may not initially agree with you, and crossing people's paths whom you would not normally associate yourself with. Some fellow travellers can be a pain or tedious, whilst others can be great companions and a walking head of knowledge. Fear is a normal part of life, however some fear is rational and some is irrational. The opportunity of a lifetime must be seized during the lifetime of the opportunity. If you don't go – you'll never know!

In regards to humanitarian work, voluntary work or travelling somewhere new, worst than fear of the unknown, is the fear of being paralysed into staying home and then spending the rest of your life with, "What if?" being run through your mind from one week to the next on a perpetual loop. If you do not go, you will never know.

You should stay away from war zones and you may wish to avoid FCO-blacklisted countries (Foreign & Commonwealth Office). The means of blacklisted countries equals: 'Sanctions and embargoes are political trade restrictions put in place against target countries with the aim of maintaining or restoring international peace and security.'[2]

Some budget travellers say you can live on $8 (£5) a day in Asia. That's only possible if you sleep in flee pit accommodation (where bedbugs, cockroaches and possibly other vermin rule); you eat from roadside food stalls, stay in one location and never take public transport. Be realistic, get a real budget and prepare for additional costs. Joe – USA.

What you can Learn on your Travels
- How other people live.
- The wonders of nature with all its biodiversity.
- Insights into your own culture and other cultures.
- About yourself, what is important and what is not.
- What you can live without and what you cannot live without.
- About others, their needs, concerns, lifestyles, language, religion and culture.
- The generosity of those who have so little.
- Your strengths, weaknesses and character. The good, the neutral and the bad, coupled with your giftings, talents, deficiencies and endurance – a mental quality.
- The world is bigger than you thought and diverse.
- Humanitarian work – working together as a team and having individual responsibilities and duties.

One evening I got chatting to two men who were staying in the same hotel as myself. They were Congolese refugees and had lived in a refugee camp for ten years! I tried to comprehend what it must have been like – having to flee your home and country to seek refuge in another, leaving everything behind and looking to others for help. Richard – Tanzania.

Chapter 2

Travel Options and Opportunities

There are many options and ideas for travel with a near infinite possible number of combinations. You may know what you want to do, but plans and circumstances can change. Options to consider:

- Go alone, with a friend, a group of friends or with a group.
- Use public transport, bus, coach, train, aeroplane or ferries, or take your own bicycle, motorbike or kayak.
- More expensive options could be taking your own car, and caravan or tent trailer, a 4x4/4wd (4 wheel drive vehicle), motorhome or sailing boat.
- Sign up with an overland bus company and travel through different countries.
- Decide where to go, what you want to do, your timeframe and your budget.
- Decide what you want to do when you travel: meet people, sample the food, see the sights, help others, charity or non-governmental organization (NGO) work, volunteer-vacation, budget cruise ships (ferry hop or island hop), go on safari, trekking, hiking, fishing, bird or seal watching, camping, rock climbing, base jumping, horse riding, exploration, Christian pilgrimage, farm-stays, relaxing on the beach, surfing, skiing, extreme sports or just chilling etc.
- Be spontaneous, following the "sea currents or the wind" – go with the flow.
- Be semi-spontaneous. Have a start and finish point (or a general idea) and discover what you'll find between your two destination points.
- Green travel – eco-friendly travels, ecotourism or low carbon to neutral footprint travel.
- Trek through a jungle with a qualified guide and see nature at its best, or hike along a mountain trail, whilst putting yourself to the test.

What Can you Do – Potential Options

- Fly to a country, buy a bicycle or motorbike and explore.
- Canoe down a section of a major river.
- Go on foot and walk and camp across a small country.
- Fly to one country and travel across a continent.

- Cycle through Europe or parts of Africa or Asia.
- Use budget airlines to travel around Europe and/or take the ferry between some countries.
- Use public transport, train, coach and bus to travel around a country.
- Walk a pilgrim route like the Camino de Santiago (Way of St. James) across Spain or travel around the Holy Land, Israel, seeing the biblical sites.
- Take a car, a 4x4, motorbike, motorhome/RV (recreational vehicle), campervan and explore a county, State, Territory or country and beyond.
- Go by coach and bus and see where you end up, or plan ahead.
- Travel on the trains across Europe.
- Cairo to the Cape (Egypt to South Africa).
- Travel down West Africa.
- Travel around Britain and stay in youth hostels, camp or sleep in your car!
- Fly into Central Africa (e.g. Kenya) and travel south.
- Travel across South-East Asia (India to Vietnam).
- Travel across China (visa extension permitting).
- Travel across America or Australia by train or an epic road trip.
- Travel around India by train and coach.
- Travel to Russia, pick up the Trans-Siberian railway and get off in Mongolia or China.
- Travel through Latin America.
- Buy an island-hop ticket for the Hebrides in Scotland (UK) and visit the remote and isolated communities in breathtaking scenery during the warmer months.
- Island-hop – in Indonesia, Greek islands, the Pacific or the Caribbean.
- Visit different Inca cities, major destinations from the old Roman Empire, sites of major WWII battles or places of other past conflicts.
- Play Pokémon Go around the world!
- Mountain bike up and down the best and knarliest trails you can find. Take your skateboard, inline skates or BMX and grind up the streets, though beware of 'forbidden' signs.
- Travel in the footsteps of explorers, like Dr. David Livingstone in Africa, Burke and Wills Expedition in Australia or the Lewis and Clark Expedition in America.
- Go to the best music festivals around the world, on a continent or across a country.

- See the film locations of a major movie or franchise. See Tataouine, Medenine, Matmata (cave dwellings) and many other Star Wars locations across Tunisia (and beyond) or where the Fast and the Furious movies were filmed.
- Buy a round-the-world ticket. Hop on and hop off at key destinations in an easterly or westerly direction.
- Use a stop over or lay over to explore a new city for a few days.
- I do not advise hitchhiking, or travelling through parts of the Middle East as independent travellers. Go with a tour company who employ locals and have experience.
- It is increasingly becoming unsafe for Western women to travel alone in Muslim countries. Western men can also be a target. However, you can also be shown the greatest hospitality as a stranger in their country, village or community. Recent political events, wars and invasions, coupled with the rise of terrorist organizations have made some destinations not as safe as they once were, whilst some should be avoided like the plague. The locals can be amazing, but a small minority of extremists, robbers or opportunists can make an area quite unsafe to be in.

Travel and Work
- Some countries offer 'working holiday visas' like Australia, New Zealand and Canada. In May 2016, Australia called for, what has been nicknamed a 'backpacker tax' for those on a working holiday visa, which was proposed at 32% on the dollar. The tourist industry and farming communities denounced this move, but in September 2016, the Australian government announced a tax of 19% will apply for working holidays on *every* dollar earned, whilst the working holiday visa was reduced by $50 AUD, $38 £24.
- Visa permitting, work your way around a country, State or Territory via farm-stays, kibbutzim (in Israel, the plural of kibbutz), fruit and vegetable farmers. This is mostly seasonal and you often work in groups, though most get paid per weight of quantity.
- You may be employed with a charity or involved in paid or voluntary non-governmental organization (NGO) work. This could be before your real travels begin or in the middle of it. It may be for one month or three, which helps offset the bills of travelling if you are paid.
- You could work with an orphanage in a developing country, many are run by religious groups or charities. Often you have to pay them, which helps offset their costs.

- As a doctor, nurse or trained medic your expertise may be wanted in many developing countries, paid or unpaid.
- You could help out at a school, as a sports coach, an English teacher in Africa, or teaching English as a foreign language (TEFL) in the Orient (China, Japan and Korea).
- You may be able to be a ski, surf or scuba diver instructor, if you have the relevant certificates and/or qualifications. This helps pay the bills as you enjoy your sport and lifestyle.
- There are a number of different seasonal jobs available at ski resorts, guides for hiking trails, translation/interpreter, working in the kitchens, security work, manual labour, odd jobs, maintenance etc.
- You may be able to get casual work here and there.
- You may be skilled in freelance work, e.g. graphic designer, proofreader, freelance editor, social media expert, App developer, computer programmer etc., and so can make money whilst on the go to assist you on your travels.
- You may be an expert or a specialist in a particular area and be able to sell your expertise whilst you are away. It may be in book form (paperback or ebook), a training course (video or Power Point) or a 'rent your brain' type consultancy.
- You may be able to write about your travels and self-publish, or compile an anthology of your travels into a paper/ hardback or an ebook. This is also possible in relation to photography.
- You could write a blog about your travels. You may have affiliate links to Amazon etc. where travel books, walking boots, penknife, waterproof jacket and other travel related items can be bought. This can bring in a little income depending on your site traffic and 'click' or 'taps' through to end purchases.
- If your site gets enough traffic, ad providers such as Google will pay 'click through' rate if the advert is clicked on or tapped through.
- You may have a YouTube channel with lots of subscribers. If a travel incident goes viral, you could participate in a share of advertising income. You may be an upcoming vlogger (video blogger), and can work as you travel. Your format could be adapted to different countries or places.
- You could be into extreme sports and film your exploits around the world. Upload onto social media sites and you could find yourself a sponsor who provides you with free equipment or payment as well.

Chapter 3

The Style of Your Trip and Timing

Each person is unique and the style of your travels can be different from one person to the next. You may want to just get away and are happy to stay in one place for the duration of your trip, a time to rest and relax. For another person, relaxing is heading off to the next city or country after a few days or weeks, whilst other people want to travel the globe on an epic adventure, jumping onto a new continent every two-three months and immersing themselves in the sights, sounds and culture. Your next trip could be the travels of a lifetime; it is good to plan, to have a focus, but also to be flexible and open to change as circumstances dictate.

> To wander about aimlessly within a country (or countries), seeing all the sights and soaking up the atmosphere can be a great travel adventure, but by being more focussed can help you get the best of your limited time away and make the most out of your money.

Style of Your Travels

- One fixed location. This is a good way to have a firm foundation in a single area if your trip is short. However, you may quickly get bored after a few weeks. You may be working with a humanitarian organization and can make friends with the locals who should be able to show you some great places, off-the-beaten-track and/or off the standard tourist trail.
- Several locations within one country. You may desire to spend multiple days, a week or two, in each city. Some cities are so large that it is possible to spend months in one place, yet see different sights and attractions each day, however, it is more interesting to move about than to take root in one place, unless you are going to live there.
- Multiple towns across one country. You have to go from A to H (perhaps you fly in and out from different locations) and therefore can spend time in A, B, C, D, E, F, G and H.
- From country to country. Travelling from one country to another can be like going from one State to another.
- Multiple countries – even across a continent. This is common, but similar to above. You may have other

objectives or wish to visit sites of historical interest or visit friends.
- Travel around the world, travel across borders or fly into different continents on a one way round-the-world ticket.

Duration of Your Travels and Timing
- Weeks, months or a year or more.
- The time of year to go, there is a big difference between summer and winter and the dry and rainy/monsoon seasons. These factors are irrelevant if you are spending a year in one place, but if it is from weeks to just a few months, then it can be a contributing factor to help hone the decision and to eliminate certain places or times of the year. How many hours of daylight are there? Do you want to see the midnight sun in Norway in summer when north of the artic circle, or the northern lights in Norway in winter?
- If you are going to a moderate secular country (as opposed to a conservative one), be aware that different religions celebrate their own festivals with their various rituals, which can heighten their emotional excitement and possibly be a threat to you. Westerners are a target in certain areas of the world.[1]

When Should I Go?
The duration and time of your trip can be determined by many factors:
- Holiday/vacation – how long is my time off from work etc.?
- Term-time – school, college or university; when are they closed and for how long?
- National holidays/vacations – the locals go away, shops shut.
- High or low season – costs increase in the high season (at peak demand) and accommodation costs varies with supply and demand.
- Weather and climate – summer, winter, dry or wet season? Monsoons can play havoc, snow can shut mountain passes, and the sun at 40°C can be unbearable. Remember, winter in the northern hemisphere is summer time in the southern hemisphere.
- The invitation – when (or if) you are invited to work with the local school, hospital, health clinic, charity, NGO etc. You may have to be proactive and contact them!
- Family considerations – will you, your parents, spouse or child need certain medical help at designated times of the

year? Is it available or too expensive? The quality, training, hygiene and equipment can vary.

- Special seasons – Christmas, Thanksgiving, Easter, Ramadan, Yom Kippur (though only one day), other religious festivals, special anniversary dates and national holidays (e.g. Chinese New Year) – from your own country or to where you are going, can hinder, disrupt, or enhance your travel plans. Flights are booked well in advance.

Questions to Ask Yourself

To aid discernment whilst narrowing down the options ask yourself the following questions:

- What languages can I speak? Do I need to speak a certain language if I am to go to —? It is not always necessary (though very helpful) to know the language.
- For humanitarian work: What can I do and what specific skills do I have? What is the neediest place? The world is needy, but where would I best be suited?
- What time commitment am I able to give for my trip? Two weeks, two months, a year?
- Can I cope with the climate? Most countries are seasonal. What about altitude or if I am based near volcanic ash – asthmatics beware! Is your skin sensitive to the sun?
- Do I have poor health? It can be dangerous to go to some countries where medical aid is much to be desired and the hospital could be several days drive away.
- Finances – how much savings do I have – can I use them? Or can I get enough money for my travels?

Things to Do

- Decide where you want to go or where you will begin (you may have flexible travel plans).
- Read travel literature and browse travel forums and websites.
- Apply for a visa.
- Buy your plane ticket and travel insurance.
- Leave contact details with your closest relatives or friend.
- Contact your credit card and debit card providers and notify them of your travels abroad. Otherwise your card may be cancelled as perceived fraudulent transactions.
- Check your local government's website for its latest travel warnings and advice. Foreign Office websites for British, American, Canadian and Australian citizens can give conflicting advice for the same area or country.

Chapter 4

Practical Preparation

Months before you depart on your travels, do your research. If you joined an organization, NGO or tour company, they will fill you in on all that you need to do (and know). Consider enrolling on an evening language course, especially if the destination you are going to speaks French, Spanish or Arabic. You can also buy a phrase book or language CDs, install them onto iTunes and put them onto your iPod or smartphone for quick reference, or get a translation App. Whilst English is spoken widely, learning another language or just essential phrases is a rewarding experience and any language study is a good investment. By putting more in now, you will get more out during your travels.

Learn some basic phrases in the local language.

- Hello, how are you?
- My name is. I am from England, America, Australia etc.
- What is your name? What is your age?
- Where is a hotel, guesthouse, campsite, cafe etc.?
- How much? Too expensive! Anything cheaper?
- Where is the toilet, restaurant, train/bus station etc.
- Thank you. Good to meet you. Goodbye.
- Numbers 1-20, 30, 40, 50…100, 1,000, 10,000, 100,000.

Buy a pocket phrasebook. Consider enrolling on a First Aid course, a little bit of basic knowledge can be a lifesaver when you are a long way from help, or at least read a First Aid book to know the basics! If you are the leader of any team or tour company then you should know the basics of First Aid or someone on your team needs to know! If you are going to an extreme or isolated place (days from civilization or in harsh terrain and weather conditions) then consider enrolling on a basic survival course, or at least read a survival book and try to take it in! If it is pocketsize, e.g. Collins Gem *SAS Survival Guide*, take it with you.

Educate yourself about the country and people you will be going to. Buy a travel guide (e.g. Lonely Planet) and read it or buy and download the relevant chapters to your destination to your ereader or smartphone. You may be interested in finding out the country's history, religion, culture, geography, climate (its seasons), cost of living, staple diet and types of accommodation if need be – each country has certain specific names, hotel, motel, B&B, inn, youth hostel, guesthouse, lodge, etc. If you feel like it, why not rent a DVD, download a travel programme or search the internet for film clips of the travel destinations you will be going to. Visit Google Earth and explore.

Physical and Mental Preparation

Make sure you are fit, your travels could be demanding, depending on where you go and what you want to do, but that is a choice that each traveller can make. You won't be expected to run a marathon, but you may have to make a quick dash to get on a bus. Your travels will not be a 9 till 5 day, sat in a swivel-chair inside an air-conditioned office, like many workplaces. Go out for a thirty-minute walk at least three times a week, do some exercise. I have known days abroad where I have been on my feet all day, from 9am-7pm, all great fun, but can make you tired. One man at a youth hostel in Rome, Italy, told my friend and I that we had visited more places in one day than he had in a week whilst being in the same city! On 6 ½ month travels from Cairo to the Cape, (22,000km on public transport) we had to take a week-out in Zanzibar to rest!

Your travels will be an amazing adventure, but if you go with the wrong attitude, a negative mindset you will miss the best. Go with the frame of mind that, "I am going to have a life changing trip – an opportunity of a lifetime!" There will be difficulties and perhaps some things that you will not like, even about yourself. Remind yourself, "I am going to go and embrace the travel experience and allow the travel experience to embrace and change me." Expect the unexpected and don't be phased by it, as the unexpected can happen! Situations may not seem fun at the time, but are all part of the experience and turn into great stories for yourself and others!

Types of Toilets

Toilets the world over are not the same. They may be Western type (the bowl and seat – though the seat is not always there), a bucket which you empty or the squat type (a hole in the ground) which are also known as long-drops. With the latter you squat down as there is no toilet seat to rest on. If there will be squat toilets in the country you're going to then practice squats to strengthen your thigh muscles and to aid balance – it will pay dividends by the time you arrive and have to use them. It may also tone your legs. The stench in some outside squat toilets can be nauseating, with flies buzzing and maggots wriggling! The floors can be slippery and often there is no light and never any toilet paper; with the idea being that you wipe yourself with the left hand (or you provide your own paper!), pour water down the hole and let water displacement take care of the rest. Some toilets are in the bush and it is customary to dig a little hole and cover up after yourself. If the bus/coach stops after a few hours on a dirt road, with no building in sight, then the men go to one side of the road and the women to the other side, and aftertime you will feel quite at home in the wilds of Africa or parts of Asia.

Other Preparation

- Make sure all your electrical gadgets work and that you know how to operate them – your new digital camera, camcorder, Tablet, ereader or smartphone etc.
- Are all your batteries charged? Do you need a spare set? Do you need a power bank for your smartphone or a foldable solar charger, USB compatible or spare cable?
- Have you bought your plug converter?
- Do you have the right clothing and the correct bag?
- If you are involved in humanitarian work then be sure to pack what equipment or tools are needed.
- Do you have a copy of all your important details. Passport number, travel insurance, flight details etc.? Has a copy been given to your nearest relatives or friend?
- If you have a return ticket and you are being picked up by a friend or relative, do they know the flight number and have they marked it on their calendar?
- Are you allergic to certain medicines or items, e.g. penicillin or plasters/Band Aids? Are you anaemic? What is your blood type? Do you have any major allergies e.g. nuts or are asthmatic? Do your travelling companions know?
- Have you been to see your doctor/physician and had the necessary injections, vaccinations, inoculations or tablets?
- Have you bought *everything* you need? See chapters 15 and 16. Chapters 8 and 10 also cover some items.
- If you are taking your own vehicle, has it gone in for a service and do you have your essential tools and spares, as well as your documentation?

We met a Japanese man on the border of Kenya who was travelling alone. He had been travelling the world for 18 months, and had no guidebook, map, camera (and this was before the era of smartphones). He travelled so light that all his possession were in a single day-bag. Long travels can become a blur, and how unfortunate I thought this man was, he had no 'visual' memory to fall back on as the years pass, or anyone else to share his adventures or difficulties with. Though I also admired him for his tenacity to go and do what he wanted to do.

Chapter 5

Things to Consider

Not every parent, guardian, sibling or spouse is thrilled with the prospect of the one they love, going travelling, taking a year out, or being away from them for two weeks or more. There may be concerns, including financial, emotional and safety issues.

Some friends are great for a Saturday night hangout, but may not be the best people to live with and travel with for weeks or months at an end. If they give you the hump after a few hours, or you get on their nerves, then travel buddies would probably not work. Travelling can easily break a friendship. The group joker is good for a laugh, but will they end up in trouble with the local police in Turkey or Cambodia and you will have to try and deal with it?

Most people have had dreams of travel – to this or that destination and with any group of friends you may have ideas or plans to travel at one time or another. When we graduate high school, college, university, during the next semester, vacation or holiday. Some dates are not good for one friend, another will not have the money for another year or two, another is in debt, another does not like the sun or cold weather etc. If you want to go, you should go! You cannot build your life around other people and wait for them to help you fulfil your own dreams. Many people only ever dream and never step further into fulfilment. If you have one good friend that you can travel with, then count your blessings, or go it alone and you will meet plenty of other people who are in the same boat as you.

The old saying goes, 'two's company but three's a crowd,' and if there is a third leg in your travel companions, there will be additional problems encountered in which just two people will not come across. Between any group of three people, there will always be a stronger bond between two of them and the third person will feel isolated on occasions. When travelling on public transport, someone will have to sit alone, whilst many rooms have two beds in them, not three, though establishments can be flexible, as long as the room is large enough. If you have to rent two rooms, will the cost be equally divided between all three friends or will the person on his or her own have to pay extra as a single traveller, or even a single supplement on some trips? I have known less than a handful of groups who travelled in threes and none were ideal. One man joined with two others in Thailand, who for some years had travelled together. The new man soon realised that one of the men found it very hard to accept him and treated him as if he was 'a threat.' It took several months before he accepted the man and the three travellers gelled as well as could be expected.

> I was the third member of a group of men travelling together, but always felt left out, as the bond between the other two was impenetrable. I could only put up with so much and without any discussion I booked my ticket, told the guys, and flew home the next day! Joseph – Ethiopia.

A person may have a work commitment which will delay their departure for their once in a lifetime trip. If you are at high school or college etc. don't go when you should be in class. Wait for term/recess time, often during summer vacation.

If you are in debt and struggle with your monthly repayments then your financial obligations will hinder you going on a trip abroad; especially if you have missed mortgage or rent payments. You may be able to stretch to two weeks away, but not a gap year or a year out travelling the globe. Defaulting on your agreement is not the best way forward.

It is advisable not to finance your travels on borrowed money because you'll have to pay it back with interest. Your £3,500 ($5,600) budget trip could end up costing you a lot more if repaid over several years, on borrowed money loaded on to credit cards. It could even double the cost or beyond, if you only paid the minimum off each month. If you are taking a year out and have a student loan then the repayment issues will vary because you have little to zero income. Can you sell your sports car to part-finance your travels? Other models which you can buy on your return are cheaper: to insure, to purchase, maintain, with greater fuel/gas economy. Can you have an advance on your trust fund or any future inheritance?

Do you have any pre-existing health issues? The medicine may not be available where you are going on your travels and the nearest hospital may be a long drive away, and ill equipped at best. Facilities in some countries or districts are very poor with no health and safety considerations.

There are those with a family to look after and you cannot just run off and leave your spouse, the children, or ageing parents (if you are their carer) to go on your extended travels. If you are married, is your spouse in full support? If you have children what will happen to their schooling if they come with you, or if they stay home with one parent? What about pre-existing health issues?

A disability may not eliminate those who desire to go travelling, but certain locations may not be appropriate or could prove difficult. Much of the developing world has little to no wheelchair access compared to the West and we still have a long way to go, whilst many places of accommodation have no lift/elevator only flights of stairs, even five storey's high. Some humanitarian organizations, NGOs or agencies may not be able to give the assistance they need or feel unable to accept their application. If you are going with a trusted and genuine friend then you should be ok, as they will be there to assist you and you will be there to help them.

There are some parts of the world where an elderly person may not be able to cope; in a cramped bus, or where you have to run for your seat or stand for five hours on public transport over potholed roads. Other elderly people put the youth to shame, in late May 2009, 65-year-old Sir Ranulph Fiennes, on his third attempt made it up Mount Everest, beating many a person half his age!

Travelling from India to Nepal was a couple and their four children, the oldest of which was about eleven and the youngest appeared to be about three. I had to wonder at the wisdom in taking months away from the children's education, on a budget travel trip, using buses and staying in accommodation which would not be permitted in Europe due to various health and safety regulation.

Avoid war zones and FCO-blacklisted countries (Foreign & Commonwealth Office). Beware of countries with hyper inflation.

Beneficial Languages

Many former European colonies speak the language of its former colonial power. English is a second language in many countries of the world and widely spoken across South-East Asia and down East Africa. French is spoken in two North African countries and in several West African countries. Spanish is widely spoken across South America except in Brazil as they speak Portuguese. English is spoken in Guyana, whilst other local or tribal languages are spoken across South America.

English is the language of business and multitudes of students or those in the tourism industry know the language well and want to practice, but this does not mean that you should not know some basic phrases in the local language. Inevitably, the longer you are immersed in one area, the quicker and easier it is to pick up the local lingo. Some destinations are merely passing through points.

In some countries outside of tourist areas, especially in east China and as I found in Dhaka, Bangladesh, it is increasingly hard to find people who speak (or understand) English, though, at least in the latter, if you give it five minutes or so (as the crowd builds) someone will come along and interpret for you!

You can download a language App, use Google Translate, whilst some countries, like Japan, have their own App financed by the tourism industry to help foreign tourist get around more easily. You can also buy handheld translation devices which have visual and audio functions. You can speak in English etc. (or pick the phrase) and the machine will speak aloud the sentence into the language of your choice (or display it on the screen). You can buy a phrase book, whilst some guide books have a language section in the back.

The World's Calendars and Time and Day

The world does not have a unified calendar which means that the calendar date, the time of day and year can all be measured differently depending on the country you are in. Crossing from one country to the next (or between States or districts) can change time zones. In some countries, the day begins at sunrise and not at one second past midnight as in the West. Greenwich Mean Time (GMT) is the standardised world time zone which is calculated as a plus (+) or minus (–) 1 hour from London, England. In Ethiopia, there is a six-hour time difference so that five o'clock is eleven o'clock and if your bus departs at 12:00-noon it is actually 6:00am in the morning, which is the normal departure time for Ethiopian buses!

British Summer Time (BST) starts on the last Sunday in March (in Spring) and ends on the last Sunday in October (in Autumn/Fall), at 1:00am GMT. In spring, the clocks go forward, losing an hour at 1:00am GMT, the UK moves to 2:00am BST. In autumn, the clocks go back, giving an extra hour at 2:00am BST, the UK moves to 1:00am GMT.

Have you considered how many hours of daylight you will get at your proposed destination? What time is sunrise and sunset in summer and winter? There is a huge difference between daylight hours in the northern (or southern hemisphere) when comparing the seasons. 16hrs of daylight is better than 6hrs if you intend to go out and about, seeing the sights in the warmer weather.

Do not book accommodation by using *only* numerals, e.g. 7/11/17 can mean the seventh of November 2017 or the eleventh of July 2017, because there is a difference between the day and the month between some countries – notably the UK and the USA. Always write the month in letters and not numerals to avoid confusion and an embarrassing situation as you may turn up at your booked accommodation early and find no rooms available, or turn up late and found you have lost your deposit.

I flew to Eastern Europe to work with an orphanage. I was greatly disturbed by everything I saw and smelt and within 24hrs of my arrival I was on the plane back home. My home church who had bought my plane ticket were very unhappy that I had wasted not only an opportunity of a lifetime, but also the church's precious resources. Ricardo – Romania.

Mental and Physical Preparation

Long before your trip commences make sure you are prepared.

- Physically – do I have health problems or a medical condition, which may exacerbate on the trip or endanger my own life? Am I unhealthy, over or under weight? Am I addicted to junk food or dependant on my fix of coffee, chocolate, medicine, cigarettes or alcohol? What medications will I need abroad and are they legal where I want to go?
- Mentality – do I know why I want to go and why I should go? If part of an humanitarian organization, NGO or charity, what is expected of me? Do I realise it is not a holiday/vacation (for humanitarian work etc.) and I may encounter some discomforts. There will be difficulties as I may be working with a group who are unknown to me, and stresses and strains are inevitable with possible personality clashes.

For independent travellers and those going with a friend:

- Do you want the extra burden of having your own vehicle or flying in to a country and buying one?
- Do you feel confident travelling alone or do you need to go with a friend?
- Have you got your finances sorted out and a general travel plan? What you want to do and where?

Valid Passport and Visa

If you do not have a passport then you need to get one soon! They cost money and take time to process. You will have to fill in an application form, send several photos and have a person (or people of repute) who will vouch for you, i.e., what you have written is true and correct and that you are not obtaining a passport fraudulently on behalf of someone else or using a fake photograph. For those who already have a passport, make sure that it will not expire whilst you are on your travels. Are there enough blank pages for Immigration and Departure stamps, and visa(s)? Some countries will expect you to have at least six months outstanding on your passport (sometimes a year) before they even allow you to enter their country or before they will issue you with a visa.

One man and his friend used to spend a year working and then a year travelling. He had already travelled Asia and America with his friend, and they were both employed and saving money to explore Australia. They lived in a bed-sit, did not own a car, had very little possessions and saved all their disposable income for their annual trips. They lived an austere lifestyle so that they could do what they liked most – travelling.

Chapter 6

Gap Year Safety

There are many dangers involved in travelling at home or abroad, as there is a danger in doing anything. One man dislocated his shoulder whilst wiping his bottom! The person who decides to stay at home has forgotten about earthquakes, typhoons, hurricanes, fires, terrorist attacks, toxic spills, floods, sink holes, landslides; most of which is beyond our control. We should not allow fear of "what might happen" to paralyse us to inaction, but we all need to be wise.

Around 200,000 to 250,000 Britons aged 16-25 annually take a gap year, before, during or after college, university or before work. A gap 'year' can be from 3-24 months.[1] Insurance data statistics reveal that one in three people who go on a gap year find that their trip is spoiled by a serious accident, illness or crime, whilst many of these are bad enough to cut the trip short.

In 2008, a coach crash in Ecuador, killed four British gap year students and a tour guide, whilst in May 2009, it emerged that Princess Eugenie of the British royal family suffered a traumatic brush with muggers in Cambodia during her year out.

In the third week of February 2009, gunmen held two hostels in Rio De Janeiro, Brazil, hostage for several hours where groups of tourists had come to celebrate the carnival week, though nobody was harmed. Official government statistics from Mexico for 2016, state that around one thousand people are kidnapped per year, however other people say it could be ten times that amount! Other countries also have kidnapping for ransom. Hostage takings are rare occurrences per head of population, though they are more likely to happen in war zones or in areas where extremists are irate at your Western presence or just because you are a foreigner.

Two months after the second Gulf War, we were in a North African country, and on the edge of one town, we had stones thrown at us and abuse shouted by the local children and teenagers. Likewise, if you go to a district that is not familiar with foreigners, they may be extra suspicious, but more often than not, you will be greeted by the kindest and friendliest people who want to lavish on you all the hospitality they can afford.

> In one town in East Africa, a tourist fell into a ditch and broke her leg. That was the end of her holiday and an accident can be the end of any gap year. John – Ethiopia.

Peter Slowe, director of the gap year company Projects Abroad, noted, "People are very concerned about safety and while we can never provide absolute safety, we can provide a certain level of reassurance," he said. "...We need to work out how to prepare people effectively. ...The second thing is they need to do some research, for example how much money they will need and what inoculations to have. If you do the basic research, which does not take long, you increase your chances of finishing your project safe and sound by 300 percent."[2]

From my doctor's surgery I picked up their quarterly newsletter and read the statistics of British people who had accidents at home. 220,000 went to hospital because of DIY accidents as compared with 290,000 injured (including fatalities) on the roads! Each year in the UK there are approximately: 87,000 injuries whilst working in the garden, including 5,300 accidents caused by flowerpots; 14,000 people injured whilst preparing vegetables (sharp knives and boiling water); 11,800 accidents involving socks, tights and stockings; 5,300 went to Accident and Emergency owing to mishaps whilst putting on a pair of trousers/pants; 760 were injured by washing-up liquid and there were 400 bra-related accidents! Need I say any more about dangers and why we should not be afraid of travelling abroad?

Each country may have its own unique difficulties that can cause problems, but these problems are a minority and incidences can be very few and far between. I have travelled to more than forty different nations and the worse I have ever encountered is diarrhoea (diarrhea), mild altitude sickness, mosquito bites, and the occasional trip-up. I have also encountered: payment renegotiations in the middle of Africa with private transport, pickpockets, drunken locals, being short-changed when exchanging money (a sleight-of hand trick), breakdowns on public transport, and once in France, a snake slithered across the footpath on a Pyrenees mountain trail which made me jump in the air and set my heartbeat thumping!

To save money, my friend and I hired a motorbike which we shared for a few days. He was much bigger than myself and when we drove on a dirt road, I lost control and we crashed. I was ok, but my friend hurt his knee. We saved money but risked our health! Papulos – Cambodia.

Travel Warnings

Since the Arab Spring, which began in December 2010 in Tunisia, North Africa, much of North Africa and the Middle East has undergone dramatic change and seen much turmoil. With the rise of the Islamic State (IS) (also known as ISIS, ISIL, Daesh and Daish) in 2014, sweeping into and taking control over large swathes of Iraq,

Syria and other parts of the Middle East; with affiliated groups in pockets in North Africa and northern Nigeria etc., multitudes of Christians, (plus Muslims, minority groups, including aid workers) have been taken hostage and endured torture, rape, mutilations etc.; many are killed, including women, children and babies. Many young women have been forced to renounce the Christian faith (or those of other faiths) to embrace Islam and are sold as sex-slaves or as brides for jihadists. The ransoming of Christian hostages in parts of Iraq is rife. These are the countries that you should avoid on your travels. Terrorist attacks have also been aimed at tourists/foreigners in Tunisia, Egypt and Mali in West Africa. In November 2015, 130 people were killed in Paris, France, and around 300 were injured in simultaneous terrorist attacks. These included gunmen/women and suicide bombers. Islamic terrorists have also struck in many other countries from Pakistan to Indonesia, and a number of incidents across Germany in the last two weeks of July 2016.

In 2007, the infamous Paris to Dhaka Rally came to an end after 28 years because of death threats against the participants by Islamic militants in West Africa.

Many governments of the world issue travel warnings to its citizens, places to avoid because of civil, political or other forms of unrest; as well as dangers because of terrorist activity and recent natural disasters. Some countries that are listed as dangerous are quite safe apart from isolated areas or certain regions in which the local government may have no control. After the attacks in Paris in November 2015, the American government issued a worldwide travel alert to its citizens.

On Friday, 1 July 2016 (during Ramadan), 20 hostages, most of them foreign (including 7 Japanese, 9 Italians, 1 American and 1 Indian) were "mercilessly killed with [a] sharp instrument" during a 12-hour siege in Dhaka, Bangladesh, so stated a Bangladeshi spokesman. They were in a cafe in the Gulshan neighbourhood when 7 terrorists attacked the Holey Artesian cafe. IS (Islamic State) claimed responsibility for the attack, though the Bangladesh authorities state that the terrorists belonged to a local militant group.

In August 2016, a 21-year-old British backpacker was stabbed and killed outside a backpackers' hostel at Home Hill, Australia, popular amongst travellers for agricultural work. She was just days into a three month trip. The attacker, a Frenchman shouted "Allahu akbar," a 30-year-old British man was injured in the attack and later died. Other terrorist attacks occurred in different cities across America the following month, including, bombs, shootings and stabbings.

From time to time, there are outbreaks of diseases, fears of epidemics, scare-mongering, actual epidemics (e.g. SARS, Ebola, Zika virus etc.) and occasional pandemics. Other preventable diseases such as Cholera, TB, Yellow Fever, Chicken Pox, Measles, Mumps etc. do break-out in parts of the world, though some, only in isolated towns or districts. These can cause myriads of deaths (or serious health issues) amongst those who are too poor to aid preventions by inoculation, immunisation or vaccination.

It would be extremely unwise to travel to an infected area (e.g. Ebola) and expose yourself or your team to life-altering consequences – that is unless you are the medical team! Sometimes these hot spots of infection only last a few months or can continue for years, whilst at other times, the whole scenario can rapidly change and a town, which could be in a state of "lock-down," can be open for business as usual within weeks.

> I was in a hotel in Jerusalem, looking out over a beautiful view. When I put on the BBC news, it showed riots in Jerusalem. I did not see them or hear them, yet I was there! Just because there is a problem in one area, does not mean the entire country is affected. Just because a forest fire rages across parts of California does not mean that the USA is going up in flames! Donald – Israel.

In mid-April 2010, a volcano erupted in Iceland and volcanic ash closed the airspace over parts of Europe for six days. Thousands of flights in and out of Europe were grounded. This stranded 100,000+ passengers across the globe, on both sides of the Atlantic and the Middle East. Some insurance policies have 'Industrial Action' and 'Volcanic Disruption' options. Finding out what your travel insurance covers before you purchase it and what it *does not cover* is essential. 'Acts of God' are an exemption clause where you are not covered!

In one country whilst aboard a busy train I was pickpocketed but upon realising the situation was able to phone up my bank and get my credit cards cancelled within twenty minutes. If my trousers'/ pants' pockets were zipped or had Velcro on them this theft would have been avoidable. It was a foolish mistake to have trousers with wide pockets, but a valuable lesson was learnt.

Watch Out – Thieves About!
In Rome, Italy, a group of four teenagers and children came around my brother and I and got in between us. When one of the teenagers put their hand over my watch, I knew something was amiss and in a flash, this robbery scene came to mind, having read it in a book. I heard my Velcro rip on my pockets and instantly got hold of the teenagers wrist, upturned it and raised their arm up high, thus pushing their body down so as to immobilise them. By this time, locals were on the scene, shouting, but as I could not say "pickpocket" in Italian, we let them go and they ran off.

In Nairobi, Kenya, known as "Nairobbery" by travellers, two Swiss girls were robbed of their bum-bags (fanny pack/belt bags). They were approached from behind in broad daylight on a busy main street. Thieves told them that they had a knife and would cut the waist straps of their bum-bags, but as long as they did not scream, they would be safe. This they did and ran off, the girls began to scream and a crowd of men went to their 'aid,' but these men were part of the same scam and hindered the girls pointing out the culprits to those who were genuinely trying to help.

On a two day bus journey in Ethiopia, one of the conductors told us that it was safe to leave our bags on the roof of the bus overnight, as it was parked in a locked bus compound. We took our bags with us only to find that the next day, the conductor of two years employment had ran away with all the bus money, equivalent to a year's wage. The driver had to borrow money so that we could get some diesel and move on, but what if we had been foolhardy and heeded the conductor's advice!

Just outside of the Vatican City, we were approached by a woman holding a baby in her arms and a large newspaper. Fortunately I had read about this scam in my guide book. She came right up to us, but we shooed her away as the paper is merely a cover so as to pickpocket you without her hands being seen. Mark – Italy.

A Stereotypical View of Westerners

In many places of the world, Western men and women are generally perceived as having loose morals, a party lifestyle, hard drinking and are all rich. The stereotypical view is broadcast by Hollywood via satellite or online streaming and enforced by some tourists. A lone woman can be seen as a target from fellow foreigners and locals alike. Consider wearing a ring on your wedding finger to help ward off unwanted attention. Being polite and friendly to some people, can sometimes be taken the wrong way. On occasions a firm brush off, or a stern talking to, can deal with the situation, or exacerbate it! On occasions, locals may come to your assistance.

I was walking along the street at the front of a group of friends. A boy on the back of a bicycle slowly rode pass, put out his hand, touched my back and stroked my blonde hair. I was so shocked, I screamed, froze to the spot and began to shout. One of the local young men heard my cry, he ran after the teenage boys who were trying to get away, pulled the culprit off the back of the bike and slapped him several times! Yvonne – Tunisia.

Chapter 7

Medical Related Issues

See your doctor/physician months before you depart. Inform him or her of where you are going and for how long. Ask what injections, vaccination, inoculation or tablets do I need? If you hope to gain access to some countries then some vaccinations are mandatory, whilst others are advisable in specific areas. Your doctor (like mine), may advise you to contact a specialist such as MASTA (in the UK) who also have an online vaccine checker list. You go through the list, print it out and take it to the doctor or local nurse to administer the vaccines.

- Potential Vaccinations and treatments so as to avoid: Hepatitis A, Hepatitis B, Yellow Fever, Malaria, Tetanus, Diphtheria, Polio, Typhoid Fever, Tick Borne Encephalitis, Rabies, Meningococcal Disease and Japanese Encephalitis. At the time of writing there are no vaccines for Ebola or the Zika Virus.
- Book your vaccinations and allow plenty of time. Some vaccines have to be taken months apart. Better to have a late vaccination than not at all.
- Have you had a Tetanus prevention injection or do you need a booster? Generally every ten years.
- Purchase your anti-malarial medication. You will probably have to pay for a private prescription so that the doctor can issue you with the correct type and number of tablets.

> I skipped some jabs at home and bought a non-effective treatment in a developing country – though I did not know it at the time! I got really sick. I saved time and money at home, but it cost me in the long run. George – Laos.

Inoculations and Jabs

Prevention is better than cure so have all the jabs and inoculations you need before you depart. If you are ill, have a disease or health problem (physical or mental), you should contact a doctor/physician to seek professional medical help before departing on your travels. The author is not a doctor/physician or counsellor. The related medical contents of this book cannot take the place of advice from a medical professional, and is not intended to, but is included as an aid and a guide. Tetanus and Hepatitis jabs are free in the UK – see your local doctor. Prices do vary between health centres for other non-NHS jabs, and only designated centres can give certain inoculations such as Yellow Fever. You must always take the accompanying Yellow Fever Certificate with you when you travel abroad as the border guards/Immigration may ask to see it. Without it, you will not be permitted to enter certain countries or be issued with a visa!

Jabs x3 against the rabies virus are expensive, around £120 ($192), but is advisable if you are going into remote jungle-like areas or if you know you will be around animals/bats within a rabies infected area. If you are bitten or scratched by an infected creature you will need another course of treatment, ideally within 24hrs which is equally expensive, but potentially life saving.

Medication and Border Health Checks

Some anti-malarial tablets are taken daily, others are taken weekly and you may have to take them two weeks before departure and two weeks after your return. There can be side effects; but you *do not want* to catch malaria. It is reported that fifty percent of local medicines (especially anti-malarial brands) in some developing countries are ineffective. Expect to pay around £50-100 ($80-160) for a six-month supply in a Western nation, plus the cost of a private prescription. If you are on the pill, some medicines can make this form of contraception less effective.

A Cholera vaccination is two sachets of powder and two containers of medicine, which are mixed with water and taken within 6 weeks of each other, £33 ($53). Can be free on the NHS.

Tick-borne encephalitis is three vaccines, two before you depart (one month apart) and one after 12 months and costs around £50-70 per dose ($80-112), or a total of between £150-210 ($240-336). I have never had this vaccine.[1]

To combat the affects of altitude sickness your doctor can prescribe DIAMOX (Acetazolamide) around £8 ($13) for 28 tablets, a two-week supply (two a day).

It is important that you keep all medicines in their original packaging with the accompanying pamphlet. These pamphlets also state the medical composition of the tablets or capsules and so make it easier for the pharmacist abroad to issue you with what you need; not all medicines are generic and Western brand names may not exist in some countries. Some medicines may require a letter from your doctor if you intend on passing through customs unhindered – ask your doctor. Some medicines in the West (e.g. codeine, for pain relief) are illegal in some countries.

Border controls can sometimes be tricky when these diseases are prevalent and in 2003, because of the threat of SARS, the

Vietnamese border guards were very nervous about tourists spreading the disease. We had to fill out additional paperwork, including the state of our health, with questions such as, 'Have you had a temperature or headache in the past week?' We had to pay on top of our visa fees for a man who wore a facemask to read our answers, tick and stamp our paper and then we were allowed to enter the country!

In 2015, the health scare was Ebola, where some people were screened, questions were asked and their temperatures taken. For 2016, it was the Zika virus, especially dangerous for women who are pregnant or for men and women who are trying to start a family.

In the last few decades, outbreaks of Foot and Mouth disease across Britain have closed public footpaths and rights-of-way across large parts of the countryside for periods of time.

In East Asia we took an overland route to cross the border which saved us $100 (£63) each. It was great travelling with the locals and the experience was more real, rather than a sanitized airport. Henry.

Developing Countries and Medical Insurance

Medical problems can be an issue in developing countries. The nearest hospital may be some distance away and the facilities may not be what you are used to, however some hospitals have incredible facilities and highly skilled staff. If you need medical assistance, try and contact your medical insurance company/travel insurance first. They may tell you to go to an approved hospital or a surgery. If this is not possible, be cautious of blood transfusions (has it been screened?). If you need an injection, is the syringe new? Have you watched the doctor or nurse take it out of its sealed package? If you are unconscious, you cannot do any of the above, but hopefully a travel friend will be able to speak to those in charge or sign the various consent forms on your behalf. Keep all receipts to be reimbursed by your insurer.

Lassa Fever and Rats

Lassa fever has seen a minimum of 400 outbreaks from 1967-2012 and is carried by the Mastomy rat which is found in parts of Africa, and like Ebola, can cause haemorrhagic fever and can be fatal. 80% of people who catch the virus either have no symptoms or those that mimic other illnesses such as malaria. There are between one hundred thousand and one million cases of Lassa fever in western sub-Sahara a year. The virus is passed through direct contact with an infected rat, by eating an infected rat, by household items or food that have been contaminated with rat urine or droppings, or contact with bodily fluids by a human who is infected.

Chapter 8

Health Related Issues

Being away from home and letting your hair down you may not be fully aware of the intensity of the sun, the dangers of insects or how quickly you can dehydrate or catch hypothermia in temperatures that you are not used to. The information within this chapter relates to personal health advice, often relating to the elements, prevention, aids, and health related items to take with you.

Cold Weather Health Related

In extremely cold weather, exposed skin but especially your nose and fingers (as well as your toes) can freeze, leading to frostbite. If the temperature is in double digits below zero, metal watchstraps in direct contact with the skin can freeze to the skin. Cold weather with piercing winds or freezing/driving rain can also cut skin. Wear lots of thin layers of clothing to help keep you warm. Do you need:

- Thermal socks and boots.
- Thermal underwear.
- Warm jacket and plenty of layers.
- Hat, gloves, mittens and a scarf.
- Protective glasses/goggles, especially when snow is around.

Sunshine and UV Rays Health Related

Sunburn, sunstroke and heatstroke can all cause major problems at home or abroad. The sun may be of much stronger intensity than what you are used to and relevant precautions should be taken. As a teenager I got sunstroke and was ill for two days; I now always wear a hat when exposed to the elements. One woman went horse riding for the day and burnt her exposed arms so badly that she had to go to hospital. After treatment she was informed that had the burns been any worse, then she would have needed skin grafts.

The sea and snow reflects and magnifies the sun's rays, and gives more exposure than if you were in the countryside or around town. Guys, remember that moisturiser and lip balm are not only for girls. Whilst you may not have had chapped lips at home, it is possible to get them abroad and in some climates, unmoisturised skin can quickly deteriorate and crack.

Cloud cover does not eliminate harmful UV rays, especially in tropical climates and those countries centred near the equator, where with no previous exposure to the sun, the average person will begin to burn within fifteen minutes. Use a high factor suncream/sunscreen, especially on your arms, nose, the back of the neck and possibly even your earlobes if they are prone to burn. If you are exposed to the sun (or just UV rays) then sunburn and/or heatstroke can cause major problems. Cover up exposed skin and drink plenty of water. Find some shade.

In 2016, a young girl was badly burnt when her mother applied a known-brand factor 50 suncream which her mum had bought in Mexico. The girl's skin began to melt as if she had been attacked with acid, which left scars down her legs. Either the 'branded' suncream was fake, or there was a manufacturing error.

- Bring a sun hat, wide rimmed to cover your ears and to help shade your face and neck.
- Sunglasses/shades with UV protection.
- Suncream and lip balm that will protect you from UVs. Don't fry yourself in the sun, cover up exposed skin to avoid sunburn and heatstroke. Umbrellas are used in many countries in summer to keep the owner in the shade.

I heard about the local swimming pool and as I had some free time from my voluntary work in a school, my wife and I paid it a visit. It was only about 20°C and I was only in the sun for a few hours, but being so close to the equator, and the fact that I did not wear my sun hat, I got badly sunburnt. Mark – Zimbabwe.

The Desert and Dehydration

The human body consists of between 45-65 percent water, depending on body size, age and gender. If you lose more than 5% of your body weight through loss of water, sweating, you will begin to deteriorate, physically and mentally. If this loss rises to 10% you will become delirious, possibly deaf and oblivious to pain. If moisture loss reaches 12% then death ensues. In hot climates you can lose 1 ½ litres/liters per hour and will need to drink up to ten litres per day! If you lose just 2.5% of your overall bodily fluids (dehydration), then your efficiency to function decreases by a staggering 25%!

To minimise water loss, avoid talking and breathe through your nose. A cyclist in sub-Sahara Africa noted that he was able to drink quite a few litres/liters less per day than what the British Army recommended because he covered his body, to keep the moisture in, which included the Arab headscarf so that only his eyes poked through. Ground temperature can be up to 30% higher than the surrounding air (just try and walk barefoot on the tarmac or on sand during summer!), so if you're in a jam and immobilised, then try to raise yourself off the ground onto a log, tree stump or ledge and be in the shade.

Thunderstorms and Lightning

A British meteorologist calculated that there are an average of forty-four lighting strikes on earth per second! Lightning strikes can kill, or seriously injure you. On 28 May 2016, at least one person was killed and more than a dozen were seriously injured in thunderstorms across Europe, in lightning strikes in Poland, Germany and France. One group of school children and their teachers were sheltering under a tree when lightning struck. They all needed medical attention. One week later, on 4 June, 71 people were injured by lightning strikes at the Rock am Ring music festival in Mendig, Germany, where 45,000 music fans had gathered.

On 21 June 2016, at least 79 people were killed by lightning strikes across four states of India. India's monsoon season runs from June to September, and from 2005, according to the National Crime Records Bureau, at least 2,000 people have died in lightning strikes in India, every year!

During thunderstorms:

- Try to get inside a building or a vehicle. A vehicle, whilst metal, will act like a Faraday cage and the voltage will go around it and not through it.
- Try to get away or off of featureless landscape (e.g. moor land) into a cave or den. If this is not possible, make yourself as small as possible. With you feet flat on the ground, crouch down into a ball and cover your head with your arms.
- Avoid conductors such as an umbrella, golf club, fishing rod, kite, metallic walking stick or trekking poles etc.
- Get out of water (sea or a lake) and as far up (or off) the beach as possible. The charge of lightning will travel through ground and water before dissipating. The closer you are to the strike, the more dangerous it is for you.

Deep Vein Thrombosis

In the past decade, Deep Vein Thrombosis (DVT) has been highlighted in the media though it was first documented in the 1950s. It is where blood clots develop in the veins of the leg and is more probable on long-haul flights, as well as other journeys where your leg movement is restricted, such as in a cramped bus.

When on a plane, but especially during a long-haul flight:

- Drink plenty of water, do not get dehydrated.
- Don't wear tight clothing, especially around the waist or lower legs.
- At regular intervals, as long as the seat-belt sign is not illuminated, walk around as much as possible. Walk up and down the different aisles, though don't get in the stewardesses way.

- Stand in the aisle at the back of the plane (near the toilets and the emergency door, where there is often more room) and gently rotate feet at the ankles, one at a time.
- If you can stretch your legs whilst seated, then the following exercise can also help reduce the risk of DVT, though getting up and walking is better; try and do both. Rotate your feet at the ankle, clockwise and then anticlockwise. Point your foot outward as you stretch your leg (you can feel the tension in your calf muscles), and move the foot back and forth slowly.
- If you are at particular risk of DVT then visit your doctor/ physician before you travel and get his or her advice. Consider purchasing some elastic compression stockings. Don't drink alcohol (as it dehydrates you) or take sleeping pills (as they will immobilise you – you will be asleep).

Insect Health Related
- Insect repellent containing DEET (diethyltoluamide, also known as diethyl-3-methylbenzamide).
- Do you need to purchase a mosquito net?
- Burning coils and plug-in insecticide vaporisers can help deal with insects, though often not if you have a fan in the room, or if you leave the window open because of the heat when there is no netting.
- Antihistamine tablets, ointments, cream or gel can help you if you suffer an allergic reaction to an insect bite.
- For the removal of leeches before they become full and drop off after drinking your blood, use a credit card to scrape them off or other flat object to break the seal of the leeches' suckers, then flick them off with your finger.

First Aid, Tablets, Medicines and Advice
- Small first-aid kit. You may want to take a sterile medical kit with you.
- Additional plasters/Band Aid in case you cut yourself.
- Antibacterial soap/gel can come in handy.
- Antiseptic cream – in case you get a cut or a scratch. The brands Sudocrem (in the UK) is an effective antiseptic healing cream, as is Germolene antiseptic cream.
- Antihistamine tablets/cream can help with allergy relief against insect bites or skin rashes.
- Tablets in case of diarrhoea (aka: Delhi belly or Bangkok blow-out). This is quite common for travellers as is the occasional upset stomach. You may wish to take some oral

dehydration tablets in case you get it bad, or make your own salt and sugar solution dissolved in water. Six tablespoons of sugar and ½ tablespoon of salt with one litre/liter of clean water = five 200ml cups.

- Mosquito repellent containing DEET (diethyltoluamide) is essential for some areas.
- Some of the world's religion expect abstention e.g. alcohol, and sexual unions outside of marriage from their followers as part of their faith. This is to honour God and protect the individual from doing something that they will later regret, or from getting pregnant or catching a sexually transmitted infection or a venereal disease. These can be life changing and can include: Syphilis, Gonorrhea, Chlamydia, Herpes, Trichomoniasis, Crabs, HIV and AIDS etc.

For other items to buy and take, including a kit list, see chapters 15 and 16. For survival items in case of extreme travel, see chapter 10.

Sex Workers and Slavery

Some Westerners use sex workers in Asia, Africa, Europe and other parts of the world. Many of the women of the night are victims of sex traffickers, poverty or under the control of a pimp. Some of the workers are also under-age yet have been told to say they are 16, 18 or 21. People are not for sale, for an hour or a lifetime and child-abuse is a crime. Modern-day slavery is most evident in the trafficking industry. Those who frequent brothels etc. to use sex workers are facilitating, exploiting, encouraging and financially supporting the modern-day slave trade, and the continual abuse of those who cannot say "No," those who cannot leave the industry they never wanted to be a part of in the first place.

Chapter 9

How to Survive Your Trip

There are dangers and hazards everywhere, but when travelling abroad we should be extra diligent because of the unfamiliar surroundings. Each country may have its own unique difficulties that can cause problems, but these problems are often a minority and incidences can be few and far between.

Unlit streets and alleyways are the norm in parts of the developing world and manhole covers may be nonexistent. Beware of potholes, raised kerbs, no sewer coverings, open sewers, ditches, uneven paving slabs and a thousand and one other obstacles in unlit areas.

Whilst you are on your travels, you may have the opportunity to participate in a sport or activity, which may be a one-off opportunity. However, be aware that safety regulations and precautions may not be as stringent in some countries as in others – this is especially true in developing countries where corners may be cut to maximise profits. At other times, the excitement of being away from home, trying to stand out, or being psyched on by other travellers, you may be brazen in your foolhardiness!

We should all be wary of extreme or adventure sports as an accident can spell the end of your travels. As a teenager I was a keen skateboarder and a lot more agile than I am now, I had bounce-ability falling over, now it is near breakability!

When it comes to extreme or adventure sports, you pay your money and take your chances. Adventure sports can include: jet-skiing, rock climbing, snowboarding or skiing, ostrich racing, buffalo riding, crocodile wrestling (just kidding!) or playing Tarzan on the vines. Extreme sports can be: bungee jumping, skiing down a near vertical mountain, white-water rafting, motocross racing, or jumping out of an aeroplane with a parachute attached etc., unless you are the daredevil skydiver, Luke Aitkins who jumped from 25,000ft without a parachute or wingsuit and landed in a 100ft^2 trampoline-like-trawler net at 120mph!

There are free versions of adrenaline pumping 'sports' which people who are away from home have been known to participate in, such as: roof-riding on buses or train surfing (standing on the top of moving transport), tomb-stoning (jumping off cliffs and high ledges into water), log walking (jumping from one floating and rotating log to another). All of these 'sports' have their own hazards and dangers which should be avoided as an accident could spell the end of your travels and a potential stay in hospital.

> I hired a powerful dirt bike and went off-road for the day. All was going well until I crashed, and I sustained some serious injuries, but after a few months I fully recovered. Ronald – France.

Crossing the Road

In the UK we have zebra crossings (black and white stripes across a road) where pedestrians can cross the road and cars have to give way and stop, however in the last decade, more and more cars do not stop, even though pedestrians have the right of way. When I was in Rome, Italy, as in other European countries, I quickly learnt that zebra crossings are a guide, that it is a designated place to cross, but you still have to dodge the bicycles, motor bikes, cars and buses! When abroad, I often try to cross the road when the locals do. I stand on the outside of them, farthest away from the oncoming traffic, when they cross, I quickly follow.

Trekking

If you are going to be trekking into some remote area or jungle then glucose tablets for an instant energy boost will be beneficial, but most importantly *always* go prepared. Take fluids and food with you as well as adequate clothing. It is better that you have a little extra equipment than to be caught out. Trekking through the jungle or in the wilderness can increase the strain on your mind and body, though the scenery can be outstanding.

The human body can go through huge extremes and when in dire circumstances, with adrenaline flowing through its system, it can really go the distance, but only for so long until the body collapses. Food, drink and rest are essential, though within each of us we have greater endurance when pushed to extremes.

If travelling with a group of friends, let them know if you are going walkabout, where you are going and when you expect to be back. This is especially true if you go hiking, even as a group, let the receptionist know. It is these people who can raise the alarm if you go missing, and hopefully you will be found. In June 2016, a 22-year-old British backpacker went missing in Vietnam after a fall down a cliff. He had injured himself, lost his way and was found dead after five days. It costs £12 ($19) per person a day to privately hire each person as part of a search party.

The Weather

Sunburn, sunstroke and heatstroke can all cause major problems. The sun may be of much stronger intensity than what you are used to and relevant precautions should be taken. The sun is at its strongest from 11am-3pm. Slip on a shirt, slop on some suncream/sunscreen and slap on a hat. In some climates, unmoisturised skin can quickly deteriorate and crack. Moisturiser and lip balm are essential, though the latter often melts!

Cloud cover does not eliminate harmful UV rays, especially in tropical climates and those countries centred near the equator. Use a high factor suncream/sunscreen, cover up, or stay in the shade, why not use an umbrella? Wear a wide rimmed hat and drink plenty of fluids.

If you lose more than 5% of your body weight through loss of water, sweating, you will begin to deteriorate, physically and mentally. For the other extreme, you also do not want to freeze in artic temperatures so wrap up when the thermometer begins to plummet. In some desert areas, the difference between day and night temperatures can be a whopping 50°C!

It is important not to underestimate the power and elements of nature. At altitude or during certain seasons, the weather can turn on a knife-edge and temperatures can plummet rapidly. Rain and piercing wind can chill you to the bone within a short space of time, and is often not noticeable until you stop moving. Be prepared!

The Dark Side of Wildlife

Each country has its own animals, insects, bugs, reptiles and rodents, some of which can cause harm. There is a reason why wildlife is called such, because it is 'wild life,' with an emphasis on the wild. You may think that it is a great idea to have a selfie with a bison, buffalo, rhino or elephant in the background, but what happens if it charges? Most animals you cannot outrun, the best you can do if the animal has not charged, but is showing signs of aggression, is to back off slowly. If you run from a lion or a tiger, you are prey and will be caught! Playing dead and protecting your head is the best course of action with a bear, assuming that you do not have bear repellent. You may be able to climb a tree, but so can bears, tigers and many other animals with claws.

In Africa, more people die because of hippos than any other creature, including tigers, lions and crocodiles. Their jaws are huge and they love to pop up from under the water and can lift canoes and small boats out of the water! Hippos can crush wooden canoes, or make them fill with water so that the occupants have to 'abandon ship.'

At the end of May 2016, a 46-year-old woman was in waist high water at Thorton Beach, Queensland, Australia, when a saltwater crocodile dragged her under. It was at night when she went for a dip with her friend. From 1970 onwards, when saltwater crocs have been protected in different territories across Australia, these tragic type of incidences have increased.

Jellyfish stings can be very painful, if not fatal. Some are no bigger than the tip of a thumb, yet their tentacles can be one metre long. One woman, a marine biologist who was stung by one of the most dangerous jellyfish in the world said, "If giving birth was as painful as this sting, then the human race would come to an end!" The woman had the maximum permitted dose of morphine and was still writhing in agony. Incidentally she got stung on her hand after she peeled off her wetsuit. In many developing countries stray dogs can be a problem; but only if they bite you! A pastor in Sudan warned, "Throw stones at them to keep them away, they carry rabies."

Insects and Reptiles

Ants are creatures so small, yet can cause devastation as they work as an army. There are many different types of ants, but if their trail is through your hut, then you could be in for trouble. The bullet ant is so named because of its bite and the pain you endure is like that of being shot by a bullet!

In 2016, a young woman died from being bitten by red ants. She had an allergic reaction and began to swell, causing difficulty in breathing. Her husband got her clothes off (the ants had got inside), but by the time the paramedics arrived it was too late.

> We arrived in the capital of Botswana having the night before slept in a cockroach-infested room on the Zambian side. We killed at least twenty of the vermin! Jack – Botswana.

If you get bitten by a snake or spider, being able to describe it to the medics (its size, colour, markings, stripes, red abdomen etc.) can help them administer the correct antivenin or medicine. Take antihistamine tablets/cream to treat insect bites or skin rashes. The brand Sudocrem (in the UK) is a very effective antiseptic healing cream.

Beware of monkeys or baboons that try to steal your food; seagulls will swoop down in some British seaside towns and take a chip or your ice-cream! Stay clear of scorpions and giant salamanders! You will be shocked at how fast a giant salamander can run when it thinks *you* are the next meal! Their claws are deadly!

Leeches can be found in tropical locations or where damp leafy-type areas are humid. They can eat through clothes and will suck all the blood they can get from you, before falling off. Scrape them off with a credit card or other flat object. A lighter will encourage them to drop off, though they may regurgitate into your wound. Beware of squeezing them as you can push their bodily contents into your wound and this can lead to an infection.

Mosquitoes can be a bane for many travellers. I have never taken a mosquito net with me on my travels, though I have slept under dozens, but I have always bought anti-malarial drugs from home when going into an area of risk. Mosquito repellent containing DEET (diethyltoluamide also known as diethyl-3-methylbenzamide) is essential and can be applied sparingly to exposed skin. DEET can irritate sensitive skin, especially on one's face. In Cairo, Egypt, I was bitten by a mosquito near my eye whilst sleeping. It swelled up, began to drag my upper cheek down and looked liked I had been punched in the face. It sorted itself out after three or four days.

Mosquito nets are useful if the place where you are staying in has the facilities to hang them! Nets that hang by one central cord are easier than those that hang by four corners; only one hook is needed rather than four. Mosquito nets are always cheaper in developing countries, though they may not have been sprayed or soaked in certain mosquito repellent liquids for additional protection.

Do not wear deodorant, perfume or aftershave in areas where malaria is common, because mosquitoes that transmit the disease are attracted by fragrance.

We were trying to get to sleep in our hut, but all night I could hear the scuttling of rodent's feet in the rafters above. I knew they were rats and I did not like them. One ran across my legs and I could not help but scream! Timothy – Papua New Guinea.

Unwanted Attention and Inappropriate Behaviour

In some countries, women, but especially foreign women can receive undue attention simply by being in public. Headscarves and flowing tops often go a long way in some cultures to reduce unwanted attention from men who are not used to seeing women 'uncovered' in public. Uncovered can include showing your legs and lower arms! In some nations, by law, women have to cover their head, e.g. Saudi Arabia and Iran, whilst in other countries coverings relate to religious places such as churches, mosques, synagogues or temples for both men and women. Some items of clothing, including jewellery, e.g. cross or crescent, and bodily markings/inking, e.g. henna tattoos, can identify you with your religion.

In the United Arab Emirates (UAE), kissing in public is deemed inappropriate behaviour with a possible prison sentence, penalty or deportation! Holding hands between unmarried couples is also inappropriate behaviour! For many years, Dubai in the UAE, has been promoted as a holiday destination and is a short hop from Europe.

Some unmarried solo women travellers have been known to wear a ring on their wedding finger, so as not to attract unwanted attention. However, like a good spy they need a cover story to respond to inquisitive questioners, "Where is your husband, how long have you been married, do you have any children?" etc.

If you are part of a humanitarian organization, charity or NGO they may be able to advise you on cultural and taboo issues in regards to relationships. They may have their own policy for the mutual benefit of all participants. Broken relationships can cause major problems if you are working or travelling as part of a team, and this can include overlanders. You may have two weeks or two months remaining of the trip working or travelling in close proximity to the one who ended the relationship and it can cause friction for yourself and others.

In many Arab countries, e.g. Saudi Arabia, Quatar, United Arab Emirates, if a woman goes to the police alleging she has been raped, there is a high probability that she will be charged for having sexual relations outside of wedlock! In many countries, women are seen as commodities to be used and abused; this is tragic, shocking, yet all too true. The reports of travellers that have been taken advantage off, to the stories that have made the headlines in Britain (and other countries) all confirm and verify this. In the last two years, there have been a number of high profile rape and murder incidents in Delhi, India, with mass demonstrations and public outcries. Tourists wearing dresses and skirts can be an issue.[1]

In 2013, a Norwegian woman in the United Arab Emirates received a 16-month prison sentence for perjury, having extramarital sex and for drinking alcohol, after she told police she had been raped. In many Islamic countries alcohol is outlawed or only available in licensed places, to accommodate foreigners and tourists. The woman was later pardoned and permitted to return to Norway.

In June 2016, a court in Qatar convicted a 22-year-old Dutch woman of sex outside of marriage after she told police she had been raped. This incident happened three months prior to the conviction. She was drinking in a hotel in Doha that was licensed to sell alcohol, when her drink was spiked. She woke up in an apartment that she did not recognise. The man stated to the police that it was consensual and received 140 lashes (100 for premarital sex and 40 for drinking alcohol). The Dutch woman received a suspended sentence, was fined $824 (£580) and was deported.

A 2014 United Nations survey revealed that 99.3% of Egyptian woman and girls have suffered verbal or physical harassment. The BBC website noted that 'Sexual harassment is widespread in Egypt and campaigners say things are getting worse.'[2] During the Arab Spring (2011) and anniversary dates connected with the uprising and subsequent protests and ousting of President Morsi of June-

July 2013, many women, including at least two western reporters were sexually assaulted or raped, especially in and around Tahrir Square, Cairo.

In the criminal code of Germany, section 177, victims should have defended themselves for an act to constitute rape. To say, "No" or "stop" is non sufficient to find the defendant guilty! However a new law, widely referred to as, "No means no" is expected to pass into law soon.[3]

> For your own safety and protection: Beware of on the spot fine by a 'policeman' who is not wearing a uniform! If a plain-clothes 'policeman' wants you to accompany him to the police station, say "No." His colleagues must pick you up dressed in uniform in a marked police car. Do not surrender your passport.

Being Robbed and Terrorist Attacks

If in the unfortunate event that you do get confronted by robbers with knives or guns, do not resist, let them take your wallet/purse, camera or mobile/cell phone if they ask for it. They are probably just as scared as you, but if you resist or refuse, they may react by instinct and you could be injured. It is not worth it, let your material possessions go and save yourself. Discretion is the better part of valour – it is often wise to refrain from seemingly brave speech or action in distressing circumstances. Report any theft to the local police and get a report filled out for an insurance claim.

In recent years there have been terrorist attacks across the globe. Apart from the common denominator of the attacks being perpetrated by jihadists, often against Westerners, if you submit and are taken hostage, you will probably be executed without mercy. The attack in the Bataclan theatre in Paris, France, in November 2015, where people went to see an American rock band revealed this execution policy. If you cannot run, hide, or play dead, and if the worst comes to the worst, then die fighting to save the lives of others. Ahead of Euro 2016, the French government released an App to alert the public in the event of a terrorist attack. See Appendix A.

> In July 2016, the United Arab Emirates (UAE) warned its citizens against wearing its traditional clothing when abroad. A UAE citizen in America, was suspected of being a terrorist, whilst dressed in his white robe and headscarf and was arrested at a hotel by armed officers. Qatar has warned its citizens to respect countries where there is a ban on full face-veils, e.g. France, Belgium, Bulgaria and some towns in Italy. Some places ban the niqābs, a full face-veil, and the burqa, a full-body covering. Some towns in France have banned the burkhini, a full body covering used when swimming.[4]

Chapter 10

Extreme and Remote Travel

The type of travel that takes you to isolated areas, remote tribes, or distant mountain ranges cost considerably more than your average budget trip, though you can tie up with specialist agencies, NGOs, charities or a specialist tour group. Tribes are often isolated in their locations, and often 4x4s or boats and motorised canoes have to be hired or rented, along with their driver/captain, as well as a guide/ interpreter. To protect your ears from noisy engines, use ear plugs or roll up tissue paper and place inside your ears! You will need to kit yourselves out with enough camping gear and food to last you (and your helpers) the duration of the trip, as well as spares and fuel. Everything adds up. Also remember that 'white man's diseases' can easily wipe out an entire tribe who have not had inoculations or vaccinations which are common to those of us in the West.

In some places, it is customary to bring presents to those who are in charge or to bring assistance to their people. Staple foods, pots and pans, matches or disposable lighters, knives, machetes, axes, clothes and blankets etc. Your guide or interpreter are always your best port of call for advice in these matters and they will probably understand the culture, customs and etiquette.

In some places, before you can camp in a village or interact with the locals, you will have to speak to the chief, village elders or patriarchal figure. Sometimes the cultural etiquette is to bring gifts for the chief, village elders or for the village at large, often for the heads of families. With those in charge on your side, your exploration in that location can begin. If you are unable to obtain the consent of the chief, then generally speaking, the villagers will be afraid to go against the express wishes of their superior. It is often better just to move on whilst still in the patriarchal's good will, rather than to offend. The leader may only be distrusting because it is the first time he has laid eyes on you. It may be possible to visit at another time, on a return trip and the door may be wide open. Do not underestimate the power of a patriarchal figure, superstition or the control and fear which witchdoctors or shamans can hold over their people.

One group were visiting an Amazonian tribe. The leader said, "They don't want any books, if they have time to read they have time to hunt! Leave them behind." In some remote locations, you and your baggage will be weighed to make sure the plane can clear the trees at the end of the runway! Please note, some tribes would rather have your friendship than for the humanitarian team to build them a house or communal building.

In some areas, the river may be the place where you wash yourself and your clothes. Locals often do a far better job at washing clothes (and a lot quicker) and are happy for the extra income. If you have to wash in a river, ask the locals to find out where the best place is and what is the best time. At certain times of day, animals may come to feed or be watered! The locals may not appreciate your soap or washing suds polluting their drinking water. Find out what creatures lurk in the river – crocodiles, hippos, piranhas etc.! If there are crocodiles, do not collect water from the same place everyday. Beware of jellyfish in the sea! Sometimes waterborne diseases or micro-organisms can be present in rivers or streams which can infect you. Common sense goes a long way, but a simple question to a local can be returned by a simple answer, thus alleviating yourself of any fears or concerns that you may have.

> I was scared in the jungle – I did not know what lurked amongst the vegetation, but I soon got used to using the woods as a toilet and washing in a cold river. Geoff – Malaysia.

An army officer came to visit our group to talk about his experiences. He informed us that out of all the safety equipments and items that you could take with you as part of a survival trip; the most important item is a mirror. It has nothing to do with vanity, but a mirror can reflect the sun's rays and be seen for many miles, alerting people to your presence. A whistle is also another handy item to take with you when going into remote areas, but water purification is essential, and takes a higher priority than food. A machete can be essential for cutting undergrowth, trees, killing animals and in skinning them!

> We trekked two days in the tropical climate to a village, which should have taken six hours. Our guide got us lost – it was tough! Our hands were badly cut on the thorns, thistles, sharp leaves and grass. My clothes of just two weeks were so badly torn and blooded that I had to throw them away and get a new set. James – Laos.

With jungle travel, be aware of your surroundings, look for vantage points, clearings, paths, signs of civilisation. If you get lost, follow a river downstream in search of civilisation, however in Africa, unless it is a huge river, follow it upstream because rivers dry up. Know where the sun is and what times it sets. Try to make camp an hour or two before the sun goes down. Be careful of where you put your hands, what you grab hold off, a prickly bush, caterpillar, spider or a snake can all cause great harm. Have a good map, GPS, a local guide and good rations and provisions. Let people know where you are going, your proposed route and when you will be back. If you are not back within a day or two, they can alert the relevant authorities or hire a search party.

Some toilets are in the bush and it is customary to dig a little hole and cover up after yourself. On one trip that consisted of a night in the desert, one person could not be bothered to dig a hole or cover their waste and another trod in it! She was very annoyed and threw away her trainers. It was a funny event, but not for the unfortunate person and the guilty party never owned up – we had our suspicions though!

I went with a small group to a rural area in Central Asia. We did our research and took some water purification tablets, though most of the time we were able to buy bottled water. One evening we used tap/faucet water with our water purification tablets to cook our Korean noodles. The water turned blue, as did our noodles, but we enjoyed them and were fine! Qday – Kyrgyzstan.

Survival Items to Consider
- Pocket mirror.
- Compass.
- Whistle.
- Survival bag.
- Space/foil blanket.
- Big knife or a machete and means to sharpen it. You may need to purchase this inside the country of destination.
- Map of the area.
- First Aid kit and bandages.
- Water purification tablets, water survival straw or mini water purification equipment.
- Food (army ration packs).
- Mess tins or Billycan to cook in.
- Glucose tablets and salt.
- Trusted lighter and lighter fuel, a flint fire starter or both.
- Satellite phone.
- Portable GPS system.
- Solar panels chargers or spare batteries.
- String and climbing rope.
- Hammock.
- Folding military shovel.
- Fishing hooks and line.

- Flashlight/head torch.
- Tarpaulin to keep the rain off at night.
- A pocketsize Collins Gem *SAS Survival Guide.*
- Ear plugs in case of noisy motorised canoe travel.
- Some people like to buy a SOS survival box which contains a little of a lot of items in case you get caught out whilst hiking or walking.

For other items to buy and take, including a kit list, see chapters 15 and 16. For health related items, see chapter 8.

I found it refreshing on my travels being away from all my familiar means of communication – a digital detox. However, after a short while, the novelty wore off and I could not wait to use the local internet. George – Lesotho.

Natural Disasters

Natural disasters can happen at any time and in these incidents, earthquake, typhoon, forest fire etc., you could be cut-off from help or stranded from days to weeks. You could have your own extreme travel for survival as you fend for yourself under trying or dire circumstances.

On Boxing Day (26 December) 2004, an undersea earthquake of the coast of Sumatra, Indonesia, triggered tsunamis along the coasts of most landmasses bordering the Indian Ocean. A reported 230,000 were killed across fourteen countries with Indonesia being the hardest-hit country, followed by Sri Lanka, India, and then Thailand. There were tens of thousands of foreign visitors at Thailand and the film and mobile phone/cell footage of the disaster that emerged was harrowing.

In January 2010, a 7.0-magnitude earthquake hit Haiti, which left 3 million homeless and more than 230,000 dead. Haiti is the poorest nation in the Western hemisphere and a popular budget travel destination. In April 2015, a 7.8-magnitude earthquake in what became known as the Gorkha earthquake in Nepal, killed more than 8,000 people and injured more than 21,000. It was the worst natural disaster to strike Nepal since an earthquake in 1934. More than a year after the 2015 earthquake, many people had still been unable to rebuild their shacks or houses which they knew as home.

Before you depart, have an emergency evacuation plan in place, not only for natural disasters and acts of terrorism, but in case of a medical emergency. Be trained in first aid, know who to phone and the options of where to go and what to do.

Chapter 11

Budgeting For Your Travels

There are a number of ways and methods of obtaining money for your travels. However, my advice is to not go into debt, by taking out a loan, putting it on credit cards, charge cards or borrowing, as this is not a budget option, nor is it wise to sell parts of your body. It is a poor investment to go into debt to travel as it will cost you so much more in the future.

Most people do not just get up and go, but plan to go abroad. It may be while they are at high school, college, university, or after a few years at work. Some people plan years ahead, for others it may be just six months or the spur of the moment! Some employers permit unpaid leave and will keep your job open for up to one year.

Financial Options

1. Live an austere lifestyle so that you can save more of your disposable income for your travels. Open up a bank account where this money is deposited and do not touch it until you travel. Cut back on travel, taxis, eating out, clothes, festivals, hot drinks (fancy coffees, cappuccinos etc.), expensive lunches, meal deals or sandwiches, make your own lunch.

2. Get a part-time job or do some overtime or extra shifts. Consider getting a second job, but don't exhaust yourself.

3. Offer your services to your neighbourhood: clean cars, dig the garden, sweep the yard, chop wood, walk the dog or baby-sit etc. Be entrepreneurial. What is the need and how can I fulfil it?

4. Use money from your savings account. If you have been given x amount for a car, your education, a deposit for a flat or to help pay for your wedding, then you should not use that designated money without consent from the giver – usually your parents or grandparents.

5. Ask your parents/family for a contribution. They may not be impressed by your decision to go travelling or could greatly surprise you by their delight that you are seeing the world. They may be glad to see the back of you for a few months or absence will make the heart grow fonder. It is wrong to expect family, friends and work colleagues to assist you on your humanitarian or religious travels if you have wasted you own resources on 'good living.'

6. If you are doing humanitarian work, why not ask your employer for a financial contribution or items/gifts for humanitarian work? The worst they can say is no. There may be a designated fund for charity work and it can be a tax write-off. Ask for financial support for materials needed for the construction of a building, a water pump or medical supplies etc.
7. Make items to sell, bake cakes or bread, make bird boxes, jewellery, model planes etc. What is the market like where you live or can you sell non-edible items over the internet.
8. Sell items you own – your car, sports equipment, jewellery, bicycle, computer games, laptop, stereo, books etc. Some items greatly depreciate in value, so if you intend to replace an item after your travels then why sell it in the first place?

The Budget

On any trip abroad there are lots of things to budget for and you do not want to cut corners or make a financial mistake as it will cost you in more ways than one. For those who are joining an organization or a tour company, all the costs will have been worked out and they will be able to inform you of any other money you may need, or what is not included in the price. If you have a Student Card you may be able to get a discount on your plane ticket or other items.

The prices below are a general guide.

- Plane ticket and travel to and from the airport, plus taxes if not included in the cost of the plane ticket.
- Visa – prices vary between countries, from nothing to $200 (£125), though most are around $50 (£31).
- Inoculations and jabs – within the UK many are free; others range from £40-60 ($60-100). Jabs x3 against the rabies virus are around £120 ($192), and need to be repeated if you get bitten by a rabies carrier. (I've never had a rabies jab).
- Medication – anti-malarial tablets from £50-100 ($80-160) for a six-month supply, plus a private prescription.
- Travel Insurance from £50-200 ($80-320) for three months to a year. Prices vary between companies.
- Cost per day – which must include accommodation, food and transport.
- If you are seeing lots of sights, museums, festivals, art galleries, gardens, theme parks or participating in skiing or go-karting etc., then add the projected cost into the budget.
- Money for guides, a translator and vehicle hire etc.
- Tools and materials for any humanitarian aid and gifts for your host or for the community etc.

- Emergency money – 10% extra on top of your calculated total, just in case!

Cost per Day

The smaller the daily budget, the more strains and tensions that will arise, especially when travelling with a group of friends. If your daily budget is tight, you may find yourself haggling over pennies and cents; a fraction of the cost of a chocolate/candy bar – and in that situation your travels can begin to lose its pleasant flavour. If your budget is slim and you get financially exploited, then it may take weeks to recover from your loss or overspend in the only overpriced hotel in town. Some towns are more expensive than others and whilst you may overspend in one place, you can make savings in others, assuming you move locations. Accommodation on the outskirts of a town is frequently cheaper than in the centre.

Based on two people sharing a room, an extra £4 ($6) per person a day in a developing country can make all the difference between a flee pit of a room and one that is adequate, whilst in Europe, the difference between adequate and nice can be an additional £25 ($40) per person (depending on location). If you are staying at a youth hostel in a dormitory then the cost per person in Europe is around £15-30 ($24-48) per night in a big city like London, Paris or Rome, but is often cheaper in other locations within the same countries. The cost in Eastern Europe is cheaper than Western Europe. Youth hostels can be cheap, however, in China, you can get better facilities and at a lower cost in many hotels!

Most rooms are only used for half a day (at night) because in the daytime you will be outside exploring the sights, unless you are semi-nocturnal and sleep most of the day. If you are based in one location for weeks or months, then it is easier to work out the cost of living. If you will be in several locations, even across countries you will need to take an average projected costing of the entire trip.

The cost per day of your travels must include: accommodation, food and transport. If you will be going in pairs (or more) you must include your budget and your friends budget to get the total daily budget. For living expenses, if the cost per day is £24 ($38) for two people, this means a personal budget of £12 ($19) per day – this includes accommodation, travel and food. £12 ($19) per person per day (going in pairs) might be ok for South-East Asia, but in parts of Africa would be a stretch and would be nigh impossible in some African countries, such as Zambia or South Africa, where £18+ ($29+) per day is more realistic. Don't forget your entertainment money, such as additional costs for a music festival, go-karts, skiing, a flight over Mount Everest, day trip to Myanmar, France or Macau etc. Sometimes for lower cost entertainment, this expense can be taken out of the daily budget, but a £200 ($320) festival ticket would be difficult to accommodate and would be an additional cost to add onto your budget.

If you are doing a lot of travel inside a country then you may need to increase your budget to accommodate the extra miles of travel on public transport or fuel for the hired bus.

If travelling with your best friend, then you'll probably be eating together at the same restaurant, fast-food outlet or roadside food stall, so you could have a common pot with all things shared; this can be an easy financial solution to paying the bills. One person is often designated as the treasurer and each person gives x amount into the money pot each week. However, disagreements can arise if your friend eats twice as much as you or only buys the expensive meals or branded fizzy drinks instead of the cheaper local ones. One person may have a real thirst and order more than you'd like. Other best friends or paired up travellers (you meet on the trip) pay for each meal individually, thus avoiding any fiscal tension.

> My friend and I spent two weeks in North Africa, seeing the sites and soaking up the sun. I enjoyed it so much I planned to go back on another occasion and asked my friend, "What would you do differently, if you went again?" "Eat better food!" he replied. Frank – Morocco.

Group Travel

If you are the designated leader of a small group of friends then you don't want to be taking them to flee pit accommodation! If you are fixed in a single location, renting an apartment for two weeks, a month or longer may be a better fiscal proposition, with amenities to cook meals. A larger budget per person may be needed for a group, unless you are renting an apartment or a complex. One group of fifteen people rented a house in Brazil with a swimming pool for two weeks and it was considerably cheaper than staying in a hotel. In a hotel it is cheaper for two people to share the same room than if you have two single rooms. Some rooms can accommodate four or more people and therefore you pay less than if you have two rooms, though with less privacy and space. However, unless you are unwell, you will probably spend less time in your room per day and more time outside, seeing the sights and enjoying yourself.

For a group, if you are a leader taking a group of people travelling then each member should be allocated some personal money per week so that they can buy a drink or a snack when they want to. Otherwise the leader or the treasurer may be pestered every ten minutes, by thirsty or hungry travellers. If you are not self-catering, set a value for each meal, then each traveller can order what they want to that value. If their meal is more expensive, they then pay the extra. If it is under, they do not pocket the difference.

You can live and eat as cheap as you want to, but cockroach and rat infested hostels and rooms will get you down after a while, and can be damaging to your health. It is a false economy and can dampen your mood, making your travels less enjoyable. Large teams cannot cope with poor accommodation. A mixed team of eight to ten people will need better accommodation and better food than just two people participating on their own travels who are more happy to go with the flow. Within any large group, there will be greater needs (the higher probability of more particular people) and by budgeting in additional finances, it will make it easier for the group and hopefully, reduce the chances of illness, bedbug bites and grumblers!

Once a daily budget has been worked out, it needs to be double and triple-checked. You cannot afford to make a mistake. Then you need to add the plane ticket, visa (if needed), travel insurance (individually or as a team), any materials you may be taking with you for humanitarian work. Members of your team may need inoculations, jabs and medication (anti-malarial tablets). As a team, you may be able to negotiate a group rate with you local doctor/physician or health clinic. You should always add ten percent on top of your total budget. This is 'emergency' or 'unforeseen circumstances' money.

Natural disasters can occur at any time. Every team leader would be wise to consider having an emergency evacuation plan for the team (or a team member), not only for medical emergencies, but in cases of terrorism and natural disasters etc.

All journeys have secret destinations of which the traveller is unaware – Martin Buber.

Travel Insurance

As a general guide, travel insurance is around £50-250 ($80-400) for three months to a year, depending on age and any previous health issues. This is assuming you will not be participating in any extreme or winter sports and you do not need your expensive electrical gadgets covered. You will probably have to get a backpackers or gap year type travel insurance as many insurance companies do not extend cover for lengthy periods of time, though you can get annual worldwide cover at a premium price. Sometimes worldwide excludes USA and Canada. Some European cover can exclude certain countries. If you're only doing your travels in one country or continent it should be cheaper than if you will be passing through several continents. If you are part of an organization or tour company, they may be able to advise you or recommend an insurer. Always check to see what you are covered for *and* what you are not covered for, and what the *excess is. *How much you have to pay for the first or each claim. If the excess is £150 ($240) and you put in a claim for £160 ($256) the insurer will only reimburse you £10 ($16). Is it worth the time and effort to recoup the value of a phone top-up? Especially, if you are only permitted to make one claim within the expiration period of the insurance.

I do not advise travelling abroad without travel insurance and be very diligent in filling out the application form. Always put in the correct details, otherwise your cover may not be valid and an undisclosed medical condition can invalidate your insurance. In late July 2009, a British woman became critically ill whilst on holiday in Barcelona, Spain. The 35-year-old mother of two collapsed with a heart attack and fell into a coma. She had booked her travel insurance online, but because the wrong dates were filled in, her insurers said she was not covered. The family faced a medical bill of thousands of pounds and it was reported that they had to pay £18,000 ($28,800) for an air ambulance to England, UK.

Shop around online for good insurance deals and remember that if you participate in extreme sports e.g. bungee jumping, cliff jumping or jet-skiing, you may not be covered. These sports can also end your travels because of injury.

'Acts of God' are not covered and this can include volcanic ash shutting down entire flight paths over many countries. Some airlines by law are responsible for their stranded passengers and 'reasonable compensation' can be claimed, e.g. hotel bill. Always read the small print (however tedious) and remember that most policies do not cover expensive electrical goods, laptops, digital cameras and only a limited amount of cash. Always keep the details of your travel insurance emergency telephone number and policy details handy. In some countries, you can have two broken legs and be lying in a hospital corridor, but you will not be treated unless you have the means to pay!

For European citizens, the free European Health Insurance Card (EHIC) entitles you to reduced cost (or sometimes free) healthcare and treatment within the European Union (EU), and the European Economic Area (EEA), which includes Switzerland and Iceland. It is not a substitute for travel insurance. The UK voted to leave the EU on 23 June 2016 and how this pans out is an uncertainty.

Chapter 12

How to Travel with Money

Nobody wants to be robbed of their possessions whilst travelling or be stuck abroad with no money. This chapter covers the methods of travelling with money; using ATMs (cash points), hard cash and other financial options. An independent traveller may have additional financial concerns, which a participant with an organization or tour company would not. If you are going on a trip across many nations for a lengthy period of time, then a selection of financial options are the best; hard cash and cash cards, so that if one option fails or is limited in one area, there is another method to fall back on. Make sure your credit card is set-up to be paid off in full every month.

I have always travelled with hard cash (American dollars and British pound sterling), alongside cash cards and credit cards. Euros are also good unless the European Union (EU) breaks up. On 23 June 2016, the UK voted to leave the EU (Brexit) and has two years to negotiate, from when it officially notifies the EU of its withdrawal.

Travelling with lots of money is all well and good, until you get robbed! Wear a money belt under your clothes, but this can be tricky at airports with the rise of jihadists and suicide belts. I do not recommend the following two methods, traveller's cheques and prepaid card, but they may be great for you.

Traveller's Cheques and Prepaid Card

Traveller's cheques have a high rate of commission and in some developing countries, they are not widely accepted or *only* certain brands can be cashed.

With a prepaid Travel Money Card (TMC), the Financial Services Compensation Scheme does not always apply; there are many restrictions on its use, and generally higher fees than a cash point transaction. I have never used this.

A Visa Prepaid CitizenCard (which you apply and buy) doubles as proof of identity and age. The minimum age is twelve. A fee of from 0-3% is taken from the amount of money put on the card (a load up) and a fee can be incurred when you withdraw money. I have never used this.

Mobile Banking and Cash Points/ATMs

Some people prefer mobile/cell banking and pay their bills by means of a phone transfer or via an App on their smartphone. In one East African country, many of its citizens use their mobiles/cell phones (not smartphones) to send and receive money, and to pay for smaller purchases. I have never used this. A number of companies like PayPal and Apple Pay also work via your laptop, Tablet, smartphone or iPhone.

Most capitals of the world have Automatic Teller Machines (ATMs), commonly referred to as cash points. Cash cards/debit cards are a great fiscal blessing for travellers. As the years tick by, cash points that accept VISA or MasterCard continue to grow and are located in more and more towns and even obscure villages. However, in some districts or countries, one or the other is not widely used, though in my experience, VISA is more widely accepted. If you are going to stay in a particular town in a developing country, search online to see if there are ATMs that will accept your cash card. Find out online or use a guidebook to discover if there are any cash points outside of the capital (or major cities). Make sure you take enough money to last you to the next cash point or beyond.

Most financial institutions charge for cash withdrawals abroad when using their VISA or MasterCard debit card. This is generally a set fee of £1 ($1.60) or more, plus 2-5% of the transaction amount. The bank ATM from which you withdraw may also charge a fee. Take out the maximum amount in each transaction rather than use the ATM twice a week. Institutions that do not charge a set fee, offset their costs via the exchange rate and that is not in your favour.

It is important that you inform your bank/building society and credit card provider that you will be using your cards abroad. Ask them to make a note on their records, as transactions out of the ordinary may be deemed as fraudulent and your card may be cancelled or swallowed by the ATM and you will not get it back! Also, make sure that your card will not expire when you are on your travels. Getting a new card shipped out by courier is expensive.

Credit Cards and American Dollars

Credit cards should be used responsibly and not to incur debt when travelling. If you are not paying your balance off *in full* every month then you should not be using them (the same with a charge card). When abroad, I use them to buy plane tickets and hire vehicles and they also carry your insurance excess if you have an accident. I have known people to go on holiday/vacation and become incredibly ill and hospitalised. One couple had to use their credit card to pay their $10,000 (£6,250) hospital bill which was later reimbursed by their travel insurance.

You can withdraw money from cash points using your credit card (a Cash Advance) but I do not recommend it. You will get charged daily interest at a high rate, and some cards also charge a transaction fee or a non-sterling fee for UK card providers. Some businesses add a handling fee when you pay by credit card. Credit cards may be swiped through the machine twice, thus charging you twice. You may not realise this until you have checked your statement at home and weeks or months could have elapsed! If you bank online, be cautious when using the internet abroad. You can ask a family member to open your mail and check your monthly statements for you.

The American dollar is a strong currency; it is stable and is widely used across the world. In many countries in South-East Asia (e.g. Cambodia, Vietnam), you can pay for your purchases (even at some restaurants) in dollars, whilst some establishments prefer it, and countries that have hyper-inflation, like Zimbabwe, where the value of a basket can be worth more than all the Zimbabwean notes you could put in it, and each note could be worth a trillion!

Most embassies will expect you to pay for their visa in American dollars and you have to pay airport taxes in developing countries in dollars, if this tax was not included in the price of your plane ticket.

I have never had denomination (bills) of higher than $50 and have travelled with mostly $20 bills. In South-East Asia, they are very keen on $1 bills and as with most foreign notes, they have to be clean and crisp. If they are marked or creased some Foreign Exchange Bureaux (FEB) or shops will not accept them. Smaller denominations of $1, $5 and $10 also occur a lesser exchange rate than larger bills. Always take a combination of bills and keep them in a waterproof money belt hidden under your clothes.

In the fourth week of January 2009, the American dollar to British pound sterling rate changed to $1.35 to the £1.00 (a 23-year low), rebounding a week later to $1.39. If a person in Britain exchanged £1,000 (as compared to the November 2008 rate, which was $2.00 to £1.00), they would have lost $650 (£406) worth of purchasing power.[1]

Street Money and Foreign Exchange Bureaux
Be very careful when exchanging money, not only at a Foreign Exchange Bureaux (FEB), but *especially* at border crossings with street money. At border crossings there are often a number of people on the street exchanging money. More often than not, they will approach you. Haggle for the best rate between the workers, but make sure you know what the *general* exchange rate is. In some places, it is very public like on one border crossing between Nepal and India, men with wads of notes sat on stools with their money on small tables. Some money exchangers work for the same boss and will tell you anything and everything so as to line their own pockets

and give you a bad deal! Do not go down a back alley or into the back of a shop when exchanging street money. You may have to be discreet, but you do not want to be hidden, just in case things turn bad. You need to be able to scream/shout and be heard or to make a public scene, not that I have had to do either, but it is better to be safe than sorry. In addition, have the amount of money you want to exchange handy, do not pull it out of your money belt or reveal that you have much more money in your wallet or purse – you could be robbed. Make sure you do the exchange rate calculations on your own calculator as some may be fixed and not in your favour! Exchange enough money for a day of travel, food, and accommodation, until you reach the next ATM. For my brother and myself, this is often $50 (£31) between us. We always have British pound sterling and American dollars on us, just in case. Looking at new money can be confusing. Take your time and count the money out, do not be hassled or rushed and check each note/bill that it is the correct denomination with the right amount of zeros on it. Beware of distraction techniques, "Police are coming!" Or "What is that?" as they point the other way, so as to take your eyes off the money. Beware of groups of men surrounding you, only deal with the person you agreed to exchange with, he may have one or two friends with him, which I have found quite standard.

With FEBs, beware of a commission rate which is deducted from your money. This can make the good exchange rate not so good as money is creamed off the top and into their pocket, not yours! Always ask for mixed denominations as a wad of pre-counted money in single bills may lack one or two notes, and you always need small notes/bills for low value purchases from little shops and food stalls. Look confident as you examine the notes, as if you know what you are doing! It is always helpful to look on the internet to see what the country's bills look like as you do not want to be handed worthless out-of-circulation notes. Whilst exchange rates vary by the minute, check online to see the *general* exchange rate and try to get the best rate.

Most major currencies can be purchased within your own country, but where and when you buy it, can vary greatly. Research has shown that it does depend on picking the right place and the right time, though the latter is not so easy to 'predict' but research in the former is easier – shop around for the best deal! In the UK, you can often get a better rate if you exchange £500+ ($800). Differences between rates can seem deceptively slim, but if it is not in your favour, it can quickly push up the cost of your budget travels! The person who exchanges 'last minute' whilst at the airport or an international train station will get the worst rate. Beware of commission! Think ahead, plan and do your research.

Receiving Money

If you are abroad and you need money quickly you can use Money Gram or Western Union, the latter having more branches where money can be sent and received. The cost of a transfer varies from one country to the next, how you intend to pay, and whether the money will be collected as cash, or go into a bank account. A £500 ($800) transfer has a typical fee of between £10-40 ($16-64).

You can also have a relative transfer money from one bank or building society account to one at home or abroad. If the sending and receiving banks are of the same company then it is generally a free service, but sending money between different banks can costs upwards of £20 ($32) and can take up to one week. The receiving bank may charge for their service and exchange rates (which fluctuate) can drop significantly within a week. A family member at home could deposit some money into your bank account, which you can withdraw via your debit card.

When we were in India, we used the HSBC ATM inside the headquarters at Delhi. It was great to be in an air-conditioned building and we took timeout to cool down and to relax on black faux leather seats, away from the noise and the hustle and bustle outside.

Selling Blood and Body Parts

I have read in some travel books that people who are really hard up can sell their blood to hospitals or clinics. I cannot recommend this. If there is poor hygiene you could end up catching a disease from a second-hand unsterilised syringe etc. You should not even consider selling part of your kidney or a lung! If you are in a bind, you can barter some of your belongings for services, or work for food and accommodation.

Good planning is the best prevention of trying to eliminate needing extra cash by working out the correct costs, the total budget and cost per person.

If you get robbed of everything, your money and cards have been taken, so has your bag, contact the police and ask them to contact your consular. The consular should be able to assist you in repatriation, or advise you on what can be done and what cannot be done, however, don't expect any money from them to carry on your travels!

In Sudan, we travelled for a time with three Japanese tourists, two of whom woefully underestimated the cost of their travels. By day three, they had phoned home, asking their families' to wire them some money. Pre-planning is essential to avoid a potential financial crisis.

Chapter 13

Make Your Money Go Further

You have saved for months, if not years, worked hard and scraped together enough money for your travels, so spend it wisely and make your money go further. Economising whilst on your travels can come in many shapes, sizes and varying ways and if you have learnt to economise at home then on your trip it should be just as easy. If you are the sort of person who blows your monthly wage before payday, then you must have restraint on your travels or you'll end up coming home early, as you will have run out of cash.

The following helpful truths will allow your money to go further and to decrease the number of times you pay over the odds for items or services. One of the best tips is to *always* ask the price before you agree to purchase; haggle and shop around for the best deal. The same principles applies to hiring a taxi, buying a coach ticket or buying from a market seller. As the old saying goes, if you look after the pennies (or cents) the pounds (or dollars) will take care of themselves. Many sellers do not have the price labels on their good and will automatically inflate the prices for foreigners, so haggling is often essential. Even the price of a tube of toothpaste in the marketplace can be cut in half if you haggle. This is not a case of taking advantage of the stall or shop owner, but the owner trying to take advantage of you! At other times, the cost of an item in the market or on the street may seem so reasonable that it is only fair to pay them what they ask without quibbling or haggling. Do not try to beat a market seller down by minute amounts (the fractional cost of a small chocolate/candy bar) when that extra will make all the difference to them and not to you.

The price of a bottle of water and food can vary from one shop to the next. The amount of money saved per bottle may seem little, but over many months it adds up! The manufacturer's recommended retail price (MRRP) may be printed on the product label but a shopkeeper may want you to pay more. Point out the correct price. If they still disagree, go to another shop and pay the correct price. The exceptions are when the product has travelled far, like a seller on the Sepic River in Papua New Guinea in the middle of the jungle, or high up on a mountain plateau in Tibet.

If the seller begins to laugh once you have handed over the money, you know that you have paid over the odds. Pay a fair price for a fair product. If you have been financially exploited by a guide or tout etc. put it down to experience and learn from it.

In India, I was taken aback at the entrance fee for tourists at the famous Taj Mahal. It seemed very high but then I realised that compared to Western prices it was about the same. It is just a bit off putting when the locals pay one sixteenth of the cost compared to a foreigner!

For some tourist attractions, you may have to pay a donation, a suggested amount to enter a museum or a religious building. If you do not have the exact amount, don't be surprised if you are not given any change! In some museums and galleries etc. you are permitted to take photos, but not flash photography. Signs will notify you of this; selfie-sticks are banned in many museums and a number of stately homes, sport events and at some theme parks. At some places you have to pay a fee to use your camera (including a mobile/cell phone camera), and an additional fee if you want to film with a camcorder. These fees are for non-commercial purposes.

Pre-Booking Tours or Transport

Pre-booking tours or transport (coach or train) through an agent is more expensive than doing it yourself, but it does save time, though problems can be encountered. I rarely pre-book accommodation if just two people are going (often my brother and I), simply because four times out of five, I have experienced problems and once you are on the ground, you can see what is available and often get the best deal. Ask the locals.

Hotels, lodges and guesthouses often display star ratings and the lower the star, the lower the price, though this is not always the case! Accommodation in some countries it appears is unregulated, except those used by tour companies. In China (and once in Mongolia) we found the local hotels cheaper and much better equipped than the youth hostel or accommodation recommended by the guidebook. The advantage of an independent group is often purchasing power – you can go to a more upmarket hotel (e.g. 2 or 3 stars) during low season and pay the same as you would in one of a lesser quality (e.g. 1 or 2 stars). Often on travels, we ask the receptionist or manager if they have any cheaper rooms or if they can do a better deal. The worst they can say is no, and the best is a discount or an upgrade. Have a poker face and be prepared to walk away. The cost of accommodation varies greatly and most towns have several hotels or guesthouses, whereas some streets are full of them.

You can rent an apartment or large house for two weeks, a month or longer. Often this is easier with a person on the ground making the arrangements. High season is holiday/vacation season or at times of religious festivals and occasionally the demand can outstrip the supply, and that is when room prices/house rentals can be greatly inflated. You spend the same amount of money, but for less quality, you may get to share your room with cockroaches and other vermin! This can be the negative side of extreme budget travel.

You may stay in many different types of accommodation, such as a hotel, motel, youth hostel, lodge, inn, B&B, guesthouse, campsite or university accommodation (outside of term time, often in the summer). If you are staying on a campsite you have to take additional gear with you (tent, sleeping bag, perhaps a cooking stove etc.) and security is not great. For those frequently on the move, you may wish to purchase some address labels, instead of having to write your name and address every time you check-in.

> One man, before he got married travelled around Europe for three months using a special rail card. He used to sleep in the train at night and wake up in the morning in a new city or a new country!

How to Save Money
When it comes to your travels there are many ways to save money, to stretch your budget. The following are suggestions to consider.
- Shop around for the best deals.
- Negotiate a discount.
- Avoid the expensive hotel restaurant.
- Buy bread and fruit from the local market.
- If with a group of friends, consider self-catering.
- Go to the local restaurant, cafe or street vendor.
- Rent or buy a second-hand bicycle when you arrive.
- Take the bus instead of a taxi around town.
- Take a coach for longer distances instead of the train, as it is frequently cheaper, though slower.
- Travel overland across borders instead of flying. It takes longer, but you'll see more.
- The cost between hotels, inns, guesthouses, lodges, B&Bs, motels and hostels do vary.
- It is considerably cheaper to have two rooms with four people in each, rather than to have four rooms with two people in each. Is renting an apartment cheaper?
- Do I really need air-conditioning (AC), a heater, a computer, a fridge or a TV in my hotel room?
- Sleep on the beach, if it is safe to.

> I have been to Nepal twice, but have never splashed out on a one hour flight to see Mount Everest. Due to weather conditions, it is a bit hit and miss and often covered in cloud.

Souvenirs and Presents
- Do you really need to buy it?
- Haggle and do not pay more than what you want to.
- If you are buying a gift for your host or new friend, make sure the item has a function, and not a mantelpiece object.
- If you are buying gifts for your family or friends back home, then make sure that they will fit into your rucksack/ backpack or suitcase and will travel well. Who wants to bring back a broken vase?

In Dhaka, we could not get off a rickshaw without the driver *always* demanding much more money than what we had agreed. On our arrival in the capital, a local businessman told us, "Only pay what you have agreed, not a *Tak more." Mark – Bangladesh. *The local currency.

A False Economy
There is a time when economising to stretch your budget is a false economy. Eating street food can be one of the best culinary experiences whilst travelling; it is frequently cheap and fulfilling, but on occasions can make you unwell. Fresh fried food I have found to be the safest option, and I have always asked the vendor to put it back in the boiling frying oil, or on the fire to burn off any germs as you don't know how long it has been sat around!

In the UK, I have never travelled first class on a train, but in developing countries I have. Sometimes it is worth paying more for peace of mind and added security whilst at other times it is merely foolish indulgence. In the case of train travel by night I have always paid the extra to have a bed and if possible a berth/compartment. At some ticket offices, it is assumed that you will have first class because you are a foreigner. For short journeys you may wish to travel 2nd or 3rd class. You can travel on a night bus or train, thus saving the cost of a room, but you may not get a good night's sleep.

When you are travelling across a country on public transport, or taking frequent journeys every few days for months on end, then these savings add up.

In the Pacific, at the end of our trip, I changed all of the team's local currency into U.S. dollars and lost lots of money because of the poor exchange rate. Only afterwards did I notice that British pound sterling was a good rate, but by then it was too late. I could have saved loads and changed the British pound sterling back in the U.S. Tim – Papua New Guinea.

Chapter 14

Time is Money – Remunerations

If the Western adage is true, 'time is money,' then those who have helped you on your travels should not be overlooked. They should receive remuneration, money or goods for their assistance and this needs to be worked into your budget. If you are part of an organization or tour group then these financial issues are not your responsibility. It is one thing for a local to give you five minutes of their time, but quite another when they go out of their way to take you where you need to go. Do not take advantage of the generosity of others. Many people live a hand-to-mouth existence. You may be looking for a specific place or have asked them where the correct bus pick-up point is and it may not be as simple as round the next block. The difficulty can be in trying to evaluate how much you should give a person who has gone out of their way to help you when you have approached them. However, if they have travelled thirty minutes from their home, it is still a thirty-minute return journey and you have encroached upon an hour of their time. What you earn in a week or just a day, may take someone in a developing country a month or more to earn. It is always helpful to find out the average income of the country you are going to. Travellers should not be cashcows, dispensing money and gifts at random.

> Around one billion people (1,000,000,000), more than one in seven people on the planet, survive on less than £1.25 ($2) a day.

Hiring a Guide or an Interpreter

You should agree on some financial remuneration before your hire your guide, driver or interpreter. If they are freelance what is their fee? Or make them an offer, you will pay x amount per hour or day. English may be their second language and they might not be tied to any particular job and could be flexible. Some people charge by the hour, half a day or a whole day.

Before hiring an interpreter or a guide, I have always had a little chat with them to make sure that I can understand them and that they can understand me – many things can get lost in translation! At the Rock Churches at Lalibela, Ethiopia, the guides work on rotation. We could not understand our designated guide and so asked for another. Before we looked around a huge temple complex in Luxor, Egypt, we asked the guide some questions about a particular pharaoh and his relation to ancient Israel to see if he knew his stuff. He was truly an expert so we employed him and his expertise to take us to the monuments and reliefs we wanted to see.

A local may have been a great assistance to you (or the team), so how can you repay them? Give them money or a present or invite them for a meal. Some locals will be hesitant, reluctant or shy to order when you take them to a cafe or food outlet; to them, the cost may be prohibitive – or just a new experience. Others are used to eating only one or two meals a day. Remind them that you are paying the bill and encourage them to order what they want. You may find that on occasions, a person may get over-excited and order too much food. In some countries, individual food items are ordered and everybody around the table (or on the floor) tucks in; there is no *individual* meal. Some out of politeness will order a plain meal, others will order more and take the remainder home for their family. If you are aware of this, then you know at least one way to bless a person who is helping you over many days. As a team, you could buy a large bag of rice, maize, potatoes or other staple food, alongside additional items that are not perishable, and give them some money so they can buy (or spend it on) what *they* deem most important.

Sometimes the person does not have the term's fees for their children's education or next month's rent. In comparison to the West, this is small in developing countries. When giving money, state who it is for, especially if the money is for personal use. If giving money to a leader or a charity, if the money is for his or her personal use make this known. If the money is for the charity, make this very clear. Some people think it is crass to hand over money – most recipients don't! If you think it is crass, you can still buy and pay for items instead of handing over money.

> In June 2016, a report stated that the 62 richest people on the earth were worth more than the poorest 50% of the world, about 3,700,000,000 (3.7 billion) people!

When to Pay

Experience has taught me that it is best to handover any money, items or an agreed wage to a person at the end of their service. However, when they are with you, you should always pay for their transport (e.g. bus and train tickets etc.) and meals, as and when the need arises. If you are employing a guide to go trekking with, make sure they have the right equipment and correct footwear. You cannot expect them to sleep under the stars while you have a tent to keep you dry. Do you expect your guide to be your cook as well or do you all participate in essential duties and chores? It is important that each person knows what is expected from them. If you have a guide or interpreter for several weeks, then he or she may prefer payment each week because they have a family who are dependant on them and bills have to be paid. Some may want half the money upfront. Agree on a fee, so that no one feels cheated at the end. You also need to ask yourself, does the interpreter have enough money to take the bus back to his own home or will he have to walk five miles every day? At times, a person may prefer to keep the money and walk because the needs of their family are great. If you have gone on a 50 mile (80km) trek do you need to buy a one-way ticket so that the guide can get home again? These are some things that need to be thought about and talked through before your trip begins.

On occasions, some guides who have been hired for just an hour (and rickshaw drivers) will have temper tantrums when you pay them – even though you agreed beforehand on the cost and destination! Be polite, hand over the money and just walk away. Don't let it sour the good time and experiences you had with the person, they are only trying to manipulate more money from you. Be strong, be firm, be polite.

Fixers

Fixers as the name suggest fix things. If you have a problem, they will deal with it or find a solution, whatever the problem. However, if you are working with an organization or local charity they will probably be able to assist. Most fixers receive payment for their help whilst many issues can be solved for free by asking someone on the street! However, top-end fixers intervene with the authorities on your behalf, like when a group needs a visa in a hurry, or a permit, when the consulate is closed or you need a land border crossing to stay open so you can get the team and its minibus through.

Chapter 15

What to Buy

You're going abroad on an adventure of a lifetime and you need to take some essential items with you. At a minimum, you will need a set of clothes and a bag; but at worse you will try to take several suitcases packed with all your favourite clothes; electrical goods and items that you 'just cannot' do without. When it comes to travel, less is best – travel light. However, some humanitarian groups take extra bags full of materials and supplies. If you are staying in one location then the contents of your bag can be heavier than if you have to carry it on your back and travel frequently on public transport.

Where you are going to and at what time of year dictates to you the type of clothing and items you will need. Where am I going to? What will the weather be like? If you know what the elements will be like then you can purchase items accordingly, however you probably have most items already. If it is hot then loose clothing is better, whereas if your location will be cold then multiple layers are more practical. Are you going in the rainy season? All these factors must be weighed and considered before you embark on your travels. Personally, I like to take clothes that wash easily (by hand) and dry quickly. I don't like wearing damp clothes and I need to know that my garments will dry well, even in winter, ideally within 8-12 hours. If you are staying in one place and there is an open-air clothesline, then it is not so much an issue. I once had to wear shorts for two days during autumn/fall whilst in Vietnam because my trousers/ pants had not dried. I since travel with two pairs.

Any humanitarian organization or tour group that you are a part off will be able to inform you of your needs and should be able to provide you with a recommended checklist of items to take, plus additional information. See chapter 16, What To Take – Kit List.

When it comes to items of clothing and a rucksack, I have always gone to a shop in person to try on the garment and examine the bag. Some items if purchased online can appear compact and light, but in reality, they can be heavy, uncomfortable or cumbersome. Like most things, if you need something in a hurry then you will probably pay over the odds for it. Ask yourself, "Will my purchase accomplish the job for that which I need it?" You may also wish to consider with electrical items: Is it lightweight, compact, reliable and do I really need it on my travels? Sometimes it's nice to have an enforced break from a WiFi enabled device or smartphone; whilst at other times, they do come in rather handy, or quite essential. A mini laptop, WiFi enabled, Tablet, iPad or smartphone can be a good asset, as many cafes, restaurants and accommodation around the globe have free WiFi. When I first went to Kathmandu, Nepal in 2003, there were lots of internet cafes and no WiFi, when I returned in 2011, most budget accommodation had free WiFi.

There are many gadgets you can take on your travels, some will enhance your trip and help you remember the people you met and the places you went to. All items can be stolen, lost or damaged and so can their power sources. Cables can easily fray and break.

Whilst most people like to look good, on travels it is advisable that you leave your bling at home. Chunky chains, gold watches, excessive jewellery, fancy handbags and designer labels are not practical, unless you are going to Monaco or Dubai, but is that really budget travel? Bling can make you standout as a target to rob.

Digital Items to Consider

It is recommended to have a spare set of rechargeable batteries for your camera, cost and weight permitting. Is your iPod or digital voice recorder only chargeable via a USB port? Remember to take a plug adaptor with you, as you can generally only find them in the capitals of developing countries in more expensive hotel rooms.

In Asia, free WiFi in cafes and accommodation is quite common. Power cuts are a regular feature of developing countries. If on the internet, write short emails and send them as soon as you can. Charge your equipment when you can, for if you procrastinate, you may find that when you want to, you cannot!

If you like photography, take enough memory cards for your digital camera so that you will not be limited in what you can shoot. More is better and whilst memories will fade, pictures can last a lifetime.

Mobile/cell phones can be a blessing but also a bane. They are great to have in an emergency, but not if you keep receiving calls or texts/SMS in the early hours of the morning, and you could end up with a whopper of a phone bill. On a trip of less than three weeks, I have generally taken a mobile/cell with me and the blessings have outweighed the disadvantages. Smartphones can also be great but be aware of huge data costs, turn off data roaming. Some Pay as you Go phones do not work outside of their designated country. If you feel that a mobile is a necessity for your trip, then you could get a new SIM with cheap overseas deals or buy a local SIM card and email your number to your friends.

In many developing nations, there are telephone shops, which consist of numerous phone booths for calling, whilst budding entrepreneurs in marketplaces use their mobile/cell phones to make money. You could buy an international phone card or stick to WiFi.

Essential or Practical Items

- Rucksack/backpack or suitcase or holdall with wheels. See the following chapter.
- A small day-bag, ideal for taking on the plane as hand/carry-on luggage with your essential items.
- Money belt, an essential safety feature to protect your excess amounts of money, your passport and cash cards. Not a bum-bag/fanny pack/belt bag. Women may prefer a neck wallet (a pouch that is hung round your neck), which is hidden under your top, a safe place for your passport or money. It is not as good as a money belt, but more practical if wearing a skirt or dress.
- Pocket calculator, which is reliable and sturdy.
- Breathable waterproof jacket (plastic raincoats make you sweat). If you are going to a cold and windy environment then you should consider it being windproof also.
- A sturdy pair of shoes or boots. If you are going into well below freezing temperatures, then specialist boots may be needed. Make sure you break any boots in before you depart. Wear them at home to get used to them.
- Scented foot insoles otherwise within a few weeks your footwear will stink! Think of your fellow room mates.
- Flip-flops/thongs for the shower or for in your room. Most budget accommodation has dirty concrete floors. You do not want to get a verruca or other foot viruses by being barefoot in the shower, or your room.
- A pair of sports sandals to give your feet breathing space if in warmer climates, can also be worn inside.
- Trousers/pants with zip-off legs are handy or a skirt with zipped or Velcro pockets (for security of your passport, wallet or purse) from any camping shop. Camouflage trousers are not advisable as you may be mistaken for military personnel and it is illegal for non-military to wear them in some African countries.
- First Aid kit. For an individual it is often better to make your own First Aid kit rather than buy an off-the-shelf one; visit your local chemist. Team leaders should buy a big one and add to it. An individual should take plenty of plasters/Band Aids, two bandages, anti-septic cream, safety pins and some medicines at a minimum. Safety pins have multiple purposes like holding your bag together, keeping your trousers/pants up if you are not good at using a needle and thread, or have just lost your button or broken your flies/zipper. If you are going to be doing a lot of trekking, consider taking fungicidal cream/antifungal cream.

- Mini Sewing Kit (matchbox size) which includes a few needles and various colours of thread.
- Small lightweight torch/flashlight. LED lights are more powerful. Headlight type torches are more practical than handheld ones because of early morning power cuts and at night, just when you are trying to pack your bag! Windup LED key ring torches are available.
- Cheap digital watch with alarm, day and date, built in light and ideally waterproof. It is easy to lose track of time and with early buses or trains to catch before sunrise, I have found a digital watch indispensable. If it does not have a light, you will be constantly waking up on the day of your departure trying to find your torch. Watches which measure altitude and temperature are interesting.
- Latest guidebook, backpackers type, I have always found useful for the cost of transport, accommodation, bus routes, places to stay, where to eat, history, scams to beware of, border crossings, area maps and visa costs etc.
- Pocket-sized phrase book. You may have a translation App on your smartphone.
- Journal – A5 spiral pad and a pen, or an iPad, Tablet or mini laptop/notebook + plug adaptor and power cable.
- Travel towel (micro-fibre type), they are very light.
- Suncream, sun hat, moisturiser & lip balm with UV protection.
- Compact umbrella to protect from rain and intense sun.
- Locks (key or combination) for your rucksack and two small ones for your side pockets, assuming you have a backpack. One medium sized lock for a hotel cupboard or for your room's door. Especially useful in cheap accommodation, for the door or an internal cupboard, though this lock is not always needed, but handy to have, just in case.
- Small pocketknife with scissors and tweezers at a minimum. This *cannot* be taken aboard a plane as hand luggage, or any sharp objects, liquids, creams and aerosols over 100ml. Do you need mosquito repellent? It should contain DEET.
- Travel sickness pills/tablets, they can also take the edge off a long journey to help you sleep.
- Toiletries: deodorants, toothbrush, creams, feminine hygiene products, razor or shaver, headache tablets, nail clippers, shampoo, toothpaste etc. Most of these items can also be bought on arrival. Share your toothpaste with a friend.
- Prescription for medicines and a spare pair of glasses. It would be unfortunate to have to wait till you return home to check your photos to see what your trip looked like in focus!

- Travel sink plug – so you can fill up your sink or bath tub.
- Small handheld mirror, a flip one is added protection.
- Small plastic or wooden doorstop to wedge on the inside of your room, when you are asleep or in the shower.

One or Other of the Following
- Silk bag liner or a lightweight 750-gram sleeping bag for basic or cold accommodation.
- Space/foil blanket, a pocket sized foil blanket that can be used in emergencies – or when cold!
- General sleeping bag, will you be camping? What rating do you need? The higher the rating the warmer and heavier the sleeping bag.

Do you Need
- A tent. A three-man tent is ideal for two people and their bags. The lighter and more compact a tent is the more expensive they are. If you both have individual tents (not recommended) then you will have to rent two pitches, a false economy.
- Do you need to take a cooking stove, *gas cylinders, plastic mug, plate and cutlery etc.? *Will it pass through security?
- Backpack cage for added security, especially if staying in a youth hostel with strangers, or on a night train. Downside is the weight, up to ½ kg.

David Livingstone was the famed missionary explorer of the mid nineteenth century who opened up central Africa to the world, exposed the vile trade of slavery and is revered in Malawi as the Father of Malawi. In 1856, he returned to England, having spent seventeen years in Africa. He had travelled over 11,000 miles; caught fever thirty times and had been endangered by seven attempts on his life! I am sure your travels will not be so extreme! Livingstone wrote: 'I have also found the art of successful travel consisted in taking as few impedimenta as possible, and not forgetting to carry my wits about me, the outfit was rather spare [sparse], and intended to be still more so when we should come to the canoe.'

Items Which you May Like to Take
Many of the items on this list are of personal preference:
- Compact video camera (+ tapes or SD cards) or smartphone.
- A digital camera and plenty of memory cards. It is better too have too many than too few.

- Rechargeable batteries for your camera (if needed), plus a spare set and a lightweight fast battery charger.
- Plug adaptor for the country you are going to and a shaver adaptor (two-pinned plug). Very important items.
- Personal Entertainment: iPod or MP3/4 player or ereader.
- Mini laptop WiFi enabled, (10 inch screen and cable can weight just 1.6 kg). An iPad, Tablet or smartphone is a lot lighter and may also be used in photography and/or video.
- Travel kettle with a plug (and not a 6-volt car adaptor). Some are supplied with two cups that fit inside the kettle. Great for tea, coffee, soups and for instant noodles.
- A rechargeable shaver, unless you prefer wet shaves.
- A hair dryer/drier, you may be able to use a friend's, so pair up with a friend and reduce the weight of your bag.

Other items to Consider
- Plastic bowl for noodles, cereals or instant soup.
- Plastic spoon and fork (as a single item) or chopsticks.
- Plastic cup, if not included with your travel kettle.
- Six pegs/clothespins, for your washing and for holding curtains closed!
- Thin string (5-8 metres) – which can be used as a washing line/clothesline or for holding things together.
- Spare pair of shoelaces for walking boots – after several hard weeks or months they can break at any time. Long shoelaces are hard to find in developing countries.
- Four A4 plastic wallets to keep documents safe and dry.
- Plastic or wooden doorstop, a great security device for when you are inside your cheap hotel room. You can also half fill a plastic bottle with tap/faucet water and put it on your door handle. If someone tries to get in, it will fall on the floor and wake you up!
- A gift(s) for your host and small gifts for when you are invited to someone's home for a meal.
- Change, so that you can phone home on your return.
- A photo of your loved one(s) who is at home, if not on your smartphone.

For medical and survival items + kit list see chapters 8, 10 and 16.

I have always been cautious of not taking too much or too few items on my travels. Unfortunately, it is often whilst you are travelling that you say, "I wish I had taken — and should have left — at home!" Long times of travelling are always a revaluation of one's possessions. James – Thailand.

Chapter 16

What to Take – Kit List

When it comes to clothes, within reason it is up to you what you want to take on your travels, though if you are going with an organization they will advise you of what you need and give a general idea of how many of each items. However, before you decide what to take; you will need a good backpack/rucksack, bag, suitcase or holdall to put it all in.

The bag that you will take on your travels is a vital component and there are many factors involved, but with some simple logical questions and answers, it will help you get the right rucksack/backpack, bag, suitcase, or holdall for you.

- Will it go as hand luggage?
- Can I carry the bag when full?
- Will I be transporting heavy materials?
- Is it more practical to carry the bag on my back?
- Will I be constantly travelling on public transport?
- Will I be staying in one place or multiple locations?

Your Bag

Rucksacks/backpacks are my preferred choice of bag for travelling abroad, but when I have to take heavy materials I use a suitcase with wheels. I have never come across the perfect backpack/rucksack. Backpack capacities are measured in litres/liters (L):

- 20-30L is a standard day-bag backpack/rucksack.
- 35+8L is what I first took to South-East Asia and it was too small and some items had to be left behind at home.
- 50+10L is what I used in Africa for 6 ½ months and on my second trip to Asia. It is my personal preferred size.

Anything above 60+10L may be too big to carry and a hindrance on public transport and anything above 80L is just excessive. However if you are in a single location and therefore not travelling regularly on public transport with your bag, it does not matter as much. If you are going on a trip to one fixed location and leaving items behind, then the weight and size of your bag, except the airline's baggage allowance is not an issue. There is nothing wrong with having a bigger bag except you may be tempted to fill it to its brim. Whatever rucksack, bag, suitcase or holdall you buy, make sure you can carry it when packed, and that it does not exceed the airline's baggage size and weight allowance! If you cannot carry it up a flight of stairs or lift it above your head to stow on a bus then you may have packed too many items. If you have a weak or bad back then a suitcase on wheels may be better, but it's no fun pulling it through the mud in the rainy season or across soft sand! If you think a suitcase is best for you then ask yourself, "Do I need wheels?" and, "Does it need to be a hard case?" Hard cases are heavier than soft cases and offer more protection for fragile items, but they have no give in them when trying to store in an overhead bus rack or under the seat and weigh more, though they can be used as a seat! Does your bag need to be lockable? Do I need compartments? Expensive luggage does not mean better or sturdier and lightweight luggage may get damaged easier.

> On my first trip, I took fresh clothes for every day. My suitcase was hard to carry, awkward on public transport and too big. Now I use a rucksack with just two sets of clothes, plus extra underwear. If I need more clothes, I buy local. Dirty clothes are normal in dusty developing countries, it's unavoidable when you travel. Nick – South America.

Airline Baggage Allowance

Airline baggage allowance varies between airlines and between countries, though 15-23 kilograms (kg) for check-in items and 5-7 kg for hand/carry-on luggage is a *general* rule. If you exceed your airline's baggage weight or size allowance, you will have to pay an excess baggage charge. This can vary considerably (from £4-34.50 ($6.50-55) per kg whilst some airlines charge a flat fee of £49.50 ($79) for up to 10 kg of additional weight! Other airlines base their charges on a percentage of the one-way economy fare, which are typically 1-1.5% of the fare per extra kg. On a long-haul flight, this fee can be large. Airlines can be flexible with charities and groups if you speak to them in advance.

Practical Clothing – Not Problematic

Remember that you are going travelling and not to a fashion show. What may be trendy or acceptable at home may not be practical or appropriate where you are going, though bring something smart to wear. Also, look presentable when passing through border crossings, otherwise you could be turned away as undesirable! There is no need to wear a suit, but just be clean, smart and polite.

The clothes you pack should reflect the type of climate you are going to. Take modest swimwear, as you never know when you may have the opportunity for a dip, use of a hot tub or a warm spring. Remember your wide rimmed sun hat if your ears are prone to burn, a long sleeved shirt to protect your arms from sunburn and by upturning your shirt's collar your neck is preserved from going red. Do you need to bring a pair of sunglasses/shades? In Africa and Asia they are frequently sold on the streets for around £1.90 ($3).

Wrong colours such as light green and light brown can show up sweat marks (or become see-through) and thus reveal, in sweaty climates patches of dark material, which can be embarrassing. Zipped pockets or with Velcro are essential as a prevention from being pickpocketed. Trousers/pants with zip off legs are handy, but set security metal detectors off!

Don't wear tight clothes and beware of having clothes that reveal too much. In some countries it is frowned upon, or even forbidden for women to reveal their shoulders or upper arms in public. Muslim countries are not enthusiastic with men wearing shorts above the knee. There are always exceptions to the rule, especially in tourist towns. Patriotic clothing, such as Union Jack shirts or the Stars and Stripes are best avoided and military clothing is a no-no. If you wear desert camouflage as the UK and US troops wore in Iraq and Afghanistan etc. and enter into some countries there may be retaliations against you. In some African countries, only military personnel are permitted to wear military style clothing. Be safe, use wisdom, be practical.

Wearable Kit List

The clothes within this kit list are a general guide and the quantity includes what you may wear on the plane, one set of clothes, your jacket and a sturdy pair of boots. I wear XXL clothes, which takes up more room than a size 14 and I travel light. Extra items that you deem most practical should be packed, but leave some space in your bag for items you purchase whilst on your trip. As a good rule of travel – pack less, wash your clothes frequently and take items that are relevant to your destination's weather conditions. The following is a lightweight list and what you should take as a minimum.

- T-shirt x 2.
- Smart shirt/blouse x 1.
- General shirt or blouse x 2.
- Trousers/pants or skirts x 2.
- Zipped fleece jumper/sweater x 1.
- Waterproof jacket x 1.
- Underwear x 4+.
- Socks x 4+.
- Hat, scarf and gloves x 1 (if applicable).
- A pair of sturdy boots (or flat canvas shoes if you prefer, but these can be uncomfortable on your soles when walking on gravel paths whilst wearing a heavy rucksack/backpack).

- A pair of sports sandals (if applicable).
- A pair of flip-flops/thongs.
- Shorts x 1.
- Swimwear x 1.
- Nightwear x 1 (or just a t-shirt and shorts).

Packing your Items and Team Materials

Before you pack, lay all your items out on your bed or on the floor, to see if you have everything (use a list and tick it off). Ideally, take two of each items: t-shirt, trousers/pants or skirts, (more for underwear), but only one jacket and one pair of flip-flops/thongs, and sandals. Remember, you will be wearing one set of clothes with you and can buy additional items whilst on your travels.

If you are part of a humanitarian organization or a religious group, you may be asked to pack some team materials in your bag. This evens out the weight and minimises loss if a bag is lost in transit.

Many items have been listed in this chapter and the previous one, but with careful packing, the vast majority of the items mentioned (excluding a tent, standard sleeping bag and video camera) can fit into a reasonably sized backpack/rucksack alongside a *small* carry-on bag. I use a micro-sleeping bag that weighs just 750 grams that will fit inside my backpack. You have to pack your bag intelligently and utilise your space. If travelling with a friend, one person packs the travel kettle, another packs the hair dryer/drier to even out the weight and space. It is not uncommon to pack and unpack your backpack or suitcase up to three times, as you juggle items and remove others. If you need two large bags to pack all your items then you have far too much! Wear heavy & bulky items on the plane.

If you have flip lids on your suncream or moisturiser and the seal has been broken, then when you travel it is advisable to tape them down and put each one inside a plastic bag. Arriving at your destination with suncream all over your clothes and equipment is not the best of starts to your travels. If you have a shaver or battery operated device which needs to be pushed up or down to turn it on, then you may wish to use tape to stop it from turning on accidentally. I was at an airport in Pakistan and I could hear this humming noise, but could not place it until I realised it was my beard trimmer which had moved in transit and the 'on' button had been knocked.

Hand Luggage/Carry-On Luggage

All essential or valuable items should be packed in a day-bag and taken on the plane as hand/carry-on luggage. Your rucksack or suitcase will be checked in at the airport. It should be at baggage reclaim when you are, but not always! You can always wear your heavier or bulky items (jeans, additional jumper/sweater, big boots, and jacket) with you onto the plane instead of packing them. Some travellers have worn multiple layers and got heatstroke!

- Passport size photos – if required for a visa on arrival.
- Medical insurance documents and any other important documents or paperwork.
- Guidebook and phrase book.
- Two to three days worth of medicines – in case your bag is waylaid or lost. Headache tablets and travel sickness pills.
- Any face creams or deodorant etc. The canister or container must be less than 100ml in size.
- Journal and pen.
- Laptop, iPad, Tablet, memory stick, and/or ereader.
- Mobile/cell phone or smartphone.
- Digital camera and/or camcorder.
- Anything else of value.

To Consider
- Some people recommend a change of clothes in case your bag is waylaid or lost. I have never needed this. For others, it is just a spare pair of underwear.
- Toothbrush, breath freshener or mints. Great for long haul flights.
- A power bank and cable for your smartphone.

Things to Take and Keep on You
- Digital watch with built-in light, alarm and date.
- Driving licence, credit card type, not a paper one for UK citizens.
- Money, money belt, debit cards and credit cards.
- Have the details of your country's Foreign and Commonwealth office to hand.
- Have a photocopy/Xerox of your passport, visa and travel details separate from the originals.
- Take your Yellow Fever Certificate and have it with your passport.

Don't Forget
- Your wallet and your money in your money belt.
- No sharp objects, such as scissors, nail file or penknife can be packed in hand luggage.
- Any canister, container or tube can hold no more than 100ml. You cannot take a 200ml tube that is half empty.
- Anything you do not want to see broken.
- Do not exceed the airline's baggage weight and size limit.

Social Networks and Big Brother

Social networks can be a good means of communication, but also an unwise means of letting the world know what you are doing, where and when. Are your settings private? Burglars love to read about people going away, the property is empty and ripe for the picking! Remember, not all your social media "friends" are genuine friends. Some contacts, you have never had face-to-face contact with. Do not vent your frustrations about a country, its leaders or beliefs on social networks. In some countries you could get arrested, fined or deported!

Many modern digital cameras are WiFi enabled (as are smartphone) and so photos can be uploaded directly to social media sites. Many digital cameras (and smartphones) also have GPS (Global Positioning System), where images are data-tagged with the latitude and longitude of your location. Be cautious of uploading data-tagged images in real-time from smartphones and digital cameras with the GPS function turned on. Turn off data roaming and automatic updates otherwise you will get a huge phone bill. Phone signals can be tracked by triangulation whilst some smartphones are the ultimate GPS tracking beacons! Big brother may be watching you!

Since the Arab Spring (2011) across parts of North Africa and some Middle East countries, the rule of law has broken down (or is in transition) and Western foreigners are more vulnerable than ever before. There are countries where I have been to in the past which are not as stable as they once were. I have been to Tunisia five times, yet more than three thousand Tunisians have left their beautiful country to join the Islamic State, (IS) also known as ISIS, ISIL, Daesh and Daish, more than any other citizens of any other country! But what about those who hold to the same beliefs, yet have stayed put, how many are lone wolves? Is it possible to track or follow you on social media, to kidnap or injure you? On 25 January 2016, the fifth anniversary of the beginning of the Egyptian revolution, an Italian student studying in Cairo, Egypt, for his PhD was abducted, tortured and killed. Nine days later his body was found. Cairo is a beautiful bustling city, I've been there, and many other cities across Egypt, but the reality is, Western travellers have to be more cautious and vigilant than ever before. In some countries there is a growing climate of suspicion around foreign visitors, often resulting in accusations of stirring up anti-government sentiment, spying or espionage! It all sounds very James Bond and to a traveller is ludicrous, but it happens.

In the wake of the Pokémon Go App, police in America had to warn players during the virtual 'treasure' hunt that they were being targeted by robbers because of the game's geolocation feature.

Chapter 17

The Plane Ticket and Review Sites

The plane ticket is often the heftiest part of any travel cost unless you are flying on a budget airline. You could pay more than £1,000 ($1,600) for a return/roundtrip trip to Australia, whereas the Orient (China, Korea or Japan can cost up to £800 ($1,300) and these prices are for economy class. However there are bargains to be had and airlines do have sales. Search on the internet or negotiate a group deal with an airline or through a travel agent/broker. During holiday and festivals (the peak season) prices increase, and will decrease during low season or as supply and demand dictates. The price of oil dramatically dropped at the end of 2015 and remained relatively low by mid-2016, reducing the cost of aviation fuel and therefore plane tickets in general.

Midweek flights are generally cheaper (Tuesday-Thursday) than at weekends as are those that depart or arrive at odd times of the day or night. Weekend flights are more expensive as is Friday and Monday. International airport departure taxes can be as high as £85 ($136) each way, unless you have a connecting flight then you pay tax on the first leg of the flight, thus reducing the cost, but increasing your travel time. If you use your credit card then a handling fee is often applied, from £3-9 ($5-14), but can be 1.5-3% of the ticket. Therefore, if your plane ticket cost £400 ($640), a 3% handling fee will be £12 ($19). Fuel duty can add an extra cost to your ticket even after you have bought it! On rare occasions, some agents will sell you a plane ticket without including airport departure tax; this you will have to pay at the airport. Some tickets are non-refundable and non-transferable. Make sure you put in the correct details, your name, time and date of departure, departing from, and arriving at, before you pay for the ticket.

Before you bag a bargain and book a plane ticket, look to see what time the flight departs and arrives before you purchase. It may depart at 10am in the morning, but can you drive the three hours to the airport (or catch the coach or train) and arrive within the two-hour check-in period, which means you will have to leave your home by 5am? But you still need to allow extra time for traffic, delays or to change a flat tyre/tire. Some evening flights mean that you arrive in the dark and will have to check straight into a hotel; unless you have pre-booked, you may pay more for your accommodation than you would like to. It can take up to 1 hour for baggage reclaim and then you have to take public transport, but often a taxi to your destination. Night-time taxis have a higher rate than day-time ones. If your proposed plane's return flight arrives late in the evening, will you be able to get a train or coach back home or be stuck at the airport until morning? Do not forget the cost of your travel to and from the airport. This may be by train, coach (minibus for a group) or by car and if it's the latter, you will need to budget the additional cost of a long stay car park/parking lot if you're going for less than three weeks. Long stay car parks/parking lots are always cheaper offsite in locked compounds than at the airport.

My evening flight into Cairo was delayed by three hours. I arrived in at 3am just as the airport was closing and there were no taxis. I had to negotiate with some of the airport workers for a lift into the city centre. I was in no hurry as finding a hotel at that time of the morning can be tricky. Newton – Egypt.

Travelling to a foreign destination is not a right, but a privilege and you may need a visa to enter the country. Some countries do not permit citizens of x country to enter their countries. Certain nationalities are barred from entry! Visa prices vary between countries and for different nationalities. Most consulates charge in U.S. dollars; the standard visa fee ranges from being free to around $200 (£125), though most are around $50 (£31) for a single entry visa. Multi-entry visas can cost considerably more and your visa may state by which method you can enter or exit the country – by land or by air, or state at which border exit. The cost of a visa can change from one month to the next, depending on diplomatic relationships and how hard-up the country is! In Asia and Africa, you *only* pay in U.S. dollars.

Some countries do not like permitting people into their country if they only have a one-way ticket. They are suspicious and think you may be a burden on their society, are up to no good or intend to overstay your visa of 10 or 28 days, one, three or six months.

When we booked a one-way flight into Cairo, Egypt, and a one-way flight from Cape Town, South Africa, back to London, UK, 28-weeks apart, the agent wanted to know if we understood how far the distance between both countries was, as she thought we had made an error. Some long-haul flights have a stopover and you may be able to spend a few days in that city (visa permitting) at no extra flight cost – it can be a cheaper option than buying two tickets for each leg of the journey. Make sure that the correct spelling of your name is on the ticket and keep the return/roundtrip ticket safe! To change the name on a ticket (or any minor detail) can incur an administration cost in excess of £100 ($160)! Confirm the time of your departure three days in advance and remind your friends!

Budget Airlines

Budget airlines, the no frills carriers are notorious for cancelling their flights when not enough seats have been sold and whilst you will get a refund, and a slim possibility of getting on the next flight, the problem is yours, not theirs. You may get a refund of the cost of the £30 ($48) early-booked budget flight, but to book another flight to the same destination could cost you in excess of £120 ($190) and all the inconvenience that delayed travel entails.

With budget airlines, real bargains can be had but you must always read the small print. Prices do not include taxes and duty, (air passenger duty), which in Britain inside Europe is presently £13 ($21) each way for economy class. The cheapest budget airline seats are sold well in advance. When the seat is "free," the taxes, duty and check-in luggage is not, nor is the handling fee and if you book over the phone this is an additional cost.

Additional budget airlines fees can include: Online payment handling fee, check-in if not done online, priority boarding fee (optional), check-in baggage per flight, as well as an additional fee for each bag. A fee for sport or musical equipment, flight change fee and a name change fee.

I have never had any problems flying with any budget airline, but their charges can considerably add up; and their 'add-on fees' alter frequently. Airport taxes have to be added onto the price of the flight which are set by the airport or government and are beyond the control of any carrier. There are no complimentary refreshments on budget airlines, but food or drink can be purchased in-flight at a good mark-up. Read the small print and the more you can do online, the cheaper it will be. Budget airlines are designed for those who travel light and who do not check-in luggage. If you can fit all your items in one bag and it is within the airline's weight and size specifications, take it as hand/carry-on luggage – it cannot get lost!

Getting a Good Deal
- Search different comparison websites.
- Speak to different travel agents.
- Do they give discount via a Student Card or for OAPs?
- Phone up and haggle for a better deal or an upgrade.
- Look on review sites to see if the good deal is actually good or will it be a let down!
- Search online for special offers and promotional codes or a discount voucher.

- Have a look at the company's social media pages for special deals or offers.

Comparison Websites and Travel Reviews

Comparison websites are a good way of looking for hotels, accommodation, flights or for hiring a vehicle, to see who can give you the best deal. Some sites cover all these aspects in one place. Other websites are solely for comparing hotel accommodation, whilst you can always rent a room in someone's home, or a place to lay your sleeping bag. You may wish to stay in a temple in Japan or in a monastery in Greece.[1]

Review websites for travel and accommodation are handy guides, but they are just guides to help you make an informed decision based on the experiences and the expectations of others. Reviews are subjective. What one person considers good value, another does not. If only negative comments are recorded or the reviews have a low rating, then the company, accommodation, home etc. should probably be avoided.

Remember, if you don't pay for 5 star travel then you should not expect it. Whilst we would like to think that all workers in the hospitality and leisure industry are there to make us feel special, they may be having a difficult day, and if we whinge, complain and are rude, then don't be surprised if they snap back or appear less than helpful! Try to be polite, calm and collective as this oils the cogs of progress much better than throwing a strop. Inconveniences arise, that's life, deal with it in a dignified manner.

Culture can also play a large factor and different things are acceptable and unacceptable from one country to the next, and the way things are done, differ. Time is important in the West, it is not so in many other countries where to turn up 1 hour late can be considered normal and is not classified as being late, but on time! In one city in South Africa, three times I had to walk down to reception to ask for a towel in this large hotel – all in the space of two hours!

In some cities, if accommodation or a place to eat has been recommended by name in a travel guide, then other establishments may change their name to muscle in! In Varanasi, India, we got a rickshaw driver to take us to Yogi Lodge as recommended by the guidebook. For a day or so, we wondered why our map did not seem to correlate with the local area, until we realised what had happened.

Chapter 18

Applying for a Visa

Do you have a valid passport and do you need a visa? Without a passport you cannot get a visa and some countries will not permit you entry unless you have a valid visa. A visa application can be turned down for a number of reasons. One student from the Republic of Korea (South Korea) was turned down from visiting Tunisia because they do not issue visas to the Democratic People's Republic of Korea (North Korea), it was an error in understanding the nationality of the applicant! Visa requirements change from one nationality to the next as do their costs. Some visas can be bought on arrival at a country, though this is more of a governmental money-making exercise because they do not check to see if you are an undesirable.

Is there enough blank pages in your passport for multiple visas, plus your Immigration and Departure stamps? If you are travelling the globe you will need a lot of blank pages; twelve countries equals twenty-four stamps (entry and exit) and potentially twelve visas. European citizens within the European Union will not have their passports stamped and do not need a visa for any European country. Some countries will expect you to have at least six months outstanding on your passport (or even a year) before they even allow you to enter their country or before they will issue you with a visa.

If you join a charity, NGO or go with a tour company, they will advise you on the type of visa needed and how to apply, what you should fill in under 'nature of your visit.' Visas can be Single Entry, Multiple Entry/Multi-Entry, Business/Work or Tourist. A Single Entry visa is often the cheapest and a Business visa the most expensive. With most countries, you can apply for your visa from your home country, some you get on arrival at the country of destination at the airport or on the border. If you are already in another country you may be able to apply for a visa from that country for your next destination. In Asia, some travel businesses will do the leg work for you and take your paperwork and passport to the embassy and bring it back. In your home country you may be able to pay a visa processing company to do this on your behalf via the postal service. Some British companies offer a visa processing service, where you post/ship your passport and completed application to them. This works well if you need two or more visas from different embassies.

Some visas are time sensitive, they begin on the day of issue and count down, from weeks to months. Forward planning is essential.

You may have to travel to the country's embassy to get a visa in person. At some embassies you have to go through an interview, this is after you have filled out the paperwork. Some embassies want to know not only your job, but that of your parents and grandparents!

On rare occasions, if abroad, some embassies will want to see a letter from your consular, for a British citizen, this costs £45 ($72)! In many respects, the embassy does not trust your passport as being genuine (or the look of the owner) and wants your own consular to confirm that the passport and the owner are genuine.

Some embassies insist on a 'letter of invite' before they will issue you with a visa. You can obtain one via email from a tour company, a hotel, an individual residing within the country or a company or organization, and print it out, so it becomes a 'letter.' Some hotels or guest houses will send you a letter of invite if you make a reservation with them, as will tour companies, when you make a booking with them; some government approved tourist companies will send you one for a fee (around $25). Some hotels will only send a letter (via email) *if* you make a reservation for three days, whilst others are not so stringent. Just email and ask for a letter of invite.

Some embassies are *only* open on certain days at certain times, and they frequently have long queues, so arrive early. Check that the correct visa has been issued to you and in your name. Some visas have been stuck in the passport of another person! Check your visa very carefully to make sure you have got what you have asked and paid for. Many years ago, to apply for a visa to India, I had to give my flight details and my ticket number. I had to buy my plane ticket *before* I could receive permission to enter the country!

We went to the Mongolian Embassy in Beijing, China, to collect our passports. It took 1 ½ hours in total. We got to the window after about a 40 minute wait (it opened from 4-5pm) and were told that we had to come back on Monday. We explained that we were told to come back on Friday. The man said as we had not done an express service it will take five day. "Yes" we said. "It has been five days!" The man began to count on his fingers whilst speaking aloud, "Monday, Tuesday, Wednesday, Thursday" – and stopped! He knew Friday (the day we were there) was the fifth day. He told us to wait, whilst he handed out other passports, and then did our visa before our eyes, alongside others who were in the same situation.

Some countries permit a transit visa for x amount of days when you are just passing through. The Russian embassy in Mongolia issues them for ten days if you are using the Trans-Siberian Railway from Ulaanbaatar, Mongolia to Moscow, Russia, which takes five days and four nights. On a transit visa, hotels in Moscow only allow you to stay two nights. If your plane does not depart until the third or fourth day, check-out after two days and check-in to a new hotel. Before we could get a Russian transit visa we had to buy our train ticket and an exit ticket out of Russia. We were told by an embassy worker that we could only spend two nights in any city and our plane ticket was for four nights in the capital. To change the dates on our plane tickets would have incurred a penalty of $170 (£106) each. We were advised by the tour operator who sold us our train ticket to submit the paperwork again the following day as 'rules' change with each worker. We got our visa without having to change our tickets.

Getting a visa can take a number of working days from when you apply for it and sometimes your passport can get lost in the system. The embassy may ask you to come back on another day. After a possible wait of a few hours and the inconvenience of having to travel to collect your passport. Be polite and persistent, tell them that you need your passport today as the working days have expired. You may have to wait an hour or two, or they may get your visa processed there and then.

Some travellers of different nationalities have been known to fly into a country, just to apply for a visa for another country because it is easy to obtain one in another capital city, other than their own country, or the country where they have come from on their travels. You can be turned down in your own country by the embassy staff for a visa for a particular country, yet be accepted when you apply in a different country!

> As Americans we took a flight detour to Poland in Europe to apply for a visa for Afghanistan. We were told it was easier to obtain one there than in Washington D.C., and it was! – William.

If you are an independent traveller then you do not need to tick the Business or Work visa box, unless you intend to work in the country at farm-stays, picking fruit and vegetables etc. For travellers, the Tourist, Visitor or Pleasure box can be ticked. Under the nature of your visit you are a tourist, unless you are signed up with a NGO or humanitarian group.

You can get visa extensions whilst inside a country (subject to the issuing staff, the embassies policies and your nationality) or often it is a case of leaving the country, which can be a simple land or sea border and re-entering on the same day, like Thailand to Myanmar and back, or within a few days or weeks. The embassy, your host or an up-to-date travel guidebook can advise on this. Policies can change without prior notice. In China in 2011, we had to book into a "government approved hotel" before we could extend our visa. We had to leave our great hotel for a pleasant stay in a youth hostel.

In Kathmandu, Nepal, we got our visa for the next country and took the bus. When we got to Dhaka, we realised that we could not leave the country by airplane unless we got our visas amended. This took half a day of travel and bureaucracy, to fill in the right forms, to get the correct stamps and the signature of the correct civil servant! Edward – Bangladesh.

In Britain, ACRO Criminal Records Office issues Police Certificates to people who want to emigrate to, or obtain a visa for, a number of countries including Australia, Belgium, Canada, Cayman Islands, New Zealand, South Africa or the United States of America. The certificate details whether or not the applicant has a criminal record in the United Kingdom and is required as part of the visa process by the respective high commission or embassy. The certificate may also include foreign criminal history information where it has been disclosed to the UK.

On ACRO you can also access application forms for Police Certificates and International Child Protection Certificates, and find out how to make a Subject Access request.[1]

Chapter 19

A Beginners Guide to Airport Etiquette

Three days before departure, check online or phone up the airline to confirm the time of the flight as sometimes they change. Make sure you know how you are getting to the airport. Do you need a map, or does the Sat Nav work? Do you need to send a SMS/text to your friends or use WhatsApp to remind them when and where to meet? Pack your bags and weigh them. Do not exceed the airline's bag and weight policy. Know which Terminal you need to be in at the airport. The entrance's between Terminal 1 and 5 could be many miles apart on the opposite side of the airport. Many larger airports run shuttle trains between Terminals.

On the day before departure, double-check your hand/carry-on luggage and that you have your passport, money and plane tickets with you. Fully charge all electronic items. If you are driving to the airport are all the tyres/tires inflated? Has the oil, coolant and screen-wash been checked? You may be able to check-in online 24hrs before departure and pick your seat on the plane. Do this with your friend(s).

On the day of departure, check you have everything with you and leave in plenty of time. It is better to wait around for three hours at the airport (you have to be there at least two hours in advance) than to miss the flight because the car broke down or the train or coach was delayed. Keep your plane ticket, money and passport on you!

Airport Arrival and Etiquette

You may have travelled abroad before, but there is always a first time at the airport. Airports are high security risk areas, do not joke about guns, bombs, terrorism or diseases. It may get you arrested, detained or barred from the flight. Do not leave luggage unattended.

- Arrive in plenty of time and look presentable.
- Do not be loud and boisterous. Do not block gangways and if with a group of friends try not to go wandering off.
- Check-in (if you have not done it online) at the airport desk with the airline you are flying with and receive your Boarding Card/Pass. (You may have an e-ticket on your smartphone and can digitally check-in, weigh your bag and print out your luggage label, alongside your Boarding Card). Your visa may be checked to see if you are entitled to enter the country you are going to. Or you may just be 'in transit' as you have to get a second flight. If

with friends, check-in as a group and ask to be seated next to each other. Even families have been split up and scattered throughout a plane because they did not ask to be seated together! Once on the plane you can ask a fellow passenger if they will swap with you so you can sit with your friend, the worst they can say is "no." Have passports and tickets to hand. If you have special dietary requirements mention it to the staff for your free meal on the plane, though food and drinks are not free on budget airlines. Check your luggage in at the same desk, your bag will be weighed. Dangerous items such as penknives, scissors, nail file, nail clippers, deodorants cans and creams and fluids in excess of 100ml should be in your check-in luggage, *not* your hand luggage. Airlines have many other restrictions and prohibited items (which change from time to time) but liquids, creams and deodorants of more than 100ml each are forbidden, though you can purchase the latter items once you have passed through the Secure Area of the airport. Do not have any loose straps on your luggage as they can get caught and rip your bag. At check-in you may be asked if you packed your own bag, and has it been left unattended. The airline worker is trying to find out if contraband items, drugs or a bomb could have been packed without your knowledge. You will receive a receipt for your bag, the airline worker at check-in may stick it to the back of your Boarding Card. This proves that you have luggage. The worker should tell you at what Gate your plane departs from, if not, look on the digital Departures Board. You may need to show your Boarding Card in the country of arrival when you depart from the airport, so keep it safe. A reminder: Do not joke about bombs, terrorism, guns, Ebola or other contagious diseases.

- If you are taking a musical instrument, e.g. your guitar, try to take it on the plane as hand/carry-on luggage, otherwise it may get damaged. If not, process it through check-in as a fragile item. If it is not in a protective case, it will probably get damaged in transit. Fragile items often have to be taken to a separate counter to be processed. You may be charged for a second bag.

A foreign musician at a British airport was asked by security what was in his violin case. The witty musician joked that it was a gun. He was duly arrested and detained for around eight hours. The police who arrested the man said, "It was no laughing matter!"

Moving Through the Airport
- Once you've checked-in and your main luggage has been taken, go through to the Secure Area of Departures. Have your passport and Boarding Card ready for inspection. There will be a

bin where all barred items, e.g. scissors, penknives etc. and creams and fluids over 100ml have to be left behind.

- Now you have to go through security. Empty your pockets and put your hand/carry-on luggage in the boxes on the conveyer belt where it will go through an x-ray machine. Camera film and tapes should be ok. You may have to turn your electronic items on (ereader, mobile/cell phone, laptop etc.). If you cannot prove that they work, you may not be permitted to take them aboard. If you are wearing boots, a jacket, belt, coat or a hat you will probably have to remove them before passing through the other side of the secure area. Staff or signs will notify you of this. Remove all coins, keys and electrical items before you walk through the metal detector/scanner (which looks like a metal doorframe). If the machine beeps, the security guard (Transportation Security Administration in the U.S., an agency of Homeland Security) will scan you with a handheld scanner and/or frisk you. You may have to empty your pockets. In April 2016, it was revealed that bras from a UK high-street retailer were setting off airport scanners due to the amount of metal in the underwire! A money belt full of wads of notes can also be an issue, just let them know what it is, and you will probably have to remove it. Do not let it out of your sight! (With the rise of terrorists and suicide belts, money belts are becoming more problematic). If the guard cannot find the offending item, you may have to go for a full body scan in a separate room. You keep your clothes on. Take your hand luggage etc. with you, which has gone through the x-ray machine. Travel/walking trousers with metal zipped pockets (I have seven zips on mine) are problematic at airports, as they always set the machine off and the guards may get nervous (as they did when I was in Pakistan). They cannot find anything and think that something is being concealed.
- You may also encounter sniffer dogs which are trained to pick up the scent of drugs, explosives or other contraband. If found with drugs at an airport you could spend decades in prison or even face execution! Western prisons are like holiday camps compared to those in developing countries and the Middle East. In some prisons, you have little to no rights and it is your responsibility to provide for yourself, e.g. food, soap etc. You may even have to pay rent for your incarceration!
- After you have passed through security, there may be time to shop, to buy a drink or have a snack.
- Get to the Departures Gate in plenty of time to board your plane. Some can be one mile (1.6km) away from check-in, so a 20 minute walk. Use the bathroom/restroom *before* you board your

plane. You will need to show your Boarding Card and passport before you can board the plane. Sometimes passengers with certain seat numbers are called first, e.g. 50-100. There will be toilets on the plane, but aircrew do not like you using them when they are on the ground and you may be 'grounded' for some time.

- Find your seat on the plane, store your hand luggage/carry-on bag in the overhead compartment. Follow the steward's safety brief and observe where the exits are.
- On the plane, you may be able to watch a movie on the in-flight entertainment system. There may be a complimentary drink and a meal or two, depending on the length of your flight. Have a good sleep if you can.
- With most countries, you will have to fill out an Arrivals Card. These are issued on the plane or at Immigration, have a pen handy. Fill in your name, passport number and answer the questions. You may have to declare how much money you are bringing in to the country. I have always been cautious about this (especially at land borders) so that I am not robbed. Under the 'Nature of Visit' (Business or Pleasure), you are a tourist unless you have a business visa for your humanitarian work. You may have to return your half of the Arrivals Card on your departure, so keep it safe, alongside your Boarding Card.

Arriving at a New Country

- Arriving at your destination by plane you will have to collect your bag and then go through Immigration. Make sure you collect your bag, and not one that looks like yours! You may be able to get a trolley to put your bag on which saves carrying it. On occasions, bags do get lost or arrive on a later plane. Contact the airline from inside the airport and they will generally forward your bag on to you.
- Go through customs and you should not have anything to declare, walk through the green channel (Nothing to Declare). If there are two gates, the other will be Items to Declare and will be red. Your bag may be checked at customs but unlikely. Often they do random searches.
- You now have to pass through Immigration where you show your passport and visa (if needed). Or just before Immigration you can buy your visa if you do not need to apply for one and/or fill in an Immigration Card.
- At Immigration, hand your passport over. The officer on duty, will look at your passport (maybe scan it) and look at you. He or she may ask you some questions, or just stamp your passport and let you into the country. Adhere to all rules and regulations.

Apart from "Hello" and "Thank you," I don't speak unless spoken to, this allows the person to do their job unhindered. If there is a health scare like Ebola, you may be screened, questions will be asked and your temperature taken.

Arriving at your destination can be exciting, but your journey through different time zones can upset your senses and dampen your emotional well-being. You may not have rested on your ten-hour night flight or you could be unwell because of turbulence.

After you clear customs and enter a new world, you should at least try to pretend that you know what you are doing; though if you are with a tour company, many pressures of finding transport and accommodation are alleviated. Try to use the bathrooms/restrooms before you leave the airport. Do you need to exchange some money at the airport, or is there an ATM/cash point where you can withdraw the local currency? The ATM is often a better option.

Foreigners are most vulnerable when they first arrive at a new destination. Be aware of your surroundings. Stepping through the airport doors with a fresh visa and stamp on your passport or when arriving at a bus, train or ferry terminal, touts and hustlers can quickly latch on to the foreigner, offering their assistance; sometimes they are helpful, at other times they are not! Be polite; do not feel obligated to enter into a conversation. Make sure *all* your luggage is with you. Do not let strangers take your bags to their transport. They may want payment for carrying your bags to an expensive taxi! Take some transport to your accommodation. There may be problems with the language, airport taxi drivers (always a few who try to take advantage), the unfamiliar surroundings and the primary object of finding a place to stay.

> Do not allow your passport to be taken from you without your consent. Without it you cannot leave the country. Do not pay an on-the-spot fine to an undercover 'policeperson' or go to 'the station' with him/her. Do not get into an unmarked 'police' vehicle.

Border crossings are the most wary places to be, but especially as you emerge from no-man's-land and into a new country where more often than not, you will be swarmed upon like bees to an open pot of jam/jelly. Do not believe everything that you are told by people who want to take your money. "The hotel is closed, the road is un-driveable, it is flooded, there are no buses till next week, I'll take you in my taxi, the taximeter is broken" etc. are comments that you may hear by people who want you to use their services.

In some countries, you cannot buy the next country's currency from a Bureau de Change or bank and so frequently have no option, but to buy money on the border. I never exchange large amounts of money, but enough for a day for two people, around $50 (£32), then I look for an ATM when inside the country. On the Kenya/Tanzania border we tried to exchange some money into the local currency, where a slight-of-hand trick cost us the best part of £34 ($54). We had not taken our eyes off the money that we handed the man; but as he suddenly dropped the exchange rate from what we had agreed, we had no choice but to return each other's money – though not all of ours came back!

In Khartoum, Sudan, we came out of yet another bank, having tried to purchase Ethiopian currency when a man approached us and told us that he could exchange the money. The bank guard moved us on and the man told us to follow him. We followed him, stopping off at several places, waiting around and after fifteen minutes, something felt really wrong and we just walked away. We eventually found a shopkeeper who could help us out.

However much you prepare for your arrival at your new destination you can be easily caught unaware, as expectation and reality can be far apart. On the journey to your accommodation there are new sights, sounds, smells and even stirred emotions, which may be hard to take in, thoughts of those you left behind and possible jetlag. Like everything, it does take time to settle in and to recover from a journey, especially if you have crossed time zones, but after a few days to a week, your body will readjust and everything will get back to normal.

You may have just arrived at your destination or after a week think that you have made a major mistake and want to go home, don't, you will regret it. If you are feeling low, look at a photo of those who are most special to you (keep it in your wallet/purse or on your smartphone) and remember the good times. You will get to see them again. Homesickness can set in after several months, but can be after just a week. You are more prone to being homesick if you have never spent time away from your family.

Check your bed sheets or sleeping bag before you get in – just in case of creepy crawlies! Shakeout your clothes in the morning and check your shoes for unwanted guests! Keep on top of your hygiene.

> The first day of travel on a different continent has always been difficult for me. The jetlag, the cold (or heat), the noise, dirt and troubles. I often ask myself, "What have I done coming here!?" However, it all works itself through within a couple of days and I embrace the travels. Derek – various places.

Chapter 20

Finding a Place to Stay

If you have not pre-booked a room in a cheap hotel or youth hostel then you need to find a place to stay. As long as the price is sensible and the area is ok, pick the first place you find, unless the street is saturated with accommodation then do a quick comparison. You will probably want to shower up, perhaps have a brief rest and then go outside and familiarise yourself with your local surroundings. Grab hold of a business card of your accommodation, just in case you get lost! Once you have a roof over your head for the first night, and assuming you are staying in the same town, see if you can stay in a cheaper place, or for the same cost with better amenities, e.g. bigger TV, Air Conditioning (AC), free WiFi or a larger room.

You can stay at many forms of accommodation on your travels: Hotel, motel, lodge, inn, B&B, youth hostel, on a campsite, in a tent off-the-beaten-track, on a beach, in a motorhome, on a night train or coach, in the back of a car, hire an apartment, rent a room in someone's home, stay at a temple or a monastery or sleep rough for a night. You can sleep at an airport, ferry terminal, on a grain truck or inside or outside a train station on the street – and I have done all five of these last options – none of which were planned.[1]

In the Pyrenees Mountain area of France, we could not find a campsite and as it was 10pm, we slept as a group on our camping mats on the pavement with our rucksacks as pillows. Sleeping outside in public is not the easiest or safest of options. It is often best to sleep with your shoes on and any bags under your head or looped through your arm. Are you sheltered if it rains? Will you be arrested for being a vagrant? Will you be robbed or beaten by a group of drunks? Things to consider.

The cost of accommodation varies greatly and most towns have several hotels or guesthouses, whereas some streets are full of them. In Ho Ch Minn City (Saigon), Vietnam, there were ten hotels within a one minute walk and by looking at all of them, we got the very best deal with quality amenities. Hotels, lodges and guesthouses often have star ratings and more often than not, the lower the star, the lower the price, though this is not always the case and the star rating can be faked. If you come from the West, you will find the cost of living whilst on your travels in the vast majority of countries in Africa, large portions of Asia and South America, is cheaper than at home.

In many places of accommodation, you have to pay daily, for each night upfront. I have found that it is a good way of breaking large notes/bills and getting smaller denominations to spend elsewhere. However, in one hotel in Tunisia, the owner was insistent that he could not change large bills (it was only 20 dinas, about £7/$11) and needed the *exact* amount each day. I found this tedious and unorthodox to my travels and so on the third day I put him to the test, I insisted that I had no change and that either he get me some change or I would pay for two nights the following day. He sent one of his workers to get change from a local shop!

In some cities in China, you have to pay the cost of each night's accommodation upfront, plus a deposit which was returned when you check-out, assuming the hotel room was left how you found it, with furniture and fittings all in one piece.

In a hotel in Lesotho, Africa, we went to pay the receptionist after we had returned from a day of exploration, but she could not be found. We went to our room and at 11pm received a knock at our door. I asked who it was and got no response, so went back to bed. After five minutes there was another knock. The receptionist had asked the security guard to knock again, I opened the door and he explained the situation. I got dressed, went downstairs and paid the receptionist. The ironic thing was that the hotel owed us x amount of loti (Lesotho unit of currency) from the previous day because they had no change.

From an email from a traveller: We just arrived in the evening and are in Kowloon, Hong Kong, staying in the expensive Salvation Army Booth Lodge on the fourteenth floor at £82 per night! We are checking out tomorrow for a cheaper place. Downtown about one mile away there are two big skyscrapers full of budget accommodation. Accommodation is at a premium and prices increase at weekends. We got a room on the fifth floor inside a shopping complex for $40 (£25) a night. It is very small and I can nearly touch both sides of the room with my fingertips! The toilet and shower are in the same 3 foot square-ish box! We have a TV and AC. Our room overlooks the road. We paid 900 HKD $120 (£75) to reserve a room for 3 days, beginning next week, which is larger than what we have and is inside the same complex.

In Cairo, Egypt, one of the night workers took our money, but apologised that he had no change and asked if it was ok? It was, because as far as we were aware, we would be in credit for the next day. However, there was a new worker on reception and there was no note of credit! It was about £2 ($3) and so we wrote it off as experience.

The receptionist was able to give us a discount on four rooms for three nights but it was still beyond the reach of our group. Our leader then spoke to the manager and asked if the hotel could be more flexible, and they were! The manager, after gentle persuasion was even kind enough to fill up the swimming pool where we relaxed in the evenings! Keumhee – Tunisia.

When we first went to Kathmandu, Nepal, we stayed in a quality hotel for a good rate as it was low season. We did not know how long we were staying for, and every few days a different worker would ask, "When are you leaving?" "We are not sure," was the reply, later we added, "Do you want to get rid of us?" "No sirs," was the polite reply. We left after ten days having been ill for a number of them and paid the night before we left. It was only in hindsight that they probably wanted us to pay our bill to-date as it was in the low season and cash-flow may have been an issue.

I went to the bathroom/restroom to have a wash and climbed into the large barrel. It was a tight fit and the water was cool. It was only afterwards that I realised that this container was not a vertical bath, but I should have scooped the water out and poured it over myself! Alan – Malaysia.

We found a beach front shack in Zanzibar and negotiated a price for three days. The man wanted three days pay up front, but we told him that we would pay for one day first, to see how it went. If it was ok (and it was) then we would pay for the next two days in advance. When we were in Beijing, China, we had great difficulty in trying to find a place to stay for a sensible amount of money. In the end we took the metro/underground and travelled many stops away from the centre and just walked around. This took 2-3 hours. One person would look after the rucksacks and the other would search. This speeded up the process and was the coolest method in 30°C humid heat! We knew we would stay in Beijing for nearly two weeks but were reluctant to pay for twelve nights in advance in case there was a cheaper or better hotel for the same money. We initially paid for five nights, then for seven and were able to negotiate a better rate for the remaining seven days. On occasions, splitting the staying time (paying in instalments) does not always work, as the hotel may receive reservations, the accommodation is booked full and you have to depart earlier than you wish to.

When we were in El-Minya, Egypt in 2008, we were only permitted to stay in a tourist hotel where there was an armed guard. When we went out in the evening for a meal he would always ask us where we were going and when we would be back. We arranged to visit some ancient tombs via the receptionist and were surprised to find that we had a policeman assigned to us for our protection. Inside the large archaeological area, where dozens of tombs were situated, with no other tourist in sight, we had two armed guards and a guide, whilst our taxi driver and policeman waited for us! Incidentally, in Egypt, most workers want bakeesh (a tip or a payment) which can become a bane, but at the time in 2008, the average civil servant got paid just £13 ($21) per month! Your little can mean a lot to them and make a difference. Also, out of Cairo, there are 'tourist trains' which travel south on certain days of the week. These trains have carriages set aside for foreigners and have additional security on them.

Some places of accommodation advertise different rates. They have a reservation price on their website e.g. $40 a room for two people, but if you turn up with no reservation the same room can cost you just $20! In Ethiopia, many of the better hotels have a cheaper price for nationals. It is the same with plane tickets. In Phuket, Thailand, by walking inland from the beach by about half a mile we found a great hotel. It was much cheaper than the beachfront hotels, about one fifth of the price, had a huge swimming pool, Air Conditioning and bathrobes for an incredible low price. They advertised for long stay guests when out of season, where one month's rent was the price of just ten nights.

I met two Asian girls on the ferry from Egypt to Sudan, where we all headed to Khartoum. They did not know how to budget their money and it soon ran out. On one occasion, they were at a campsite and could only afford a bed in the open air! They phoned home and their parents wired them the money to fly back to Japan. Chuck – Sudan.

Things to Know
Many hostels and places of accommodation have a shelf or shelves of books in different languages which can be exchanged or swapped. You hand over your book and you can take another. Check first though, as it may be a complimentary shelf of books for the guests to borrow, not to swap or keep.

Accommodation like B&Bs and some youth hostels have periods of the day when you may not be permitted to enter the accommodation, a "lock-out". The proprietor will expect you to depart at a certain time in the morning, e.g. from 9am-12 midday and not to come back until a certain time, e.g. from 4-6pm. Some establishments have a curfew where the gate or main door is locked, e.g. from 9pm-midnight and will not re-open until 6-7am.

Do you need a TV, fridge, Air Conditioning (AC), or computer in your room? Many establishments charge extra for these items. You should be cautious of having the AC set too low, so that it makes it difficult to acclimatise; you may catch a chill at night. If it is 35°C outside, and you set the AC to 20°C (room temperature in the UK), 15°C difference may be too difficult to cope with, consider setting it to 25°C. Some hotel key cards are placed in a slot by the door, so that when you remove the key card, the lights and AC turn off. You can sometimes override this by placing a ruler in the slot. This is best done after the maid has done the room, i.e. you have come back after lunch, and are going out again.

If you want to try and keep liquids cool without having a fridge, fill the sink with water. If you've forgotten your travel sink plug, stuff the hole with tissue, a polythene bag or upturn a glass or ceramic mug.

If you have a water boiler in your room, you may need to switch it on an hour or two before you intend on having a hot bath.

Some accommodation is not automatically cleaned on a regular basis. Sometimes you need to hand the room key in at reception when you go out, so that the staff know that the room is empty. On occasions you have to ask at reception for your room to be cleaned and for the majority of places it is a free service, included in the cost of accommodation. You may need to ask to get your bin/trash can emptied or to provide you with toilet paper, (or a towel when you check-in).

Treat the maid and accommodation workers with the greatest of respect. Many countries do not have a minimum wage and you may consider leaving them something on departure. In a developing country just $1-5 (£0.60-3.00) depending on the length of stay in basic accommodation would mean much more to them than to you. In Axum, Ethiopia, we went on to the hotel rooftop to film the sunset over the town. The manager came to see us to find out what we were doing. After explaining, and letting him look through the camera lens' eyepiece, we asked him what the round wooden huts were in the grounds of the hotel, (though sectioned off from the guests' side of the hotel) – it was where the workers lived.

Chapter 21

Reservations and Accommodation Checks

I rarely make reservations, pre-booking accommodation, unless it is a short trip or if I need a base for a single night. It often does not end well or match expectations, and my expectations for budget accommodation is low. I am not paying the earth, so I don't expect greatness, just adequate to ok. I am more happy to go with the flow by not pre-booking and discover where I will end up, which for me, is part of the fun of travel. Good deals can be found when using comparison or last minute hotel websites, or phone up the hotel direct. Remember, accommodation reviews are subjective and should be used as a guide, not as authoritative.

In Dublin, Ireland, the hotel was over-booked so we got turned away and put into another, less desirable hotel! When we flew into Switzerland, I had incorrectly written down the name of the road by missing out just one letter, yet a road of that name existed! Our hotel was on the other side of the city and this mistake cost us nearly 2 ½ hours! On another occasion, we pre-booked inside the country for the next town and when we arrived, the accommodation was filthy and grotty and was likened to a $1 a night hotel! Our only condition when we booked was that the room had to be clean and even the tour guide worker was embarrassed at the hotel he had to take us to, as it was the worst in town! We phoned the tour owner who told us it was our problem! For many people in poor or developing countries, the philosophy is that as you're rich, it's your problem and even though it's not your fault, you have to pay for it!

We got a lift on the back of a 4x4 pickup. Our other passenger was a large bristly pig. It was tied by its legs and squealed all the way as we bounced along the mud road to our next destination. Rodney – Laos.

In some areas, often near train stations, workers hand out flyers for accommodation. In many cities, but especially in developing countries, what you see on a flyer, glossy brochure or a website, often does not match reality. These 'informative' photos may have been taken a decade ago and the room has since seen a lot of wear and tear. Some images may have been digitally enhanced.

When we were in Nepal for the second time, we contacted a youth hostel in Ulaanbaatar, Mongolia, and arranged to stay with them for three days. The hostel had a free pickup service if you stayed with them for three days or more, and as the plane arrived in the early hours, it seemed the best option. The pickup never arrived, so we took a taxi, banged on the door, were let in, but no room had been reserved for us! We stayed a second night and then checked into a great hotel for less than the cost of the hostel!

If you are couchsurfing (staying on people's couches/sofas) then you may want to let them know when you will be arriving, or if you are renting a place. If you are using a home or area-space rentals website such as Airbnb, then you need to pre-book to claim your space, your bed, room, shed, pitch for your tent, apartment etc. If you are on a walking holiday, or pilgrimage, you should try to pre-book, even if phoning ahead to the next place the day before. If a place is full, they often suggest other places to stay, some will even phone up on your behalf if you ask, to see if they have a vacancy.

Accommodation Checks

With most places of accommodation, it is wise to view the room before you check-in or pay for a week up-front.

- Does the room look clean enough at first glance?
- Are there any flies or mosquitoes in the room? Do the walls have blood splats on them? This is a sign of mosquitoes that have sucked blood and have been swotted!
- Are there signs of dust and dirt? Rub your finger over the wooden table or window ledge.
- Are there signs of any insects, e.g. ants or cockroaches, or rodents droppings in the corners or edges of the room? If there is an ant trail, the ants will stick to their path and avoid you, but it is still not pleasant.
- Is there a window in the room? Some rooms are windowless and without a breeze can be stifling hot.
- Have you got a room with a view, do you want one? Pull back the curtain and you may see a wall or a guest looking back at you. On the other side of the building may be a view of a lake and the price per room may be the same.
- Is there glass in the window frame and a pair of curtains? Does the window open or does the frame look rotted?
- Does the door and its lock look secure? (You can wedge the back of a chair under the door handle or use a wedge).
- Is there a bed and a sheet or duvet?
- Is there a ceiling fan and does it work?
- Does the light work? Is the bulb bright enough?
- If there was a fire, is there more than one exit?
- Does the worker (or workers) look trustworthy or sly?

- Is there a chair? Good for hanging your clothes on. In most places, you do not want to leave items of clothing on the floor for insects to crawl into.
- If there is a balcony, does it look safe and sturdy. Can my room on the second floor of a backstreet be broken into via the balcony?
- Does the TV and AC work? Does the heater work?
- Do they have a plug socket or sockets so that you can charge all your electronic items?
- Is there a major trip hazard. One hotel had a one foot step between the bathroom and the bedroom. At night this could have caused an accident when you are half asleep.
- Is there a broken tile on the floor which you could trip over and injure yourself?
- Is there a shower, a sink or a bath? Is there a sink or bath plug? Does the bath look generally clean? Is there a mirror? Do they provide towels for free?
- Does the toilet work – will it flush? Is there a toilet seat?
- If you don't like the room you have viewed, you can ask to see another, or ask if there are different types of rooms on different floors. The cost can vary considerably.
- What time is check-out?
- Is breakfast included?
- When do I pay?
- Is there free WiFi?
- Do they have a swimming pool and is it filled with water?

Hostel Checks
- Are there male and female toilets/showers? In one hostel in Budapest, Hungary, there was a unisex toilet and shower complex. Each shower cubicle had a lino shower door which you pulled across, but your clothes and towel hook was on the outside, four feet away from the bathroom communal area!
- Is there a glass door for the toilet door or for the room's main door? You may value your privacy but other countries and cultures have a different view on these things.
- Is there a lock-out time?
- Is there a secure locker designated to each person?
- How many people to a dormitory?
- Are the bunk beds all connected together? If one person moves, all the beds may move! If you don't want a top bunk, is there a lower bunk available?
- Is it a mixed dormitory or for males or females only?

- Is there a communal area, a place to cook or watch TV?
- Is there a computer so you can use the internet or free WiFi?
- Are there any perks? Baguette and butter for breakfast, plus a cup of tea or coffee, or free pancakes at 3pm.
- Do the workers appear friendly and helpful or off-putting?
- Is there any 'small print' I need to know about?

Types of Toilets

Toilets the world over are not the same. They may be Western type, the bowl and seat – though the seat is not always there, a bucket which you empty, like in old prisons, or the squat type, a hole in the ground, which are also known as long-drops. If you remember doing squats thrusts in your physical education class at school then this is close to how you use squat toilets – you squat down, but without bouncing back up every few seconds. There is great pressure on your thighs, (impossible to read your iPhone7) and the stench in some outside squat toilets is nauseating – quite literally, with flies buzzing and maggots crawling!

When I was in Sudan, I urged and urged in a squat toilet and had to stuff toilet paper up my nostrils and tell myself to get over it and get used to it. If you're wearing trousers/pants, be careful that you pull them down low enough; otherwise you can make a mess in them! With your trousers being inverted, your coins and other items in your pockets are liable to fall out – a good reason why you should have zipped or Velcro pockets! Months before I went of to Africa, I began practicing squats to strengthen my thigh muscles and to aid balance – it paid dividends. Not all is bad though, if you make it to Japan, you may have the pleasure of sitting on an all-singing, all-dancing (not literally) electronic throne of thrones!

I needed to go to number two and found directions to the toilet. All that was there was a hole in the ground. I looked at it and pondered how it should be used, as there was no porcelain throne or toilet seat. I quickly sussed it out and pulled my trousers (pants) down and sat over the hole. Nobody told me that it was designed for squatting over! Jack – Thailand.

Chapter 22

Personal Hygiene and Scams

I know I am not your mum, but if you want to stay healthy to maximise your travels, you must keep up your personal hygiene, wash your body regularly and don't forget your clothes. If you can stand your trouser/pants up in the corner of the room, or your t-shirt is like cardboard, then it has too much grime on it! Whilst travelling, virtually everyday I have been able to take a shower or at least wash in a bowl. Some countries are so hot and humid that after you have dried yourself, you begin to perspire again.

Personal hygiene varies from one person to the next. In many developing countries of the world, the priority is to get food on the table and everything else takes second place, even purchasing soap. Deodorants are available in developing countries, especially in the capitals, though their prices are often the same as in the West, which for many nationals is too expensive. In areas where malaria is common, mosquitoes that transmit the disease are attracted by fragrance e.g. perfume, aftershave or deodorant, so why wear it? You may meet people who smell (and they may think the same about you), but it is more often than not because they have done a hard day's work and have yet to return home and wash. In some countries, water is precious and having enough for the family and their herd is the top priority, whilst tens of millions of homes do not have running water. Washing can be a luxury, but we must be careful to maintain our personal hygiene on our travels

I have always taken a can of deodorant with me whilst on travels and when it runs out, it runs out and I only replace it a few weeks before I depart for home – I do not want to smell on the plane! Remember: deodorant cans *cannot* be taken on a plane as hand/ carry-on luggage, so spray up before departure. If you don't care, your friend might!

Scented foot insoles or insoles impregnated with charcoal help mask smelly footwear. If you are able to leave your footwear outside on a balcony or by an open window at night, where they will not get stolen or wet, then do it.

Washing your Clothes

To save money on my budget travels I used to wash my clothes by hand, I either used the sink or a bath, ran the hot water, or near boiled the kettle and added the powder. The powder could be bought in single sachet or a 250-500 gram bag. I used to wear washing-up gloves because the chemicals can have a negative impact on sensitive skin. Rinse with plenty of water and wring your clothes out well. With socks, you can spin them around like a windmill and see the droplets fly off. If we had a balcony, the washed clothes used to be placed over that to dry in the sun and air, or put on the back of a chair; whilst t-shirts were hung from a coat hanger, or a washing/clothesline was strung across the room, near an air vent, open window or a fan if possible. Don't put wet or damp clothes on lacquered furniture as it can lift.

In some places, washing is charged by the kilogram, by the bag, a set fee for different items and garments, or you pay for a full load with a washing machine. Some hotels charge by the garment and the cost is quite shocking – using locals instead of a hotel is cheaper. In Gondar, Ethiopia, one teenager said his mother could do our washing for us. We did not take him up on the offer, as we did not know where he lived and we thought our clothes would go missing. In a guest house in Lusaka, Zambia, we were told that they did not do any washing. I explained to the owner that we did not want it done for free, but would pay a worker to do it, and a worker quickly came forward for the extra income.

In Kenya, after travelling for about 18 hours on the back of a grain truck from the border with Sudan, our clothes were covered with dirt and dust from head to toe. We checked into a cheap hotel and asked the cost of washing a *very* dirty bag of clothes. The worker gave the price, but it was only right that I showed her the state of our apparel in case she wanted to increase the price. No price increase was forthcoming.

At a hotel in Kenya, the worker told us he could not wash underwear because it was a Muslim establishment. We explained that we are all men together and that he could put them on the rooftop in the sun, whereas we could not. The worker relented and we paid the going rate.

Many places of accommodation offer clothes washing services and subcontract it to someone outside, and take a cut for themselves. If the hotel charges $1.50 a kilogram and you can get it direct for $1 a kilogram, I know which one I will take. Some places let you drop it of in the morning and collect it at night, or you drop it off before 1 or 2pm and collect it the next day after 9am. In Hong Kong, I thought one of my t-shirts did not come back from the home launderette and so asked the worker to search. It transpired, that I found the t-shirt in my rucksack and had to go and make an apology. After that, each time my washing was handed in, it was counted in and counted out!

I have never paid for my washing to be ironed, though some services do this for free. In Kathmandu, Nepal, one launderette worker said they charged extra for ironing, which we declined. However, our washing was always ironed, and we wondered if the man was trying to take something extra for himself.

Some youth hostels and other forms of budget accommodation have washing machines where you pay a set fee for a single load. They can be coin or token operated, or you pay one of the workers. Sometimes, to have the clothes spun 'dry' is a bit extra. Washing powder may or may not be included in the price. There will be a public washing/clothesline and often you have to search for space to hang your clothes. Take your clothes in as soon as they are dry or someone else may take a fancy to them and help themselves! You can put the washing on in the morning and often within one hour or so, you can hang them on the clothesline, go out for the day, come back and collect your washing. In some parts of the world when it is around 25-30°C, you can do your washing in the early evening, and even if there is no sun, your washing is often dry before you go to bed at midnight.

Dubious Incidents and Scams

When someone says to you that they can get a good deal, you should consider that the "good deal" is probably for their benefit and *not* for you! In Malawi, we wanted to see a waterfall which was off-the-beaten-track, and had been made famous by its discovery to the world by Dr. David Livingstone. The lodge owner had a taxi driver friend and told us, "I can get you a really good deal" and the next day came back with a price. The price was no better than if we stopped a driver on the street, in fact, in was not a good deal, but an expensive excursion for a few hours where the lodge evidently would have taken a cut, if we had taken him up on his "really good deal." Incidentally, the same lodge owner wanted to sell us some gems as "that is what Africa is renowned for and known for," he said. I told him that I had not seen a single gem in Africa and had travelled 10,000km. I am convinced that if we had bought "gems" from this man they would have been costume jewellery at best or worthless tat at worst!

Getting off the ferry at Zanzibar, we were bombarded with offers of help, taxis, hotel reps (self-employed touts), before we had even completed our stroll down the gangplank and got our passports stamped! After politely declining all offers, a man continued with us (several fell away as we continued ignoring them) and followed us into a lodge as recommended by the guidebook. The man tried to get money from the hotel as commission, but we told the hotelier that we did not know the man and that he followed us in. If the man had got commission (for doing nothing), we would not have been able to negotiate a price for the room and get a discount.

In India, you get people who want to 'practice' their English and as you walk around the backstreets, you'll end up at the 'family business,' a carpet or silk shop. "Let's go inside," the son will say, who is unrelated to the owner, "you can see the family business." You are taken into a room with blankets and silks and other goods stacked all around you, and given a seat in the corner, farthest away from the door. You are offered a free drink by the 'father' who begins showing you the family's craftsmanship; you look around and your unofficial I-want-to-practice-my-English "guide" has disappeared, whilst silk scarves and cotton blankets are strewn on the ground to block your exit, and you get to witness high pressure sales techniques!

Some sellers will pester you for a purchase or play the sympathy, "feel sorry for me" card. The concept is, if they pester the foreigner long enough some will give in, or if they tell you're their woes, some foreigner will capitulate. On the Zambia/Zimbabwe border by Victoria Falls, we passed the border check post to have a view of the Falls on the Zimbabwean side. A man wanted to sell us a Zimbabwean trillion note/bill. I do not collect foreign money and knew because of their high inflation that it was practically worthless. The man went from $10, $5 to $1. Each time, I told him that I do not want to buy and walked away; to admire the view and to take some more photos. Each time he came back with a new offer. In the end he told me politely that I was wasting his time as he could go and sell it to other foreigners and that if he did not sell it, he could not feed his family and would have to go and steal instead.

We hired a guide for thirty minutes to take us to three specific tombs scattered amongst a wide area. Upon payment, the guide was very unhappy, angry and sullen and demanded more. I thought that perhaps I had underpaid him and after careful consideration gave him some extra, but still he was not happy and demanded an outrageous amount, which his friends agreed with. I realised that I had been manipulated into paying the man more than I should have done, but he never got the outrageous amount he wanted! Newton – Egypt.

There are some people who want you to read out a printed letter on their behalf, which they probably typed themselves at the internet cafe. The letter, on A4 paper, which is sometimes laminated, goes on to explain that this person should be employed as a guide or similar, or that the person needs financial help, with a recommendation from John Smith of England, or Joe Bloggs of America. Other people claim to be collecting money for charity, whilst some beggars can find a foreigner amongst a crowd of hundreds. Some people do need help and maybe you can make a difference with your loose change, on the other hand, indiscriminate giving to some people may do more harm than good.

I have read reports of peep holes in cheap accommodation, especially in Thailand. With today's technology, hidden cameras can be an issue, even in more upmarket accommodation with a rogue worker, instances have been reported to management and the police.

In China, if you are a man you may get invited to visit a tea shop by a pretty Chinese woman (or vice versa for a woman, a man will invite you, or two women for two men etc.). She probably works for the shop and gets a commission by getting customers through the doors of these traditional tea shops with their elaborate ceremonies, which is quite an experience. She will probably flatter you both and encourage you to buy some tea for yourselves, and some for your families at home, as a present, and it is a lot more expensive than your local brew at home. Once payment has been made, she will be gone and will look for the next unwitting customer. If you want to experiment, if you are approached and invited to drink some tea (e.g. along the Bund, in Shanghai or in Beijing), politely decline and see how quickly they move on to the next foreigner. It is a real and thriving industry. A similar technique is used in Soho, London and other places of the world, to get you into a bar where the drinks are four times the standard price, or you have to pay a hefty entrance fee. Some establishments employ promoters.

> I met this man as we were returning to our hotel and we went for a coffee. It was a good opportunity to practice my language skills. After a few hours, he walked me back to where we met up and then demanded money! I was confused and explained that I do not pay for friendship, but to no avail, I walked off in disgust. My friends who were too tired to come out that night and stayed around the pool instead, said that he might have been a rent boy (male prostitute)! Mark – North Africa.

A common swindle in Kathmandu, Nepal, is for mothers with babies in their arms, to ask you to buy powdered milk for their baby. The mother is in collusion with the shopkeeper and once you have disappeared, she returns the goods to the shop, both seller and mother get a percentage. In other countries, a child asks for a bottle of milk which later gets returned. Some beggars also work for pimps who pay them a wage whilst the pimp gets the larger proportion.

I have heard about some mothers who expose their babies to tropical heat so as to elicit more money. The baby looks dehydrated, exhausted and potentially sunburnt. As one woman author noted, no loving mother would ever expose her baby to such tropical heat, but would wish to protect him/her and put them in the shade. One man in Wales, claimed that his grandfather had died and he needed money to get back to Ireland for the funeral. I twice heard the story from the same man in two different years! He specialised in preying on students and foreigners!

In Tunisia, a common scam was for people to allege that they worked at the hotel that you are staying at to gain your confidence so that you would buy from them or use their services. We would always ask them, which hotel is that? If they guessed correctly (and in some towns they had a 33.3% chance of getting it right), then they would have to tell us who the manager was, which nobody knew!

Be careful if you buy electrical goods at an airport. Many years ago, when the latest iPhone was released, they were being sold at an airport in Beijing, China, for a cheaper price than in the West. The problem was they had no internal electronics, it was just a shell of a smartphone with good packaging, and they could not be returned!

I was on the Trans-Mongolian Railway which joined the Trans-Siberian train line for five days and four nights. A Mongolian passenger from another carriage borrowed my travel-plug adaptor and assured me of its return. I never saw it again nor the borrower. Whilst it was of little value, I wish I had taken a photo of the person concerned as the item was used most days.

Fellow Travellers – I've been Robbed

You may come across a fellow traveller who claims to have been robbed and needs money to get to their embassy in the capital. It may be genuine, it may be false. Some travellers prey on the generosity and compassionate nature of fellow travellers. If you hand over any money, don't expect to get it back or to hear from the person again. However, you may be able to get an item in exchange for the money (like a guaranteed loan, you get their camera or gold necklace etc. and when they reimburse you, you return the item), this is assuming they were not robbed of all their possessions. If they have been robbed it should have been reported to the police and they will have paperwork to prove it. If their passport has been stolen the person should contact their embassy, ASAP. Embassies are not banks and do not financially bail their citizens out or make loans, though they can help in many other ways. The traveller should contact relatives or friends back in their home country who should be able to help him/her, as well as their travel insurance provider. If the person was not travelling solo, why have their friend(s) not helped the person out?

Chapter 23

Settling In

There are many things to do when you are in the country of your destination, but a few things to do once you have found your accommodation.

- Familiarise yourself with your local surroundings. Look for landmarks.
- Acclimatise to the heat or altitude. This may take some days to a few weeks.
- Try the local cuisine, though ease yourself in gently if you have a sensitive stomach.
- Go out and see the sights and meet the locals.
- If you need some items, go and haggle with street sellers. However, don't exploit your buying power, get a discount, but remember, they need to make a profit to live.
- Listen to the local radio, if there is one available.
- Watch the local TV programmes if possible, but especially the news and local affairs programmes.
- Having your hair cut in another country is always interesting and is good for social interaction. But be aware that your words may get lost in translation and your hair style could drastically alter with a single snip of the scissors!

Journal and Daily Budgeting

I would encourage anybody who goes travelling to keep a journal, however brief, even if just a short paragraph per day. The weakest ink is better than the strongest memory. In my A5 spiral bound journals (a new one for each trip), I keep a daily record of all the places that I have been, what I have eaten or seen, observations, how I feel and the day's expenses. A journal is interesting to read when you go through what you did each day, one year on from your travels and after several years, you can pick it up as a travel adventure and the memories will come flooding back.

Daily, I tally up the expenses (accommodation, food, drink, travel, and entrance fees) and then add them together to form the week's expenses and then add up the monthly budget. I can keep a tight tab of the budget and if we have overspent one week, we have to make cuts the following week. The monthly tallies are recorded at the back of my journal alongside all the money exchanged and withdrawals at cash points/ATMs. I have found that this method is the most practical when it comes to balancing the books. Due to exchange rates there are always minor differences.

> For my first few months in Africa, I tried to avoid staying in accommodation that had a TV. I wanted to live life in Africa, and not see fictional life in the West on TV every evening. William – Zambia.

Your Room – Your Home
Try to keep your accommodation tidy. Mum/mom will not be there to clean up behind you. Even if you are in a hotel or guesthouse; use the bin/trash can and do not *expect* the cleaners to pick up your rubbish because you could not be bothered to put it in the bin. Remember, you don't know who will pay you a visit or just pop in. The same applies for when you rent an apartment or house. The quality of furniture varies from place to place and the bench that can hold four petite Asian women may not hold two burly Westerners. Don't put damp clothes on varnished furniture because the lacquer may lift. Don't tramp mud through the home or your room.

It is unwise to leave valuables lying around – do not tempt the cleaner or others. I have stayed in 100s of different places and only once was something stolen from my room – lip balm. Someone had a greater need than myself and I was able to laugh it off. In hostels (amongst fellow foreigners), things go missing; and are more likely to. There are always rogue opportunists.

> Charles Caleb Colton (1780–1832) wrote: 'Those who visit foreign nations, but associate only with their own country-men, change their climate, but not their customs. They see new meridians, but the same men; and with heads as empty as their pockets, return home with travelled bodies, but untravelled minds.'

Beware of
- The dangers of familiarity as it can breed contempt.
- Doing the right things for the wrong motives.
- Being outwardly submissive but inwardly rebellious.
- Making promises that you have no intention of keeping.
- Deliberately rocking the boat to draw attention to yourself or playing the fool.
- Usurping authority or not being submissive to the charity or NGO leaders.
- Breaking the rules – they are there for a reason.

More Effective than Defective
To be more effective than defective on our travels we need to:

- Be prepared – financially, physically and have the correct mentality – be positive.
- Be flexible – change happens, the best of plans can fall through.
- Be wise in all you do and say.
- Be kind and considerate to others.
- Wear the right clothing and be sensible.
- Have a willingness to learn and to be taught.
- When working with others, ask the right questions in the right way – inquire rather than condemn or accuse.
- Try to fit in – assimilate, mingle and interact appropriately with the locals.
- Be humble, kind and courteous.
- Look after yourself. It is easy to throw money into bottomless pits or to let one's self go when away from a familiar routine.

Power cuts are a regular feature of developing countries (from 10 minutes to 12 hours) and at other times electricity is sporadic, sparse or is turned on and off at certain times of the day or night. From May into June 2008, Zanzibar in Africa, was without electricity for over two weeks! Charge your equipment when you can, as if you procrastinate, you may find that when you want to, you cannot! You and your friend might be vying for the only plug socket in the room.

Travel Frustrations and Inconveniences
- People who blatantly lie to you and try to deceive.
- People who deliberately try and short-change you.
- When you are charged a *lot more* than the locals for goods or services because you are a foreigner.
- When you are asked for money, a tip (bakeesh in Egypt) or a gift, for no reason whatsoever.
- When a worker *demands* more money even though you have agreed a price with them beforehand. Even more so when the worker has not been helpful; you pay the agreed sum and then the worker gets angry and demands more, (which you should not pay).
- People who try to renegotiate the cost of private transport when you're half way to your destination.
- Delayed transport, the ten hour train journey should have left at 6am but did not leave until 3pm!
- Accommodation that has been pre-booked, but is not as described. It is a lot worse.
- Having to run around a capital city trying to obtain a visa, when the consulate only opens for one hour, two days a

week. Dozens of people may be in the queue. (Sometimes you need proof of your onward travel before a visa is issued and/or a letter of invite from within that country).
- Pickpockets – those who steal from you.

Characters and Knowledge

Whilst travelling, you will meet some great characters and probably some odd ones as well! These can be fellow travellers or just workers at a hostel, hotel, cafe or local restaurant. You may come across some great places to enjoy yourself. Lots of knowledge can be gleaned from fellow travellers (receptionists and taxi drivers), recommendations, places to stay, where to eat, what to avoid, what to try, scams to beware off etc. Sometimes you just have to ask, what is there to do around here? Is there any...? Where is the best place to...? Can you recommend any cheap...?

Individuals may try and tag along with you, it may work well or it may not. If you want to say no, then politely say "No." On a camping trip in Wales, I met a man whose wife refused to 'rough it' under canvas. The man was going to visit some place and asked if I wanted to go with him. I had other plans and told him I was busy. The next day, he told me that he had postponed his visit and would I like to see the place today. I politely declined.

I was in a youth hostel in Rome, Italy, with my friend when we got chatting to another traveller. We later told him we were going for ice cream and he invited himself along! We had a great time together, the man turned out to be a barrel of laughs.

In Budapest, Hungary, I met two Korean travellers, a young man and a young woman who had teamed up with each other in Europe, for the financial benefit of travelling in pairs, for safety and because of language issues. Their budget was on a shoestring and in the mornings they only had bread for breakfast and bought a small cheap evening meal.

In Cambodia and in one east African country we came across a go-kart track with petrol engine go-karts. It was a good chunk out of the budget for just 5-10 minutes of speed, but seriously great fun!

In El-Minya, Egypt, we were invited to pay for a one hour trip on the Nile in a traditional felucca alongside many Egyptians. The price seemed excessively high so we declined. At Luxor, Egypt, we were able to hire an entire felucca and its captain for one hour at a cheaper rate that two single seats at El-Minya.

Chapter 24

A Foreign Language

Language difficulties during your travels abroad combined with unfamiliar social and cultural cues can make communication problematic even on a basic level. Frustration can set in when you are unable to express yourself fully. Learn to laugh at your mistakes. Be aware of your mannerisms and hand gestures. Speak slower than your conversational speech; the person may not be familiar with your accent. You may be speaking in a second language or they may be listening to a second language.

If part of a humanitarian group, NGO or charity you may need to use an interpreter. When using an interpreter, there may be misunderstandings and miscommunication. It is important that your interpreter *understands* English and the language that he or she is interpreting into! Use plain English; avoid big words, speak slowly, clearly and precisely. Keep sentences short. Avoid slang and phrases or words that are only relevant to your culture. Do not use words which have a double meaning, or of the opposite intended; i.e. wicked – to mean evil or good? Sick – to mean great, vomit/barf or unwell? Keep clear of idioms, colloquialisms, modern sayings or catchphrases, which will only make your interpreter raise his or her arms and give you a blank look.

> When dealing with people from abroad you need to use "export English" – Lord Alan Sugar, British entrepreneur. Slow down (to give the person time to think) and keep it simple.

Jokes rarely bridge cultural divides and can be hard to interpret. Do not speak about politics, democracy or against tyrannical leaders as you could endanger your hosts or cause great offence and harm. Do not discuss these subjects in public places as 'loose talk costs lives,' as the old war saying goes. Poems and songs are also difficult to interpret and rarely if ever make sense to the interpreter or those listening. As a foreigner you may be asked to speak at a school or to a youth group. Local English teachers are often looking for English speakers to take their class (or assembly), to interact with a real native of the language and to engage the children. If telling a story, make it relevant and with younger children, raise and lower the tone of your voice and try to act it out, gesture with your hands and use exaggerated facial expressions. If you are not tied to a microphone then try and walk around to help act out the story. Make it exciting for your young audience, and hopefully funny in places.

You may encounter a time when you wish to communicate with another person, but your interpreter is not around. One solution is by the use of a dual language book where the two languages are printed on opposite pages. If you have a phrase book, you may not be able to pronounce what you want to say, but you can point to the text and let the other person read it. If they can find the answer in the phrase book, then they can point the answer back to yourself and you can read it.

When Language is Problematic

- Hand gestures often help, you need your room cleaned (pretend to vacuum). You need to drink (cup your hand, bring to your mouth and pour/shake). You need a place to sleep (hands together on their side and put your head on them).
- If you are not sure of the local name for an item, like toilet paper, take a piece with you. Or with your phrase book, point to the relevant item or phrase.
- You can take a clear photo of a destination sign and show it to a taxi or bus driver, or point to it in your guidebook.
- Ask someone who understands you (waiter, receptionist etc.) to write out the destination in the local language – especially if the script is different than your own, like Chinese, Korean, Japanese, Russian, Tamil, Urdu, Hebrew or Arabic.
- Take a dual language book with you. These have two languages printed on opposite pages making it much easier to communicate.
- Dual language Bibles are an excellent aid for Christian travellers when they cannot speak the language, yet with prepared selected passages of Scripture, they can still communicate with Christians from the host nation.[1]

In communicating via a second language you need to be understood; not misunderstood, which is a very important point.

The Sounds of Language – Pronunciation

Citizens of different countries struggle with certain sounds, simply because they are unfamiliar with them. Koreans cannot pronounce the letter 'Z,' the Chinese and Koreans cannot sound the letter 'L' which is very similar to the letter 'R' – hence why they say, "Melly Chlistmas" and not Merry Christmas. This use of 'L' for 'R' is known as lambdacisms, and the Japanese on the other hand, substitute the letter 'R,' for the letter 'L'. The English cannot hear the difference between some French words with their acute accents, whereas some people from the Orient can hear the difference between wool and wall, yet are unable to pronounce them as two individual words. Many African languages use 'clicks' where the tongue hits the roof of the mouth to produce various words. Just try it.

Language Tales in China

The following is a series of emails written by my brother[2] when we travelled around China and the issues encountered with the Mandarin language:

We went to the bus station to buy a ticket to move on to the next city. I tried to speak in Chinese again. "I would like to buy a ticket to go to Yangshuo." I'm not sure if anyone understood what I said, as the tones of Mandarin Chinese are hard to grasp – "Woou sheunnggg mai piaowoo ccheeeew Yanngshoooo" – "I would like to buy a ticket to Yangshou." However, with my few words and our phrase book, the people got the idea. Everyone looked a little out-of-their-depth as they did not understand us and we did not understand them. Crowds of people came around and one woman spoke to me. I looked at her and said, "Woow tingg boouu donggg" – "I don't understand." The lady and her friend laughed as they recognised what I said and they spoke to each other. "I don't understand!" Finally a man said to us in Chinese go from "Zhaoqing, to Wuzhou, to Guilin, to Yangshuo." We understood the simplicity of his statements. I said in Chinese, "Gee dinana chewwww?" – "What time does it leave?" He looked at me puzzled. I said again, "Geeeee diaanna cheeeew?" He looked puzzled again. "Gheee diannn chheww." He smiled and said in Chinese, "Oh, what time does it leave!" "Barr dian." 'Barr dian,' what does that mean again? In Chinese: 1, 2, 3, 4, 5, 6, 7, 8. But we still could not get there until someone managed to write it down as a figure eight and my friend saw it. They use the English numbers on their notes etc., so they are familiar with it.

We had planned to spend one night in this city and move on, but as we had had a real problem buying tickets to get out and the hotel was so nice, we spent another day. We looked for the old city wall, but could not find it. A Chinese man said, "Hello, how are you" in English, so I went over to him and showed him the book and pointed to the Chinese writing of old city wall. He pointed the way and in Chinese I repeated his directions, "Straight on, then, turn left." I was feeling a little better that two years of private study of Chinese was not wasted.

At a tea shop, a man told me that it was cold in Beijing, so I said in Chinese, "It's really cold." The Chinese woman selling the tea looked surprised and said, "He speaks Chinese." She then asked in

Chinese, "How long have you been learning Chinese?" I understood the first few words, but she spoke very fast. So through our Chinese friend, we explained that I only knew some phrases and was like a young child in speaking the language. However, this experience of hearing me gave her confidence to spend the next 15 minutes speaking to us in Chinese, even though we mostly understood by her hand gestures and by translation.

As for the Chinese language skills, all I can say is that I have good days and bad days. On a good day, it seems like almost everything I say in Chinese is understood. On a bad day, I speak to someone in Chinese and they look at me and say, "I don't understand...I don't speak English." I think, "I'm not speaking English...is my Chinese that bad!" This situation is complicated by the fact that Mandarin (the official language) is taught as a second language in many areas of China, because there are numerous Chinese languages and numerous tones, types and variations of these languages! The list goes on and on! One morning we were checking out of a hotel and I said, "Please can we have the receipt." "Qhing Ga Wo Midan." The women looked very confused at me. Then ten seconds later I realised that I had said, "Please can I have the menu" instead of receipt!" – Midan is menu, Sidan is receipt.

We manage to get by with the language by finding English speakers (some of the young people), by using the phrase book (pointing to the Chinese/English text) and by my limited knowledge. As an example, when we were buying tickets, the lady was talking and I understood very little. Then I heard, "Mingtian." I knew that meant "tomorrow" and she was asking if we wanted to buy the tickets for tomorrow. Immediately I said, "Mingtian. Yes. Mingtian." Or in Chinese "no" would be, "Bu Mingtian" – not tomorrow. I feel good when I understand and realise how little I know when I don't! The Chinese language is so different from European ones. The sentences are often constructed very differently. For example, "Ni shir na guoren?" means "What country are you from?" But the literal translation is, "You are what country person." This has given birth to a language which people jokingly called Chinglish. It's the Chinese version of English. So it is normal to see signs saying: 'You use toilet correctly' – meaning, 'Please keep the toilet clean,' or 'The green grass is afraid of your foot' – 'Please keep off the grass,' and 'Slip carefully' – 'Be careful, the floor is wet.' In a fast food restaurant, we walked up the stairs. The sign could read: 'Beware of slipping' but instead in Chinglish it was: 'Beware of landslide.' In our hotel, there is a sign that is trying to state: 'If you want clean towels, please place them in the basin.' In Chinglish it reads: 'If you need to be replaced on a towel, please wash basin!' Another sign for 'slippery' reads, 'Carefully slide.'

Chapter 25

Be Smart and Shrewd

Entering into a new country you have to learn to be streetwise, to be smart and shrewd. If you are with an organization, stick close to your leader and keep an eye out for your fellow team members. Border crossings are the most wary places to be, but especially if you emerge from no-man's-land into a new country. In some countries, you cannot buy the next country's currency from a Bureau de Change or bank and so frequently have no option, but to buy money on the border. A slight-of-hand trick or a rigged calculator (so use your own) can cost you. Sometimes a zero or two is knocked off the end figure! Instead of getting 200,000, you may get 20,000! In some places there may be a black market, a better rate compared with the set rate of exchange. I have never used it, though many travellers have been exploited, even with out-of-circulation notes/bills or the money exchanger is an undercover police officer.

If you use facilities at a border town (e.g. a hotel or coach station), you need to know not only the cost, but clarify the currency as well. Don't assume prices are in the currency of the country you are in!

In many places of the world people *want* to carry your bag; it is unlikely that they will run off with a fully laden rucksack/backpack, but they *will* expect payment or take you to their preferred choice of bus, taxi, or hotel where you will end up indirectly paying for it. If you ask, "Where is the nearest hotel?" in developing countries, some people will want to take you to it and expect financial recompense! Just ask to be pointed in the right direction. Others will take you to a hotel and ignore the guesthouse, campsite, hostel, lodge, B&B and other accommodation because you asked for *a hotel*. If they have gone out of their way then give them something for their time and don't let them run off with your wallet or purse! Keep some coins or small notes/bills handy.

I have found that in both Africa and Asia, children love to touch your skin, stroke your arms, and sometimes even adults, especially if you have hairs on them as Africans and Asians generally do not. Africans are fascinated with straight soft hair, especially blonde-haired people, and do not be surprised if someone tries to stroke your hair or arms. Adults may ask, and it is nothing to be afraid of, but if you are a woman, be aware of men and rebuke them firmly if the occasion requires it! In China, many people wanted to take our photo, with them standing next to us – selfie! Others would try to do it discreetly, and we would stop and pose for them which made them very happy. Be a good ambassador for your country.

Christians in developing countries have informed me that in their countries, just walking alongside a foreigner bolsters their own status, but to talk with one is far better. It is a good opportunity to practise your language skill or to learn new things, whilst some people are best kept at arms length because you *know* they are up to no good, you may feel uncomfortable in their presence. Others are after a free meal, your contact details or will be friendly with you in an attempt to get closer to members of the opposite sex within the group. Always be ready to help a member of the team who may be pestered or harassed by a local – "We have to go, goodbye," and walk off together. A good test of the 'sincerity' of a local man speaking to a female member of your group is: Does he stay around when a male member of the team introduces himself and joins in the conversation?

Be aware of your surroundings. Be cautious who you go with or follow, if they have approached you, offering to show you something. They may lead you into a dark or quiet alley to rob you. Others may get you lost, and will *only* take you to your accommodation for a sum of money. Be shrewd in the discernment of people's motives. Your tour company, organization, NGO or charity will advise you of no-go areas and places to avoid.

If you are a prankster, or like to have a laugh, be careful that the joke does not backfire on you. In September 2016, the Australian state of Victoria made it a criminal offence to moon (mooning), streak or expose yourself in public. The Summary Offences Act also outlaws singing "an obscene song or ballard" and behaving in a riotous, indecent, offensive or insulting manner." First-time offenders can face up to two months in jail.

In some places it is best not to reveal where you are staying, in which hotel or guest house etc., just be vague, if asked, "over there" and point in a general direction. In one town in Kenya, a man tried to enter our hotel claiming to be our friend (presumably to get access to our room). The security guard was wise enough to remove him from the hotel and reported the incident to us. We had only arrived the day before, only spoken to a few people, and told no one where we were staying.

Getting Your Attention

In Africa, to get your attention people will hiss as it is rude to shout, but in South-East Asia the customary, "You, YOU!" or "Oi!" yelled at the top of their lungs by a seller is common. Others try to get your attention by saying, "I want to show you something," or "I want to tell you something." You can be in the midst of a conversation and a person will interrupt, tug on your sleeve or even slap you gently on your arm to get your attention! As much as these instances may be a nuisance, remember that these people are only trying to make a living and the quality of your life compared to theirs is huge. If you were in their circumstances, you would probably do the same. Be polite and smile. Some sellers have some handy items, knickknacks or snacks (especially at bus stations) and you will be thankful that they approached you, whilst some guides are real gems of local knowledge and can take you into areas where you would have never trod.

Scams and Warnings

Additional food that you did not order can appear on your table and you will be charged for it, though in some places in North Africa, mint tea is freely served after the meal. Ask before you sip, otherwise it is too late and it goes on the bill! On rare occasions, bottled water can be delivered to your table and the seal may be broken. Always reject it, as it is tap/faucet water at best or stream water at worse and could make you unwell.

Students who desire to practise their English may also approach you. A good opportunity to meet new people, but be cautious if they invite you to a cafe or restaurant, as it may be their job to drum up customers into expensive establishments. On the other hand, I have been in a restaurant having a meal with a group of local students and when the bill arrived, the locals vehemently complained to the owner over the inflated foreigner's bill!

Some calculators are set to deceive people. They can be known as trick calculators and are used by con artists, especially when calculating money in foreign exchange. For example, one calculator's total for 5 x 4 was not 20 but 16! To get this sum the owner pressed 5 x 4 x and the total would be 16 (notice the x sign). But if 5 x 4 = was pressed (notice the = sign) then the total would be 20. Take your own pocket calculator, it is essential.

Not everything that is labelled or touted as handmade is handmade. Just because someone puts a 'present' in your hand and tells you it's free does not mean that it will cost you nothing! At other times, sellers will put items in your hand and refuse to take it back, yet expect money for it. If you don't want the item and they refuse to take it from you, then place it on the ground or somewhere safe and just walk away. Don't be emotionally manipulated into buying items you don't want or parting with more money than you want to.

If travelling on public transport, know where your bag is at all times. You don't want to fall asleep on a long journey and find that somebody has taken your bag. If on a train, use your rucksack/backpack straps and clasps to tie it down to the overhead rack, this will also prevent it from rolling off onto your head or the lap of another passenger! On most minibus taxis, if you sit on the front row there is room to put your bag in front of you. Having your bag on your lap is not ideal, but can be better than having it on the back seat where a unscrupulous passenger has knifed the side of your rucksack and is taking your valuables. In one country, the window was open and a man put his hand inside and tried to pickpocket me. I was sat next to the conductor and the locals thought it was hilarious, but he represented all the other passengers as they were the same nationality. In another country, a six-fingered man got on to the coach and wanted to show off his additional finger with pride whilst with the other hand he tried to steal items.

A dual British/Australian citizen, living in Dubai, United Arab Emirates (UAE), with his wife and children was arrested and held for twenty-two days in prison before being charged in August 2016. He was only allowed to change his clothes once a week and had to pay for his water whilst incarcerated. On Facebook he had promoted a crowd-funding campaign to raise money for a U.S. charity that provide blankets, clothes and tarpaulins for refugee children in Afghanistan. Under UAE law, it prohibits donations or advertising fundraising campaigns without prior permission from Islamic Affairs Charitable Activities Department in Dubai.

Free WiFi at Cafes and Restaurants and Internet Banking
When I first went abroad as a teenager there was no such thing as the internet or mobile/cell phones and planes had a smoking section! In 2011, I purchased a Mini laptop with a 10-inch screen, WiFi enabled with 6hrs battery life specifically for a 3 ½ month trip in Asia to assist me with work as I travelled. You may prefer a Tablet, iPad or smartphone. Many countries have free WiFi hotspots and it was the first time abroad that I did not have to pay to use the internet! Some hotels have internet cables in their rooms or in their lounge or lobby area, which you can plug into your laptop. Other establishments advertise their free WiFi zone within their cafe, restaurant or museum. However, they do not always work, or the staff are unsure of the network or password. Check that the WiFi works before you order a drink or a meal! Li-Fi, a light-based data delivery method may replace WiFi in the future.
You may want to let your friends and followers know of your trip via social networking sites, micro-blogs or vlogging (video blogging).

Beware that social networking sites do not become your master and you become its slave. You have gone abroad to travel and to have new experiences – enjoy!

I have been on many computers in internet cafes and have been quite surprised at what I have found in Documents, the personal files that people have written and left on the computer's hard drive; business proposals, completed job interview forms etc. If you write a file on a public computer, save onto a USB memory stick and delete the file on the computer, and empty the Recycle Bin/Trash Can.

You should be very cautious of using online banking from an internet cafe (especially in developing countries) or cheap hotel and try to avoid making purchases online. A programme could be collecting all your details. If you have your own laptop, Tablet, iPad or smartphone then it is safer but not immune to cyber attacks, ransomware or malware. Keep your own antivirus software up-to-date. Avoid clicking through on pop-up boxes. You are not the millionth visitor to a website and will not win a prize – do not try and claim it! Do not get paranoid, just be aware of these things.

If you are not using your own device, then remember to 'Log Out' after all applications where you have had to enter a password to access information, even your email account. Do not click, 'Remember Me.' Or, 'Keep Me Signed In,' unclick the button if it automatically defaults to that setting. After you have logged out, you should delete the computer's history, information that remains within the computer's memory such as websites visited and passwords. With your internet browser open, delete your browsing history, temporary internet files, form data and passwords etc. At one internet cafe, ironically, opposite the National Electricity headquarters there was a power cut! We went outside until the power came back, the computer restarted itself and opened up all my browsers, including my email account!

In October 2016, nine Australians were arrested for stripping off to their swimming trunks (Budgie smugglers) after the F1 Malaysian Grand Prix. Their swimwear was decorated with the Malaysian flag. They were charged with public nuisance and fined, but could have been jailed. The previous year, four tourists were jailed in Malaysia for stripping off at the peak of Mount Kinabalu and taking naked photos of themselves which were uploaded to social media.

In October 2016, a Dutch backpacker in Myanmar was sentenced to three months in prison for unplugging an amplifier which was blasting out a Buddhist sermon, disturbing his sleep. He walked into the temple with his shoes on at 10pm, on 23 September, nearly causing a riot! Wearing shoes inside a temple is forbidden and a fine was paid (£50 $80) instead of having to serve a longer sentence.

Chapter 26

The Laws of the Land and Be Safe

Wherever you go to in the world, even outside of your own front door you could encounter trouble, but wisdom and caution are the best line of defence; whether at home or abroad. On occasions, countries or some areas can break out into political instability, so it pays to scan the local news headlines, international papers and look on your government's website as they issue travel warnings to its citizens. In many places of the world Westerners are targets.

Curiosity can override common sense, but avoid political rallies and demonstrations as they can turn nasty and you could end up in the middle of it. Tear gas, rubber bullets, and flying missiles (rocks and stones) make no distinction on whom they hit or affect. Keep away from drunken crowds. Football/soccer matches can be an issue, especially if rival fans go on the rampage as seen during Euro 2016 across France.

Handbags and bum-bags (fanny packs/belt bags) are magnets for thieves. If you can loop your gadgets (e.g. digital camera or mobile/cell phone) on your belt covered by a long shirt or jumper/sweater then this is better, or inside a day-bag. Zipped or Velcro pockets on trousers/pants or skirts are very good for wallets, purses and passports. Some people have their passport and excess money in a pouch which is hung around the neck and tucked into one's top – out of sight, out of mind. Money belts are very good. Handbags can be easily snatched off the arm and can cause injury. Beware if people bump into you as they may be trying to steal from you, grope you, or coming between you as a group to pickpocket; or distracting you at a restaurant or cafe, someone else takes your bag from under (or on top of) your table or chair etc. Hook your day-bag round your chair leg or through the arm of your chair. Large crowds at bus and train stations can be a pickpocketer's paradise.

It is unwise to invite a stranger into your hotel room as they may be a sex worker; regardless of the fact that they are the same sex as you. Most hotels do not permit room calls/visits because of this very problem.

Don't invite trouble and be sensible in what you wear and where you go, especially in religious countries. In some places it is sensible not to go out alone, especially in a foreign country where you will feel more vulnerable. If you are travelling alone, you don't have to be a hermit, but make new friends, whether locals or foreigners. As in your home country there are some places where it is advisable not to walk alone and not to go after dark. We have common sense and it should be applied. Look after yourself and lookout for your friends.

Every once and a while I have encountered problem people whilst travelling. It may be the guy who is intoxicated or high on drugs; the criminal who is envious or who despises your presence in *their* neighbourhood, those who are unbalanced in mind and those in groups who are boisterous, being egged on by the crowd. In these circumstances, it is best not to be confrontational or aggressive, but to walk away. In Dhaka, Bangladesh, due to an incident, we walked into a photographic shop and stayed inside until the crowd had dispersed.

Political tension has revealed to the world the inflamed anger of some indigenous people in certain areas of a minority of countries. At other times, if you hold a certain passport, you may be denied a visa or forbidden access to enter a country, whilst a change of regime or government can change their ruling at a whim. In some countries, because of war, economic sanctions or the countries colonial past, some foreign citizens may face added danger or disdain, thus hindering and possibly endangering those with them.

Ignorance of the Law

There is a saying that goes, 'Ignorance of the law is no defence' and being in a different country than your own with unfamiliar laws does not mean that prosecution will be less swift if you break the law, nor will you have immunity because you are a foreigner.

Laws which may differ from your own country can be:
- The forbidding of taking photographs of military installations or bridges.
- The forbidding of importing foods, plants or other.
- What you can wear in public.
- What you can say in public; religious or political, even comments on social media, about leaders, royalty, and even blasphemy and swearing/cursing.
- Public interaction with members of the opposite sex, even when married. Kissing or holding hands etc.
- The forbidding or distribution of illegal or unauthorised literature. At tourist attractions around China, there were a number of signs relating to this. It could be: workers' rights, religious rights, literature or proselytizing. Standing up to or opposing the government or local leaders, dissent.
- Various driving or travel regulations, including where pedestrians can cross a road, jaywalking in the USA is illegal, but not in the UK. Other countries state that

jaywalking is illegal if a designated crossing is within 100 metres of where you cross.
- Drinking alcohol in private or public. In the USA you have to be 21 to drink alcohol in bars, in the UK it is 18.
- Age related laws, what you can or cannot do until a certain age. As above, but also driving, establishments you can enter, what you can view, own or buy.
- Some laws relate to what you can take in or out of a country. National treasures, works of art or antiquities.

Be careful what you Write or Say

Just before Christmas 2008, two Scottish missionaries to Gambia, David Fulton (aged 60) and his wife Fiona (aged 46) were arrested and charged with sedition (inciting rebellion against the authority). They had written emails critical of the country's president and sent them to friends and organizations in the West, the content of which Gambia deemed seditious. In court, at the capital Banjul, they pleaded guilty in the hope that a lighter sentence would be given, but on 30 December 2008, they were sentenced to a year's hard labour in Gambia and were each fined £6,250 ($9,250). The court stated that the emails, which the Fulton's insisted were harmless, incited 'hatred or contempt against the president or the government.'

In January 2009, Australian writer, Harry Nicolaides was sentenced to three years in prison under Thailand's draconian lese-majesty laws, which forbid criticism of the king, which is seen as an attempt by the government to stifle dissent. Other people since then have been arrested in Thailand and in other countries, based on similar laws. Some are just immediately deported. This includes comments made on social media about the government and/or its policies.

In most countries, Western tourism is too important to imperil by locking up travellers for minor offences though policies differ between tourist and rural areas. If the police stop foreigners, it is usually to give a firm but polite telling off but this is not the case in countries that are not dependant on tourism such as Iran, Burma, Bhutan, Sudan, Somalia and North Korea. In March 2016, Otto Warmbier, an American college student was sentenced to fifteen years hard labour, for 'crimes against the state' allegedly trying to steal a political banner whilst on an organised tour in North Korea.

Other countries have laws against defacing the monarch or president, the burning of flags, flags have to be illuminated at night, speaking or writing against those in leadership, or changing the words to the national anthem, even in a parody. In the USA, The Flag Code states: 'The flag may be displayed 24 hours a day if properly illuminated during the hours of darkness.' However the term 'properly illuminated' does not go into specifics.

Since 2014, almost two thousand people in Turkey have been prosecuted (including children and celebrities) for insulting President Erdogan. This includes sharing posts that "insult a public official." You do not need to be the originator of the article or image, but merely sharing it can lead to a fourteen month suspended jail sentence, as a former Turkey beauty queen received in 2016. On the night of Friday, 15 July 2016, there was a military coup in Turkey, which failed. More than 200 people were injured, around 160 were initially shot dead and more than 17,000 people arrested with 35,000 detained. At least 81,000 workers were fired or suspended.[1]

In some countries, swearing via social media or messenger services can land you with a fine!

Stimulants and Narcotics

Be careful of what you are offered to chew or drink. If you are offered a substance to chew, except chewing gum, then in all probability it will be a narcotic type stimulant. It may be perfectly legal and culturally acceptable, or perhaps even expected, but it is advisable to politely decline. Other stimulants are snorted and any of the above, can really mess with your stomach and bowels, or head to produce a drug-like effect, hallucinations, evil dreams or nightmares. It may be beetle gum in India, chat or chad in Africa, or the more common known narcotics in Thailand, with their dozens of Western names. What you have been given may also relax your mind and body so that you can be robbed or taken advantage of – it also makes it easier to kidnap you as you are in a docile state. Beware of having a pill or tablet dropped into your drink as you may wake up somewhere where you do not know and discover that something happened that you did not consent to.

Don't become an unwitting drugs mule or a drug mule full stop! If you are offered a free flight and some money to take a bag to another destination, decline and get out of there quickly. A free flight and $500 (£312) may sound great, but there is a catch, it is breaking the law and can lead to many years (or decades) in prison, and in some countries, the death penalty. Prison in developing countries are often Dickensian in their mode and manner – that is, they are like a debtor's prison from the Victorian era. Dark, dirty, unsafe to be in and you are expected to pay for your own incarceration! In addition, you may have met some travelling companions along the way, do not pack any of their belongings in your bag, and do not carry their bag (even a day-bag) across any border. If there is anything illicit, it will be your bag and your companion will vow that he or she does not know you!

People who have arrived in Dubai, in United Arab Emirates (UAE), via Amsterdam in the Netherlands have been arrested at the airport because automatic narcotic detectors have found traces of illegal substances on the soles of their footwear; traces so small that it cannot been seen with the naked eye! As one reporter noted, if you are walking through Amsterdam, it is highly probable that you will pick up minute traces of narcotics. Codeine found in some Western painkillers is also illegal in UAE.

Across Britain it is illegal to smoke in public places such as hotels, cafes, restaurants, pubs/bars, nightclubs, shops and workplaces. Some places will have designated places where smoking is permitted, for many bars, it is outside the doors. Some places have also banned e-cigs/vapours. The signage will tell you what is not permitted. You can also received a fine if you litter – dropping your rubbish on the floor, or flicking your cigarettes away.

Since 1992, Singapore has had a ban on chewing gum, to help clean up the country's public spaces. Revised in 2004, travellers can bring their own personal supplies of medicated or dental benefit gum. Dispose of it in the correct way, or you'll be in trouble!

Potions and Alcohol

All cultures have strange, weird, wonderful food and beverages, but some are not so good for you as others. Yak butter tea in Tibet may be greasy, but is not alcoholic or considered dangerous nor will it alter your state of being, and it is these latter beverages that you must be very cautious of. Local brew can be very potent and more often than not, you may be offered a drink without knowing its true contents. Juice from palm trees ferments within hours in hot climates and has a high alcohol content.

If you get invited out for a drink or a meal by some locals, don't be surprised if you end up paying for everything! They may be employed by the cafe, bar or the restaurant to drum up customers; many young women are in this employment, even in Western cities. They will have a great time at your expense. You may enjoy yourself as well, but it could be an expensive night out for a budget traveller and why should you pay for friendship? You don't have to think negative about the locals or fellow travellers, just be cautious and not naïve. Ask yourself, "Why have they approached me, and what do they want, or expect to get from me?" Remember, you can walk away at any time or start as you mean to go on, buy yourself a coffee or a meal, and decline offers from others.

In many Islamic countries, alcohol is outlawed or only available in licensed places, to accommodate foreigners and tourists. In America, you can learn to drive a car at 16½, be on the frontline in the military at 18, buy a gun at 18 (younger for a rifle or shotgun) and drink alcohol at 21. In many public places across Britain, drinking is an offence under local bylaws and fines can be issued.

Chapter 27

Food, Glorious Food

The world has much to offer in the realm of culinary delight. If you are with a humanitarian organization, NGO or charity, hopefully you will be well looked after, but it may take time for your taste buds to adapt! On your travels you rarely have to go without, unless you live frugally which is often a false economy. At other times you may pine for certain food. When I first went to India, I really wanted a cheese and pickle sandwich, but could not get one!

The global market has much to offer and whilst travelling, it is always interesting to try different foods. Dining out, you may encounter on your local menu, the familiar and unfamiliar! From rats, bats, cats, dogs, hogs and frogs, ants or plants, grubs or shrubs, snake or hake, rice or mice, snail or quail and crocodile eyes to vegetarian pies. Other foods you may encounter could be: Monkey, kangaroo, hippo, ostrich, yak, guinea pig, pigeon, rabbit, various rodents, reptiles and insects; grasshoppers, worms, grubs, bees, lizards, fish, shark, crab, shell fish and a whole host of birds and foul. Remember to have water handy to wash it down or milk to douse the hot spices!

Back in 2011, relating to Zhaoqing, China, I wrote: 'We ate in a local buffet restaurant today. We just pointed and they put it on the plate. Half the stuff was not what I thought it was! However it was good. We bought some fruit from a street vendor – don't know what it is, but he gave us a sample, so we bought about a dozen of these little fruits which have a large stone and need to be peeled. They are nearly transparent in colour and taste a little of citrus.'

In one town in Vietnam I ordered a chicken salad. I recognised the strips of chicken, but all of the greens just looked like garden weeds! In many restaurants in China, the fish or sea creatures are so fresh that it is like going to an aquarium. You pick your fish, squid, eel, turtle etc. and the chef will go and prepare it!

Beware of overdosing on your country's staple food that you have not eaten in months. One Korean student had not eaten rice since she arrived in Britain. When, after many months it was placed before her, she ate and ate as if there would be no tomorrow. The rice swelled up in her stomach, causing her excruciating pain and she had to be taken to hospital.

In most major cities, there may be familiar fast food chains, or a local imitation, which you may not appreciate! The fast food may taste great, like at home, but you can not live for months eating it without consequences – there is a reason why it is called *junk* food! High in calories with little nutritional value, get some fruit and vegetables inside of you as you travel.

We checked-in late at night and found that the hotel menu had one set price (expensive) for a buffet meal, which did not even look appetising. We took a taxi to a fast-food joint, had a great meal, took a taxi back to our hotel and all this was cheaper than the hotel buffet! John – Swaziland.

Some countries' carnivorous food may well be a pet from home. For some it is a delicacy, like dogs in Korea and China, horses in France or donkey in parts of Italy. In some countries, my brother and I have decided not to talk about our food, but just to eat it, without knowing what meat or part of the body it is! If you think it may be x part of the body, it can put you off your food entirely.

In Indonesia, monkeys harvest coconuts for their masters and on a good day can pick three hundred! Otters in Bangladesh and cormorants in China are used to catch fish, whilst ferrets are used in Britain to catch rabbits.

Prince Philip, husband of HRH Queen Elizabeth II is well known for his verbal gaffes. Whilst in China in 1986, Prince Philip said, "If it has got four legs and it is not a chair, if it has got two wings and it flies but is not an aeroplane, and if it swims and it is not a submarine, the Cantonese will eat it."

British chef, Jamie Oliver was in Whyomy, USA, cattle raising country, where he spent a few days on a working ranch. After the bull calves were castrated; the testicles were peeled, cooked in batter and eaten. The rancher informed his guest, "Nothing gets wasted," and after tasting the 'cowboy cuisine,' even Jamie with joy and a look of glee said, "It tastes like scampi!"

In the West, we go to the supermarket or order online and have a sanitized view of pre-packaged meat, whereas in much of the developing world, you go to the market, buy your meat fresh e.g. chicken, kill it and prepare it.

I spent a year in an African country teaching English, but I was the one who received an education! The culture, customs, accommodation, the people and the food was all an experience for me. The usual staple diet of matooke, rice, beans, posho, cassava, chapattis, tomatoes, onions, green peppers, grasshoppers and ants were common. Those who had a little more money could afford beef, but chicken, turkey and pork can be quite expensive. You usually have to kill it yourself though! Russell – Uganda.

Food Allergies and Food Hygiene

If you are allergic to certain food types, you need to be extra cautious when travelling. If you have a nut allergy, ground nut are often used in curries. If you were to ask the server, waiter or waitress, "Does it contain nuts?" If English is a second language, it may be taken as a statement, "I like nuts" or a request for nuts! In many countries, most servers, waiters or waitresses would not be able to tell you all of the ingredients in every dish on the menu. In many countries there can be a high level of cross-contamination as the same spoon or ladle is used in multiple dishes. In addition, the workers may not have washed their hands after using the bathroom.

Hygiene, refrigeration and pasteurisation may not be as good as at home. This means that some foods (or drinks) especially in hot climates may make you unwell. Raw meat and fish, cream, mayonnaise and cooked food that has been left around in humid temperatures can make you ill. Even salads, fruit and vegetables washed in local water may be problematic. One saying is: 'Boil it, cook it, peel it or forget it,' but this is not always practical or possible. A distinction should be made for those who are abroad for two weeks or three months. You cannot avoid most types of food on your travels, but you do not want to be ill for a week when your trip is only two weeks in duration! Self-catering groups can wash vegetables, fruit and salad items in water with chlorine or iodine to help kill germs. Frying food in very hot oil helps kill germs.

For longer trips, you can try eating small amounts of different types of food, or taking a sip of the local water, to see how it affects you and to help build up your immune system. It may not be the food that is the problem, but the restaurant where it is prepared and sold. In some food establishments, to reach the toilet you have to pass through the kitchen. Having seen the kitchen in some places has put me off some of the meals I have ordered as the hygiene and general cleanliness appeared to be nonexistent.

Some people when abroad, *only* use bottled water to brush their teeth with, I am not one of them, though if the place is grotty, the pipe-work looks in poor condition, is made of lead, or if the 'tap/faucet water' is collected from the roof when it rains, then I avoid it or boil it in my travel kettle. One traveller who we met on the back of a pick-up truck in Zambia, was in his late 50s. He told us that when he travels he never buys bottled water, but drinks the local water, direct from the tap/faucet. "Occasionally I get a stomach upset," he said, "But that is part of travelling."

In some African countries, we found it difficult to purchase milk that had not gone off. When it came in a container, you could often sniff the lid top, to try and check (or just open the lid), but when it came in sealed 250ml sized triangle-shaped plastic packaging, you bought your milk and took a chance. In our room, we always smelt the milk before we poured it into our tea or bowl of cereals. It is good to have a taste from home, once in a while as a treat. If the milk was off, we poured it down the sink; whilst to keep it cool, we put the lid on or pegged the corner and filled the sink with water. Once opened, it cannot be left around for days in a hot environment and most of the time should be used within 12-24 hours. Have a glass of milk.

Food Advice
- Wash your hands after going to the toilet/bathroom and before handling food. Some public toilets are so dirty that you have more risk of catching something from turning on/off the tap/faucet if you are only doing a number one. Hand sanitizers or gel come in useful in these instances.
- Buy bottled water with sealed tops, not ones that have been refilled and the safety seal glued back on!
- Tap/faucet or stream water can be boiled or sterilised.
- Carbonated drinks (fizzy) are generally safe to drink as is fruit juice, unless it has fermented and gone off.
- Milk can go off quick if it has not been refrigerated. You will be able to smell it or at least taste it.
- Boil unpasteurised milk.
- Be cautious of yogurt, mayonnaise and ice cream. They can be breeding ground for bacteria and if ice cream has melted and been refrozen there can be major issues. If you can taste ice, this is a good indicator that is has melted and been refrozen – better to throw it away, than to be unwell.
- Avoid ice in drinks as it is probably tap/faucet water.
- Avoid warm food or food that has been exposed to flies.
- Avoid uncooked food in countries where hygiene is poor.
- Cheap uncooked meat can be an issue. It may be off, been sat around for some time, or could even be road-kill.
- Fish and shell fish, especially when uncooked can be hazardous in some countries. If it is fresh it should be ok, but it may have travelled a day on the back of a pick-up truck in scorching heat and in direct sunlight.
- Watermelons may have been pricked and left in the local river to 'juice up.' Other slices of melon are sprinkled with water to keep them moist.
- Can it be boiled, cooked or peeled? If not, avoid it.

Food Etiquette
In many countries, you only eat with your right hand. Trying to separate meat with only one hand and no utensils is a real bind and

tricky, that is why in Japan, meat is cut into portions to enable you to pick them up with your chopsticks; but have you ever tried to eat Korean seaweed or pick up thinly sliced vegetables from your plate with chopsticks? It's a real challenge. And how do you eat a spring roll when you have no knife? Your eating utensils and accompanying food 'plate' could be: A knife and fork, spoon, chopsticks or by hand. Your food could be placed on a paper, plastic, wooden or ceramic plate, or saucepan lid; served on the table, in a tray, on a banana leaf or in yesterdays newspaper.

You may be invited into a home as the guest of honour, what they set before you may be a much larger portion than what they serve themselves, or an expensive speciality food. To refuse may be seen as an insult, whereas at other times, if you eat it all, you could be deemed greedy! Take small portions and eat slowly. You may get first pick of the bowl and when you have eaten, the host and/or his or her children will be permitted to tuck in. You could be served lamb's head in Morocco, sheep's testicles in Mongolia, bats in Borneo, baby sparrows or a snake's heart in Vietnam or duck's tongue or pig's intestines in China! In Alaska, your diet could consist of: Maktak (raw whale meat), Beluga whale, caribou, seal, owl, polar bear or walrus!

> I had a meal of sago for the first time. It's a powdery starch that is found in certain sago palms (the pulp of a tree). I ate it and smiled; it looked like wallpaper paste and tasted like it! Charlie – Papua New Guinea.

In some cultures, you leave some food on the plate as a sign you're full, at other times you eat it all! In some cultures you accept a little food, move it around your plate and it's ok, in other places it would be frowned upon as playing with your food! Sometimes refusing drinks is rude, but you can accept it, put it to your lips without drinking any and then place it on the floor or table without offending your host. Whatever is put before you partake of it, unless your conscience or religious beliefs denote otherwise, regardless of how unpalatable it looks, imagine it is your favourite food, be positive. If you are a particular eater, a good rule of thumb is: don't ask what it is! Try to be thankful and grateful, and look as if you are enjoying it. Remember, in many cultures it is customary to bring a gift for your host or when invited to a home for a meal.

To burp in India after a meal is considered a compliment, but not in Britain where it is rude, as is blowing your nose at the meal table in Korea. If in India, you were to dip your japatti (bread) into the main dish, those eating with you would not be able to participate of that dish and it would have to be returned to the kitchen. Whereas in the south of Tunisia, our group got invited into a Muslim home where the host set before us a very large bowl of couscous. We sat cross-legged in the courtyard and each person had a spoon and tucked in; whilst the cooks; the women (who do not eat with men that are unrelated to them) watched from a respectful distance.

Watch and observe the locals who are always forgiving of foreigners and will more often than not, laugh at you if you get it wrong, rather than rebuke you! It is good practice to laugh with them, not at them, as a curved smile sets a lot of crooked things straight!

Vegetarian Meals

Being a vegetarian by choice is not the norm in most countries and in places where you can buy vegetarian dishes it may not be vegetarian enough! Encountering indigenous 'vegetarians' is often because they are too poor to eat meat, or because of religious reasons (e.g. India or Nepal), or the Dreads of Domenica (similar to Rastafarians). Buddhist cuisine is primarily vegetarian, in order to keep with the general Buddhist precept of ahimsa (non-violence – no fly swatting allowed!), though some sects eat meat. The ahimsa ideal had its development in Hinduism. Many Sikhs maintain their right to eat meat, but only vegetarian meals are served in the Langar (free refectories which are maintained by Sikh Gurdwaras) to avoid controversy.

I ordered a vegetarian curry in Ulaanbaatar, Mongolia, and the server asked if I was a vegetarian. I said, "No." The curry that was put before me had several tasty lumps of tender beef with freshly cut chunks of carrots!

We went to the local cafe and ordered a cold drink. The cafe worker got a bottle of coke and took the top off. He told me it was two dinnars. I do not read Arabic, but I could see that the highest price on the drinks board was 0.50 dinnars. A fellow traveller expostulated with the waiter, and pointed to the menu; the waiter shook his head and I had to give in. Always ask, "How much?" before you order! Nicholas – Tunisia.

Tea in China

On our sightseeing tour of Guilin in China, we visited two ancient pagodas where we met a Chinese man who was on holiday. He had excellent English and was an avid bodybuilder. We spent around three hours with him, walking and talking about many things. He took us to a local restaurant where we ordered three different dishes and drank copious amounts of green tea. The food is all shared and people take a selection. Our friend, kept on filling up our tea glass and serving us food and teaching us culture and custom, whilst my brother was able to practice about eighty percent of his vocabulary – the man was impressed, as have been the shop keepers.

Our new friend invited us to a tea shop as he was going to buy some tea for his father as a present – it cost £28 ($45) per kilo and was made from yellow flowers! It was fascinating to see the hundreds of glass jars filled with flower petals and plants, a cacophony of colours vying for our attention. However, before he bought the tea he said, "You must always try the tea first." We sat at the back of the shop where four little tea pots were filled with four different types and colours of tea. The water was put on to boil whilst the ritual of warming the tea micro-cups, rinsing and washing began, which probably only held about 15ml. A ceramic test tube-like china tea vessel was filled with tea and the tea cup put on top. This was then turned over and placed in front of you on a square wooden saucer. You lift up the test tube and so the tea pours into your micro-cup. You smell the test tube and if it is too hot you roll it between your fingers, thus displacing the heat. The micro-cup was filled and filled and refilled on copious occasions and we were taught that you have to smell the tea, before you taste it. It was only when I was so full that our friend turned his cup upside down which symbolises "enough" otherwise the tea seller will keep refilling all day! Tea pouring in China is a ritual and the best tea can cost £200 ($320) per kilo and is also used for its medicinal properties.

Chapter 28

Keeping a Journal

When travelling it is a good idea to keep a journal, however brief. I use a new A5 spiral bound lined journal for each trip, you may prefer a leather-bound non-lined journal, a roll-up journal or a digital form, on your laptop or Tablet, remember to save a backup copy. Daily I keep records of the places that I have been to, observations, notes, facts, figures, what I have eaten, how I feel, who we met, and the cost for each day. Your journal can become your very own travel adventure when you read it in later life (in 1, 5 or 10 years time) and the memories, sights and smells can come flooding back.

At the back of my journal is where I keep the accounts. The cost per week and per month, exchange rates, the cost of plane tickets, car hire, cash withdrawals and any other large expenditure.

For your Journal

You can write a lot in your journal, or you may write a brief paragraph, doodle or sketch. The following are suggestions.

- First impressions of each country or city.
- The character traits of a country and its people.
- Name of your accommodation and cost per night.
- What you enjoyed, liked or disliked.
- Where you went and what you did.
- Distances travelled between cities.
- How far you walked or for how long.
- What wildlife, birds, animals, reptiles or mammals you saw.
- Salient points and memorable incidents and people.
- What did you taste, smell and experience?
- What caught your eye or moved you?
- The food you ate and its cost. Was it a local cuisine?
- Any local phrases or words you have picked up.
- Have you any anecdotes?
- Was there a pertinent or striking experience?
- Facts or statistics you read or heard?
- Daily, weekly and monthly expenditure.
- How much money your withdrew at each cash point (ATM) and the exchange rate.
- What items would have been great to take and what you should have left at home.

Excerpts of Four Days from a Travel Journal

May 2011. (Day 1). We caught the coach at 3:45pm to London, Heathrow terminal 4 and arrived at 6:00pm, earlier than expected. Our flight to Jeddah, Saudi Arabia departed at 8:40pm. Check-in asked about our visa to Pakistan but we told them that it was ok and they let us through. Very tight security. Off with shoes, belt and empty all pockets. Sensors still went off and after a pat down [frisk], we both had a full body scan, front and back in a separate room! This was the scan where they see you naked. We first thought that it was a strip room, the man who came behind us (only one person in the room at the time), looked really worried. Had no food on the flight, just drank and must have slept a few hours.

Day 2. We arrived at 4.40am (plus 2 hrs from the UK) at Jeddah airport, Saudi Arabia. It was 25°C on arrival! Another security check, off with boots and belt. Spent some US dollars in the airport on drinks. Later brought up some of my Pepsi in the toilet! I think it may have been local water with the Pepsi syrup as it was not bottled, plus lack of sleep did not help.

We left Saudi at 9.25am and arrived in Islamabad, Pakistan, at about 4pm (plus another 2 hrs from UK GMT). We have now passed four time zones. We were in Pakistan with no visa! And to get to departures you had to leave the airport (an airport porter assisted us, for a fee of course, but well worth it). It was 34°C when we arrived. We could not enter departures for a further 3 hours, so we said goodbye to the porter and $5 (£3) and sat outside the airport, no visa, officially in Pakistan, yet unofficially! We kept telling all security people inside that we were in transit, hence no visa was needed! We took a few photos. About 30 minutes before we were going to go inside departures, security personal approached us and wanted to know who were, what we were doing etc. Checked our passports, not happy that we had no visa, but we explained that we could not get into departures and the security man on the door confirmed this. They wanted to know if we had been taking photos etc. Got to remember that Osama Bin Laden was killed just last week about an hour away from Islamabad. We flew out at 10pm and arrived at midnight in Karachi, south-west of Pakistan.

Day 3. It was 36°C when we arrived at midnight! The Pakistan Airline had a hotel room arranged for us (alongside other passengers), but we explained that we could not go outside of the airport as we had no visa. "It's ok," said one of the officials and so off we went. No visa and yet we travelled about five minutes to a hotel near the airport. Tight security in and out of the airport complex and hotel. Had a shower and slept on a bed for 5 hours. What a blessing as we thought we would be sleeping in the airport. Had breakfast, 2 eggs and 3 buttered toast. You cannot believe how good it tasted, because for the last 24 hours we had eaten so little, just a nibble of one airplane meal.

The airline shuttle bus took us to the airport, machinegun posts, armed guards, bollards in road etc., waited outside for 30 minutes or so. Had three security checks inside which with queues took about two hours. Empty entire rucksack (virtually), everyone not happy that we had no visa – in transit. We changed £60 at the airport for Nepalese rupees at 108r to £1. [In the Nepalese airport it was just 70r to £1!]. One of the top immigration officials said that we should have never left the airport, but that it was not our fault.

We arrived at Katmandu, Nepal, at about 4pm (plus 45 minutes), so now 4 hours 45 minutes in front of UK GMT. $40 each for a visa which took 5 minutes, collected our baggage, negotiated a taxi into Thamel district and a taxi tout took us to his recommended hotel. Blue Horizon Hotel. And it is good! £10 a night 4th floor, 2 beds, ones a double, AC, TV, shower, toilet and free WiFi! Went out about 5.10pm to get food and supplies. About 27°C. We are at 4,400 feet, that is 4,100 feet higher then where I live! Tired. We intend to spend at least a week here, to arrange visas etc. and to begin acclimatisation for Tibet.

May 2011 (Day 4). Today we went out to source a ticket to Tibet. We looked around at all the options, but because of the political tensions, they are not letting anyone in without being on a tour. So there is little freedom and because it is a tour, it is very expensive. The first few days here I was fine, but my body is struggling to adjust; going up another 10,000 feet does not seem wise and we would be tied to two people, a driver and a guide, as part of a group.

A Day Trip to Macau from Hong Kong

We left our guest room at about 8.50am and took the subway to the ferry terminal where we booked on the 10.15am ferry – they depart every 15 minutes, but this was the first one we could get on. The ride to Macau was smooth, about 1 hour in duration – 65km west of Hong Kong. Immigration took nearly 1 hour – a dozen long queues! We took a taxi to the Old Protestant Cemetery, where Robert Morrison (1782-1834), the first Protestant missionary to China, is buried. There were a few other notable people buried in the small graveyard, from surgeons, authors, sailors and those from the East India Company. One American helped set up the first electric telegraph service in Japan.

In Macau, they have their own system of money which is pegged to the Hong Kong Dollar, so you can pay in either currency – this makes it easier. There are many Unesco World Heritage sites, including the front remains of St Paul's Church, destroyed by fire in 1835 – with a massive flight of stairs up to the entrance, which dates to the 1580s, inside and down below is a small museum of sacred art and artefacts. Macau was a Portuguese Colony, given by the Chinese for their help in ridding the area of pirates in 1557. There was the first western style theatre in China, Pedro V Theatre (1850s) in pastel green and along the shoreline, a massive casino presence – huge buildings! We went inside one of them (a first) and it all looked a bit baffling – lots of tables, slots machines and other gambling tools. In the lobby, were two massive diamonds and a world-record brass animal head which sold at Sotheby's for £6.9 million and was brought back to China – lots of people were taking photos – 1,000s of Chinese visitors.

We also went down Street of Happiness which was used in 'Indiana Jones and the Temple of Doom' – which is at the beginning of the film where Shorty (Chinese boy) is driving Dr. Jones and a woman, Willie, the nightclub singer in a white dress through 'Shanghai' after escaping through a window. There are red shutters on the upper level. Other scenes were shot here also.

We took a bus back to the ferry terminal at about 4pm where we were able to go on standby and departed an hour earlier at 4.30pm. We had booked for 6pm departure, because after this time, tickets doubled in price and we were concerned that we may be caught [and have to pay double]. In Macau, it felt more Chinese than what we had seen so far, more of what it will be like within a few days and beyond. Strange food, little English signs etc. and squat toilets.

Chapter 29

How People Tick – Culture

Culture defines who you are, your social queues, familiar references and defines how things are done; because that is the way they have always been done. It is the way a group of inhabitants do things; their attitude, behaviour and values. Culture changes from people group to people group and from country to country. Culture can be broken into smaller segments within a country or even a county (or State) of how those in the north differ from those in the south, or east from west.

The culture of another can be simply observed from an outsider's perspective, but the closer you get the more complex it is! Culture within the same nationality can also change depending on one's upbringing or between generations. The best way to see or observe culture is to go to an ethnic group other than your own; ideally, one that is outside of your own country. You will see the differences between yourself and them, and how you react to the way they do things or how they react to the way you do things!

Every culture has its good and bad points, though ethnic members of each culture may not be able to see certain negative aspects until they are confronted with the culture of another. Culture is the norm of life, the way things are done and therefore each culture thinks that its understanding of the right, good and the true is best – if only because it has always been done that way. Other options may have never been considered or the tradition is just too strong to break. Some cultures do not use the Western idea of personal space or privacy and what may appear 'in your face' is normal behaviour to others.

Regardless of our nationality and cultural traits, we all need to be careful how we 'come across' when we interact with others, but as foreigners we must be aware that we do not present ourselves as loud and boisterous, especially on public transport and when in public places. Be cautious how you interact with members of the opposite sex. You may be accustomed to giving strangers big warm hugs (or air kisses) as part of your introduction/greetings, but at times, it would be more appropriate to smile, say hello and just put out your hand, though in some places even this is a step too far! Being too friendly in some cultures is an indication of wanting to have a sexual relationship with them and that western glance may land you in trouble! In different metros/subways of the world, you avoid eye contact! In Russia, you don't smile at strangers as it is considered as insincere, whilst some people will think you are a strange person or up to no good. For Russians, smiling is between friends.

Culture Shock and Culture Fatigue

Arriving at a new destination on your travels can be a culture shock. It is often an immediate reaction when you pass through the airport doors onto the street or within a day or two when you venture out and about. It is when all your usual references have been taken away producing sensory overload and things can become a blur or a shock!

Flying into Delhi, India, was my first encounter with Asia, apart from eating in Indian and Chinese restaurants in the UK, which does not count! I was away from the familiar surroundings of Europe and had stepped into a location, which was alien to me. It was extreme culture shock, in which the mind and body struggled to cope, trying to adjust to the sounds, the sights, the smell, the noise, the traffic and the temperature. I had heard about culture shock, but you have to experience it for yourself to truly understand its meaning! Matthew – India.

Your surroundings, the different language and culture, alongside different foods, the temperature can all affect your mental wellbeing and perception, which can leave you feeling low or having a case of the blues. If you are part of a humanitarian organization, NGO or charity, as you begin to settle into a routine and the weeks or months pass by, you can begin to have culture fatigue, it happens over a period of time when you begin to get fed up with everything. You become tired, wearisome of your host, the people or your host country. You begin to criticize, complain, moan and whinge – "Why do they do it like this!?" You may feel frustrated over the language, troubled by the bland staple food or overpowered by the local spices, tired of the cold showers, lack of privacy, early mornings or late nights, the cold, humidity, the heat, dirt floors, the bugs, insects, flies, the inner city exhaust fumes, the people, the smells, anything and everything!

The disorientation of culture fatigue can manifest itself in many ways: stress and anxiety can make you feel less able to cope with your new surroundings and even minor incidents can seem like insurmountable hurdles. Stress can cause you to become irritable, angry, frustrated, tired and anxious and often leaves you unable to sleep soundly. Sometimes you can start to dislike the local people, believing that your culture is right and that theirs is deeply flawed.

You may even resent the fact that you have to go home! Where possible, talk the situation over privately with someone of your own nationality, a friend, a fellow traveller or an NGO worker etc. Do not post your grievances on social networks. Bad feelings can disappear more easily, when you no longer dwell on them – think positive and look on the brighter side of life.

There are also some practical remedies to help combat culture fatigue. Relax and if possible, with your NGO leader's permission, take some time-out, as you may be over-doing it. Appreciate the beauty of your surroundings and do some exercise, as it is good to get the body moving. Catch up on lost sleep and missed meals. Go to bed earlier and you should not be too busy to eat. Sometimes we can be caught in the rut, like in a 9-5 job, where everything seems the same, as every other day and sometimes we all need a new challenge, which can help us refocus our efforts. Culture shock or culture fatigue does not affect all people – some people are not fazed by anything!

Culture Confusion

You may encounter culture confusion where you can see the good points in your host's culture and the weaknesses in your own (and vice versa) and have trouble trying to reconcile two cultures into one. It can be like standing at a set of crossroads unsure of where to go and not knowing which direction to take or how best to go about it.

A Ghanaian proverb states: 'Rather let your children starve than have a guest go hungry.' In Western culture, this proverb is difficult to fathom in practice, but it brings to light the importance of hospitality. In the West we put our aged parents in nursing homes, whereas in many cultures to pass over the responsibility of those who brought us into the world and took care of us as a child is considered wrong. A number of cultures have more than a nuclear family (parents and children) living under the same roof, often it is three generations. We do not enter into the culture of another whilst on our travels to judge them or condemn them, and we certainly cannot demand or expect them to enter into Western culture with all its flaws and weaknesses.

Chapter 30

Being Culturally Sensitive

On your travels you should be culturally sensitive to those around you so as not to cause offence, or a scene. Outside of your own country or continent you can quickly discover that your concept of time and space differs, people dress and look differently, interaction with members of the opposite sex may be very different than what you are used to and values and beliefs change. Being culturally sensitive means that we should be aware of the basic cultural do's, or more importantly, the don'ts (cultural faux pas – a slip up), and where possible find out the taboos – what to avoid, what not to discuss and abide by them! Nobody expects you to be an expert on all things cultural, but a few essential basics are well – essential! The locals will more than likely chuckle by minor misdemeanours, but may not be so forgiving on major issues of culture, especially in the context of relationships, religion and politics.

Travellers when talking to the locals should avoid talking about their possessions and wealth, unless you are in Monaco or amongst millionaires of London, New York, Sydney, Shanghai or Beijing. What you earn in a day may take a month of hard labour for the local worker; don't be insensitive. A local in a developing country may struggle to give two nutritious meals to their children a day.

Be careful of your mannerism and gestures, as body signals mean different things around the world. If you're in Brazil and give the thumbs up sign 'its ok, it's good,' it means you want to have sex. In the Middle East, crossing your legs and showing the soles of your feet is disrespectful. Be very careful wherever you are with eye contact with the opposite sex, and how you greet them, if at all. A Western glance in an Eastern setting may be taboo!

Some cultures do not use the Western idea of personal space. When conversing they stand so close that you may get their verbal 'spray' on your face; whilst others have bad breath! Try not to be repulsed! In many African countries, you may sit at a table or at a booth to eat your meal, but it is not exclusively yours and others may use the spare seating to enjoy their meal.

An Englishman in Pakistan was told by a local, "You have all the watches, but we have all the time!"

In Hindu and Muslim cultures, the left hand is considered unclean, so be careful what you touch and do not eat with your left hand! But how do you hold your veggie burger? In China, do not stick your chopsticks vertically into a bowl of rice and leave them there. It is like incense sticks, honouring dead ancestors. Also when you finish your meal, place your chopsticks on top of your bowl, but do not have the sticks pointing to anybody else on the table.

On a ferry from Jersey, we met two men of retirement age who in the 1970s, in a small campervan had driven from Europe across the Middle East and into Asia and back. They told us of an incident when they accidentally knocked a boy down who had run out in front of their vehicle. They knew that if they had stopped, they would have been killed by the locals who were enraged and so drove on until they found the police. The police acted as mediators to the family and negotiated a penalty which the travellers had to pay. After payment was settled, the men were free to carry on their travels.

A principal of a teacher training college in Kenya, said that part of African culture was, "There is no harm in asking." He went on to explain that if you gave someone a pair of shoes, you should not be surprised if they ask for socks, because "there is no harm in asking!"

In some cultures and more often than not in isolated communities, far from modern civilisation, it is perfectly normal for women not to cover their breasts. Especially in Africa and tribes located off the Amazon River in South America or on Western beaches. In fact, in some parts of Africa, it is more acceptable to show one's breasts than one's legs! Up until quite recently in some parts of Papua New Guinea, it was just as common to see a woman breastfeeding her baby as it was her piglets!

In Africa, the people have a slapstick type humour, like Laurel and Hardy or Charlie Chaplin, someone falls off their bike and everyone laughs, including the thrown rider! It was very evident in many African countries that jokes and funny incidents would travel down the length of a bus and have all the passengers laughing or talking about it. Whilst disgruntled passengers would club together as a group and as one body, put pressure on the conductor or driver for their misdemeanours or delays.

In American culture, to say, "Thank you" to someone who has helped or served you requires a response, often, "You're welcome." I have also heard this response in a few Asian countries. To say that a place is "homely" in America will be received as an insult (this place is plain or ugly), but a complement in Britain (this place is cosy)! In America, the word homey is preferable however with pronunciation and accents you may make a faux pas and get it wrong! The phrase 'wash up' in Britain means to 'clean the dishes' however to 'wash up' in America means 'go wash your hands' – the meal is about to be served. To 'crack a window' in America means to open it a little, not to damage it! One foreign student was helping the principal of a college and was asked to paint the window. The student reiterated what the principal has said to confirm that he had heard it correctly – and proceeded to paint the glass (not the frame), as that was the window!

In many societies, men and women do not sit together in public places. If you are invited to sit on a raised platform or at the front facing a group or an audience (both an honour), be careful how you sit – legs crossed can be a no-no and legs apart *is* a no-no. Look around and observe.

In Calcutta, the cost of our hotel for four nights in 2003 was the equivalent of a month's rent for one local man. It was the cheapest hotel we could find with a Western style toilet and cost us just £4 ($6) per-night! Mark – India.

Religion

In relation to religion and worship. In the East, people take off their shoes, but in the West, they take off their hats. However, in a synagogue you must wear a covering for your head. Being culturally sensitive also borders between different countries and varying communities. What is acceptable in a tourist town in one country may be frowned upon in the next town.

A hijab is a headscarf worn by Muslim women; concealing the hair and neck and may or may not have a face veil. A jilbab is an Islamic ankle length garment for women (though I have heard the term used to describe the male equivalent), whilst a thawb or thobe is an ankle length garment worn by Muslim men with short or long sleeves. One man in North Africa bought what he thought was a thawb. He was tying to blend in with the locals, but received many funny looks. It turned out to be a nightgown!

Hindus, Muslims and Jews are all forbidden by their religions to eat pork – pigs are considered unclean, so you will do well to leave your bacon bap, ham sandwich or Hawaiian pizza (ham and pineapple) alone or avoid them altogether! If you are in an Islamic country or area during Ramadan (40-day fast), avoid eating or drinking in the presence of Muslims during daylight hours. It should be ok in tourist areas, but can cause problems in other areas.

In the Arab world a dog is unclean, in the West it is a family pet, a guard dog, or a guide dog, whereas in Korea it is a delicacy, though some Koreans do keep them as pets, but they're also bred as food in China. Showing a picture to an Arab of you and Lassie embracing as 'man's best friend' will not help you become friends! In many parts of the world, a horse is a work-animal, for pulling carts, carrying loads or a means of transport, in France it is also food.

In India, the cow is sacred as is the monkey and they wander freely everywhere. For Hindus, all life is sacred, so don't go swatting flies or stamping on cockroaches in their presence. Some sects of Hinduism revere the rat and have them running around their temples where you have to take off your shoes to enter – so wear thick socks and beware of nibbled toes! Some worshipers will even drink milk from the same bowls as the rats and to feed them is an honour, whilst millions of Indians live far below the poverty line and many beg outside the temples and beyond.

In India or Nepal, you may come across 'holy men,' naked Sarduhs who sit around their followers and smoke cannabis as they try to attain a state of enlightenment. Going into some temples or shrines you will see depictions and graven images of their gods, some of whom are connected with fertility rites. Whilst other Sarduhs publicly display their deadness to sexual desires by lifting heavy loads with their genitals and dance around in wild frenzies during festival times.

We had some free time so I headed to the local oasis for a dip in the refreshing water. Five minutes later, the team leader arrived and told me that I should not have gone into the 'locals' pool whilst only wearing my swimming costume. I should have known better, it was a Muslim country and all the men were staring wide-eyed. Yvonne – Tunisia.

In the Arab world and in Hindu custom, henna tattoos are part of culture, religion and ceremonies, where different patterns on various parts of the body represent or announce certain things. Henna tattoos are non-permanent and last several weeks. If Tattoos/inking are problematic, you can wear long sleeves or long trousers to cover up. In Judeo-Christian belief, flesh piercings, flesh tunnels and cuttings in the Bible are linked with those involved in occult practice and devotion to the dead.[1] In some countries, curious locals may want to know why some travellers have gone back to their ancestral tribal past with body piercings, flesh tunnels or tattoos, especially across Africa, in Papua New Guinea or some Islands of the Pacific.

I once asked a middle-aged man in Sudan, if his dad had been a cannibal, "No" replied the man, "But my grandfather was!"

Other cultural sensitive factors can be:
- What you can or cannot do in public or behind closed doors.
- The consumption and use of tobacco or alcohol.
- The wearing of flesh tunnels and nose bones.
- Other body piercings and jewellery, even crosses.
- Type, style and cut of clothes – what is acceptable and what is not – is it too revealing or too tight?
- Long hair versus short hair, for both men and women.

- Makeup, lipstick, and nail varnish, even on your toes.
- Unnatural hair colouring, pink, green or blue etc.
- Mixed bathing – in swimming baths, lakes or in the sea or in a sauna or hot tub. Some places have different opening times or days for men and for women, to keep the sexes apart.
- Types of swim wear – is it modest? Or is it banned like the burkhini in some towns or beach resorts in France.

Superiority and Pride

Superiority and pride should not be entertained, but especially when travelling. Looking down upon others is wrong. Many people are less fortunate than ourselves. We could have been born in a different country and into a culture where education, social, religious or political spheres could have been very different than our present one. On your travels, many minor things may annoy you; don't let it get you down. If things are going hard in a developing country, you may want to tell yourself that you are from the *West* and they are from the *third-world* and thus try to make you feel better by having an attitude of superiority, enabling you to rise above your discouragements by putting others down. This is exactly what a school bully does, he or she puts others down to raise their own self-esteem.

It is not uncommon for humans to laugh at, or at worst, look down upon others who cannot perform or do what is second nature to us. In the West, the vast majority of people can use a washing machine, set the HD TV box, or use a smartphone etc., but often if we go to a developing country, we can be like fish out of water. What is normal to one community can be seen as an unusual custom for another. Foreigners in a developing country are often deemed 'uneducated' because they do not have the basic life-skills of cultivating and tilling the ground or knowledge of how to pluck, gut and cook a chicken. Others are squeamish over the sight of an animal being killed to celebrate a festival, which will be a feast for the village.

Chapter 31

The Oppressed and the Exploited

On your travels you may encounter some unpleasant sights, the oppressed and the exploited, from animals to humans, the overworked and underpaid. In many countries of the world females are deemed not as important as the male and are treated as second-class citizens. Frequently in developing countries, the indigenous women have a much harder time in life than men. They are often at the beck and call of their husbands, other male members of the family or the wider family circle. They are also expected to work longer and harder than their male counterparts do, though they nearly always patiently endure it as their lot in life.

The history of exploration is etched with the sad stories of polygamy, the buying and selling of daughters and wives, and the oppression of the female sex. Whilst there are double standards for the male who is frequently unfaithful, who negates his responsibility to look after, provide for or be faithful to the one he is married to, and his children.

In Arab countries, many women have to fully cover themselves and have never experienced the wind blowing through their hair. Others are not permitted outside in public without a chaperone or a male member of the family accompanying them; some are beaten or reprimanded for showing their hands. Many are shut up at home in an incarcerated-like existence and not permitted to find employment outside of the family home.

The sight of an African girl or wife, pounding the family's food, cutting the maize by hand, or doing menial tasks for little or no reward, out of duty or compulsion can be difficult to observe, whilst the son of the house receives an education, often his sister will not.

Asia is the sweatshop capital of the world where underage children and poorly paid adults work excessive hours under difficult circumstances for little fruit for their labour. It is often in these factories under these circumstances that household brands have their goods manufactured and sold in the Western market at superstores and designer outlets.

In many countries, children have to work, but more often than not, if a family encounters financial difficulties, the son will continue his education but the daughter will have to earn her keep. Seeing a child of any age, carrying, dragging or lugging a full twenty-gallon container of water on their backs is a heart-wrenching sight.

It was in North Africa nearly two decades ago when I first encountered child labour. The taxi drove past half a dozen children selling traditional bread; each spaced out dozens of metres from each other on a main highway. The team leader asked the driver to pull over and we bought several 'loaves.' We gave the girl a note and told her to keep the change. Her eyes lit up and a broad smile came across her grubby face. We drove off. The girl was about six years old, the same age as my sister and that was when child labour 'hit me,' I had a point of reference that I could identify with.

In some countries in Africa, South America and Asia, often the children have to contribute to the family income, more often than not this means that the children help in the fields or in the family business. This may be before or after school, but in some cases, they do not go to school. In many ways it is like eighteenth century Britain where children were integral to the labour force of the Industrial Revolution and later, Victorian England.

We went into this two-story restaurant in Asia. A girl of eleven or twelve, the waitress, took our order. She spoke good English. The food was served at the same time as the school children were let out. We observed the child waitress peer over the balcony and look with longing eyes on her contemporaries who were dressed in their clean neat school uniforms. She longed to be with them, but, even at her tender age had responsibilities which were of greater importance. Stuart – Cambodia.

'A righteous man regards the life of his animal, but the tender mercies of the wicked are cruel' (Proverbs 12:10, the Bible). On your travels you may see heavily laden animals; horses, camels or donkeys; or those being whipped and beaten, the malnourished or overworked animals with scars and open sores to homeless, gaunt, street dogs, cows and cats. In many places of the world these are unfortunate sights from the animal kingdom, but a fact of reality.

One man noted: 'I saw fishermen using cormorants to catch fish. This ingenious method of catching fish in China has been carried on for nearly three centuries, but I thought it was cruel. The birds had rings on their necks to restrict their gullet. Thus, only small fish can pass through their gullet whilst the larger ones are collected in their distensible pouch for the fishermen.'

We spent a few hours in the national zoo. Being a developing nation, the animals were not well kept. I think the tiger had been driven mad as he just paced back and forth in his small cage, with nothing to do. It was quite sad to see this once mighty beast, broken in mind and neglected in body. Toby – Nepal.

Chapter 32

Travel Writing and Photography

If you are an experienced writer, you may be able to write about your travels and the articles may be good enough to sell to a magazine, newspaper, website or in-house travel brochure as seen in airplanes' back seat pockets. Many publications expect you to have an agent to represent you and your work, as unsolicited mail is often thrown away. Some editors like good photos with an article and are more likely to buy the article if you have quality up-to-date images. Or an editor will commission photographs or use an agency for the stock images they require.

Your travel story could be considered for publication, but this will mean a lot of hard work and if the publisher will not actively advertise your work and promote it, it could leave bookshop's shelves within six weeks and never reappear. A publisher will ask, why is this book worth publishing and distributing? Is there a big enough audience to make a print run a viable financial option?

If you are not confident, why not have a go at writing a travel blog, you could get spotted or discovered for your talent or be able to advertise the books and products of others and receive a commission or referral fee, like Amazon's associate programme. Your writing or photography may not be good literature or art, but friends, family and other travellers may enjoy it. Consider self-publishing, do it yourself. Remember, how one person speaks, may not be the correct use of written syntax. Our phraseology and verbiage is often plumbed from our culture, our area, groups of friends and our upbringing. See Appendix B.

If you don't enjoy writing, you may enjoy photography and be skilled in the art of capturing a memorable image imprinted in a moment of time. Practice makes perfect. It takes months or years of practice to play a musical instrument to a proficient level, but you have to start somewhere, the same with writing and photography. You may not have the best written article on a particular location, but combined with stunning photographs, it could clinch the deal and sway an editor.

Self-Publishing

You can also consider self-publishing a book about your travels. Whether it is an eBook for Kindle, Nook, iBook or Kobo etc., or a physical paperback via CreateSpace, an Amazon company, or via

IngramSpark. The book can be about your adventures or a pictorial book of photographs with just a line or two of text for each image. You may not make much money, or you could be surprised. Income that is generated by sales does have to be declared to the tax man/IRS. However, see publishing as a legacy and do it because you enjoy it, not as a way to make a living, as most authors cannot.

As a word of caution, do not expect other people to finance your dreams (a publisher) and don't spend more money than you are prepared to lose! See Appendix C.

Travel Photography

Since having a digital camera, I have always taken a lot of photos to capture moments in time. Before digital, I had an automatic 35mm camera and had to be more selective with my shots due to the cost of processing the film. I am not a professional photographer, though my images have been used on a few book covers, inside books (colour and black and white images) and on websites. For myself, for every one hundred photographs I take, one or two are really good. The others could be improved and enhanced with post-processing. When I went to Africa for 6 ½ months, I took nearly 10,000 images in twelve nations. When I was in Asia for 3 ½ months, I took nearly 6,000 images in seven nations. Back in 2008, I bought 2gb SD cards, now I buy 32gb SD cards. Photography is important to me and so for each lengthy trip aboard I have always bought a new digital camera, with a greater zoom lens and more megapixels. To go abroad and to have my camera pack-up would be most unfortunate.

You can also sale or license your images through licensing companies. For some, you can set the price and the company gets a commission. The golden hours of dawn and dusk are ideal for photography, otherwise the sun can be too harsh and begins to drain colours. Shadows can also be an issue, though also part of a good image. See Appendix D.

Beware of viewing your world *only* through a 3x2 inch LCD screen. Let your eyes enjoy what your camera lens also sees.

In Tanzania, I ran low on memory cards. I went on the internet, ordered them from a British company and got them sent out by courier – all of which was cheaper than buying them in Dar es salaam, the largest city in Tanzania. I have never made the same mistake twice of having to buy additional memory cards whilst travelling.

In the north of Vietnam, we went on an organized tour as part of a day trip to the demilitarized zone, which included walking through an indigenous tribe's village. The tour guide said that he did not understand the local dialect, but he was convinced that they understood him. The group began to take photographs, until "One dollar!" was demanded from each tourist for a photo from every indigenous person. A member of the group asked the tour guide, "Why should we have to pay when we have paid you, what does the company give to these people?" "Nothing" was the short reply. At the time, the average daily wage in Vietnam was just $1 (£0.60).

Not everybody enjoys being photographed, or what they are doing. One travel photographer barely escaped with his life after he was spotted taking photos of a sky burial in Tibet, where a human corpse is chopped up and then eaten by scavenging animals or carrion birds. Whilst he was using a zoom lens, the sun glinted on the glass and gave his presence away. More recently, in August 2016, a tourist took a photo of a woman in a burkhini in a little bay at Sisco, on the island of Corsica, France, which resulted in a large brawl where five people were hospitalised!

At Ujiji, made famous by H. M. Stanley who 'found' Dr. David Livingstone, we were taking photos and filming. A woman came up the hill, shouting and hollering at us, stating that we could not take her picture. We were focussing on the trees and the shoreline and not in her direction! The locals thought it was funny, we were not sure if she was just having a bad day or had mental health issues.

In some museums, galleries and stately homes, you are permitted to take photos, but not allowed to use a flash. Some establishments will charge a fee for you to use your camera (including a mobile/cell phone camera), and an additional fee if you want to film with a camcorder. These fees are for non-commercial purposes. To film in the Egyptian museum in Cairo used to cost £1,000 ($1,600) per hour, plus extra if you needed to use the electricity for your lighting equipment! Selfie-sticks are banned in many enclosed places, but also includes some theme parks and sporting events as they can injure or annoy fellow patrons. Signs will notify you of this.

Chapter 33

Transportation – Buses, Trains, Taxis etc.

Travelling on public transport in developing countries should carry its own health and safety warnings. Many public vehicles have bald or under inflated tyres/tires, many with chunks of rubber missing! Weak and worn brakes are also common and can be frightening! In Vietnam, before descending down a high mountain, the coach pulled over and the driver removed the wheels and checked the brakes – this was reassuring. In northern Ethiopia, we saw many trucks and some coaches at the bottom of gorges! It appeared that most had gone over the edge on hairpin bends, unable to stop.

Weaving in and out of traffic is standard practice across many developing countries as the race to the end destination is of prime importance. Some long-distance drivers alleviate fatigue by chewing narcotic type stimulants. As a passenger, you are unsure if it is reassuring or not – they are trying to stay awake, but they are not entirely on this earth!

As a passenger you can also fall off the back of a pickup, be bounced out of a truck or slide off the roof of a bus or a train, and you would not be the first! I do not advise travelling on the roof of a coach, bus or a train. When it rains, the driver will not stop for you to come inside and if the driver has to do an emergency stop, you will slide off! If you sleep on the top of a train, you may roll off on a bend and encounter a hard thud as you hit the ground at speed.

> I was travelling on the top of a vehicle and decided that I would impress my friend by doing press-ups on the roof rail of the moving truck. I would clap my hands between each push-up, but as I later realised, if I got it wrong, my teeth would have been smashed! Charles – India.

When travelling abroad you will inevitably need to use public transport to get around, unless you have your own vehicle. Some countries have "skin tax" as one Asian pastor informed me whilst laughing profusely! On occasions, locals have arranged transport for us and bought the tickets on our behalf because they pay the going rate. Most guidebooks give approximate prices for various services and foreigners generally pay more than the locals.

In some countries they have 'women only carriages' on trains or areas designated for women only. This can be in a train station, seats on buses, a section of the restaurant etc. In Dhaka, Bangladesh, the restaurant we frequently visited had booths with curtains for women or for married couples only. This was so the wife could take her veil off and eat unhindered in public, yet private way.

Buses and Coaches
In some places, the words 'bus' and 'coach' are used interchangeably. Some drivers will take you to the agent or ticket office of their choice as they get a cut. Some agents sell tickets for transport that does not even exist! Whilst others will try to sell you a ticket to anywhere; even if it is in the opposite direction to where you are going! Have a map handy and know where you want to go or in which general direction.

In some places, there is a metal box with a slot on public transport where you place your money, like on trams in Hong Kong or buses in Beijing. In Geneva, Switzerland, and in the Netherlands, you buy strips of tickets and each destination will cost you x amount of ticket. In the Netherlands you hand them over to the conductor, whilst in Switzerland we had to put them into a slot.

Many years ago, I was at London Victoria coach station with a friend from Italy. We were taking the night coach to Utrecht, Netherlands. My friends said, "Mathew, all our fellow passengers will be Europeans, we do not queue (in an orderly line like the British). When the doors open, run to the front of the queue and just make your way to the coach door. If you don't, you will be sitting where you don't want to all night!"

I crossed over the border into an East African country and a teenage boy helped us find the correct bus. I gave him what seemed a fair financial recompense. He took the money with a sullen look on his face and said that I should give him double the amount. Back on the bus, after contemplation, the boy had wanted the equivalent of several hours pay for just ten minutes work! John – Ethiopia.

If your coach journey takes more than a day and parks in a coach stop overnight, the dozens of vehicles may look similar. Take a photo of the coach, its designated number e.g. 332 or its number/license plate, this will make it easier to find in the morning. Also look around to find a reference point within the coach stop, the vehicle is near x hotel, or by a lamppost in the corner etc. Remember the driver's face and that of the conductor. If you still have trouble finding the vehicle in the morning, the conductor may come and find you! In some countries commercial vehicles by law have the owner's name and address on the side of the door. If the driver gives you any serious trouble, e.g. you have hired the vehicle and its driver and he/she wants to renegotiate the price in the desert, or your bag has gone missing from the roof, take a photo of door or any identifying number and the driver and tell them you will be reporting them to the police. Their whole attitude will soon change for the better! In August 2016, the Tourism Minister for India recommended that all women tourists should take a photo of the taxi and its license plate they are getting in and send it to a friend before they depart.

In Nepal, sometimes the driver's friend will charge you for putting your rucksack on the roof, when all of the bags go on top and are tied down. Often they are covered with tarpaulin to keep the rain off and thieves away.

The bus arrived in the dark halfway through our two-day journey. A non-governmental organization (NGO) worker who was on the bus suggested that we got a fixer to find us a place to stay (one who fixes problems for a fee). It was not necessary; we looked out of the window as we drove into town and knew where the accommodation was! The next morning, before sunrise, we boarded the bus by 6am and saw the NGO who had been there since 5am. His fixer had given him the wrong departure time, whereas we just asked the bus driver! Jason – Kenya.

In Ethiopia, the roads in the north of the country in 2008 were mostly gravel and dirt, and the buses were old; you get to feel all the stones in the road as you are rattled, rocked and rolled about in your seat and sometimes into the aisle! After an eight or twelve hour journey of just 150-250 km you are glad to arrive at your destination! One Korean traveller unwisely took a two day consecutive journey which made her unwell for two days and was incapacitated during that time. If time is money, and some say it is, then that was two days lost from her already short schedule, and if your vacation is only two or three weeks then that is a big percentage of your schedule disrupted, so learn to be flexible, and take travel sickness pills, and/or rest in a city for the day.

In a number of African countries, the long-distance buses or coaches were stopped at check-points and the passengers had to show their identity cards or passports to the relevant authorities, often the police or the military. As a foreigner, the person who is looking at your passport wants to make sure that you are not in the country illegally. To speed up the process, we would have our passports ready and open on the visa page. Some personnel do not understand how a visa works or what it looks like. As a foreigner, your documents are not always checked and often you are passed by, whilst on occasions, other people are taken off the vehicle.

Major Transport Hubs

In some larger cities there can be multiple coach, bus and train stations. If you have to leave early in the morning, try to work out which station you have to leave from, even if that means visiting the terminal a day or two before. If you want to go to A to C, the bus may not depart until 3:30pm. However, as in one city in Asia, we could get on an 8:30am coach from A to B and when we arrived in B, we were able to get a coach that left for C within 30 minutes of our arrival. Some countries have major public transport hubs to get around within the country. These hubs e.g. London, Cardiff, Manchester and Glasgow in the UK, may not be the shortest route, or the fastest way, but are major connecting hubs for a coach or train company. If you are in the South West of England and want to go to Cardiff, Wales, via National Express coaches, the hub takes you to London first (to the east), where you pickup a second coach which goes slightly north and then west to Cardiff. By car or by train you can take a more direct route.

Trains

In Britain, the railway lines are operated by different companies. Going from A to H you could travel on a number of differently franchised train lines. Sometimes it is cheaper if going from A to C to buy two tickets for each leg of the one-way journey (A-B and B-C), because the tracks you could be travelling on can be operated by different companies. In some cases, you would not even have to get off your seat because you would be travelling on the same lines.[1]

India has the largest rail network in the world, compliments of Britain's imperial past, and employs more than 1.3 million people! However, entering into some of the huge train stations, such as at Delhi or Calcutta can be daunting, with thirty or so counters to choose from, and often dozens or even hundreds of people in each queue. In larger cities there are often a 'tourist' or 'foreigner' counter which is dedicated to non-citizens. Search for it and use it. There is nothing worse than waiting one hour to buy a ticket and to be told at the counter that you are in the wrong queue! In X'ian, China, at the end of the Silk Road, there were about twenty counters with queues of people four or five wide, many of which were going out of the station doors into the pick-up and drop-off area! Literally, more than a thousand people waiting to buy their tickets. It was all too confusing, so we asked the youth hostel staff for their advice. They looked on their computer and told us the times and prices and offered a free service, where one of their workers does the queuing and buying on your behalf! You just hand over the money up front and write out your details. Pre-booking trains (or any tour) through an agent is more expensive than doing it yourself, but it does save time, though problems can be encountered. In India, the agent informed us that the train that we will be travelling on arrives and departs from the same city, but at two different train stations. What he failed to inform us was that the distance between these two stations was greater than the span across the English Channel; from England to France! It was a two-hour bus ride, but it took us three hours to find the correct pickup point as the bus did not stop at either of the two bus stations in town!

Travelling from a border town in Sudan into Khartoum was a two-day journey so we went first class. To our dismay, the carriage had no beds, the seats were hard and dusty, the fan did not work and the sliding door to our compartment fell off! The train carriage came from the latter part of the nineteenth century, but we counted our blessings. We travelled with friends, thus we knew our belongings were safe, and third class had wooden slated benches; that would not have been a pleasant journey! At some ticket offices, it is assumed that you will have first class because you are a foreigner, so it pays to ask if there is a cheaper option.

Taxis and Rickshaws

Most places of the world I have travelled to, taxis have been cheap compared to the UK. The only exception is in Mongolia, where anybody with a vehicle can be a taxi. This was before Uber came onto the market. If you stand on the road, point you arm and wave your hand, within no time a driver will have stopped for you. The driver may or may not speak English and a short journey can soon add up. We quickly learnt to take the bus around Ulaanbaatar.

Taxi drivers often have the best local knowledge for cheap accommodation and you can save a small fortune. However, some taxi drivers or rickshaw drivers (notably in India) will take you to their preferred hotel or shop because they are paid to bring tourists there. On occasions, I have taken a taxi or rickshaw to the booking office for the train or coach, only later to find out, it was an agent who charged me four times the actual cost of the ticket on public transport! In Tunisia, many taxis want to charge extra for your rucksacks or suitcases.

If you take a taxi use the meter (if it works) or agree on a price beforehand if this is possible, otherwise any crazy figure could be given at the end of the journey. The danger with the meter is that you may be taken the long route. Some rickshaw drivers on arrival at your destination will ask or even demand more money than what you negotiated and agreed before departing! Pay what you have agreed unless the driver has been exceptionally helpful, then give a good tip, or if they have had to go out of their way, thus the journey took longer than anticipated. A rickshaw is often a three-wheeled vehicle, know as tuk-tuk in Thailand and many other names in different countries. In 2003, in Calcutta, India, they had hand-pulled rickshaws (a two wheeled cart), which was one of the last places on the planet and a left over from the Victorian era of the British Empire, however you can still find them in some places in Japan. Some taxis are peddle powered as seen in some city centres across the world. In and around Oxford Street, London, some riders charge the earth! Often £7 per person per minute! At present it is largely unregulated but as long as the prices are displayed they are within the law, though often the police have to intervene because unwitting tourists are being financially exploited and call the police. What group of three people wants to pay £180 ($288) for a 20-minute ride? Some taxis are bicycles with a rack over the back wheel, which is the seat and small metal pegs to rest your feet on.

Minibuses and Long Distance Taxis

Some taxi ranks are like bus stations where the 7-seat car or 10-seat minibuses are lined up under different destinations, often competing owners. Many have workers whose job function is to direct you to where you need to go. They help fill up the vehicle so that it can depart when full and receive money from the company or driver.

Some taxis pick up people en route and in many African countries this is common. Your agreed price may only include your seat (not the entire taxi) to your destination and a five-seat car may take six or seven passengers with two people on the front seat! It is common to be charged more than the locals. Sometimes they ask if you would like to pay for two seats, I never have, though on a rickshaw in India, I was charged for two seats as the driver said I was too big! The cost of the ride was less than half a dollar for "both" of me, it was dark, I had been travelling all day, I was very tired and it was not worth spending time to discuss the issue with the driver.

Long distance taxi drivers (which may be a minibus taxi, especially in Africa) upon arriving in town will often drop people off at the depot/taxi rank or set stops or along a route. The driver may take you to a hotel, or a selection of hotels, but naturally, you will have to pay extra if this is out of the way. In Ethiopia, one conductor (money collector) was most helpful and walked us to the next taxi depot so we could catch a ride to the next town. In South Africa, one minibus taxi booked us on to two additional taxis (without our knowledge) because we wanted to travel to a particular city. We were not aware that the single taxi could not travel there in a single journey. After 16 hours or so of travel on three different minibuses it was great to arrive in Cape Town, where the driver spent two hours dropping people off at their preferred destinations.

Chapter 34

Overlander – Your Own Vehicle

You may be adventurous enough to want to take your own vehicle with you as you travel the open road, or you may fly into a country and buy a vehicle. Budget travel does not often involve buying a vehicle in Asia, Africa or Latin America, as public transport is relatively cheap and often safer. However, if you are living out of your vehicle, then you can make savings on accommodation. Certain countries are cheaper than others if you intend to buy a 4x4 (4 wheel drive vehicle/4WD), or just a car, but you need to take into consideration, where you will be driving to and over what type of terrain and for how long. Do you know how to drive a 4x4 off-road? If not consider going on a day course where a professional instructor will guide you through and over some extreme obstacles.

On the Nepal/India border a couple were driving a Citroen 2CV, a small 2WD car with a little engine, but with great suspension and a retractable central canvas roof. At border crossings, you have to fill-in additional paperwork, and can be waiting a long time for bureaucrats to grant you permission to enter their country with your vehicle. They may wish to dismantle or strip down your vehicle in search of contraband, whilst some guards may expect payment of some kind to help oil the cogs of progress. They may take a liking to some of your spares, luggage or clothing, or state that they collect notes/bills from other countries as a hobby! Be naïve and play dumb or give them a small gift.

In April 2016, the UN Ambassador's motorcade of Samantha Powell, hit and killed a 7-year old boy in Cameroon. Two months later, the US paid in Central African Francs the equivalent of £1,260 ($2,016), plus two cows, food and supplies, as part of a compensation package commensurate with local customs.

Buying a Vehicle

If you are going to buy a vehicle, what will you do with it at the end of the journey, sell it on or scrap it? Is it worth flying 500 miles out of your way to buy a cheaper vehicle, knowing you'll have to drive it to your 'starting' destination, which will cost x amount and take you a number of days over hard roads. Is your vehicle economical on fuel? Your vehicle may not have the original engine in it and could be downsized, from a 3.0L petrol/gas to a 2.4L diesel and may not have the torque needed to get you where you need to go. The seller will tell you want you want to hear, once it is driven off the lot and paid for, the vehicle will be your problem! Is the vehicle big enough for all the passengers and your equipment? Most people who buy used vehicles in poorer nations spend hours on roadside verges, trying to fix an issue, or waiting some weeks to get a more serious problem fixed.

Take the vehicle for a test drive, use the gears and turn left and right, some owners only want you to go in a certain direction, on a brief drive round the block and this should set alarm bells ringing. Is the seat adjustable, are you too big or too small for the vehicle? Is there much travel in the clutch? Do the gears sync easily? Does reverse and fifth gear work? Some sellers may put a different gear knob on the gear stick and you may not have a fifth gear or overdrive. What does the vehicle sound like to drive? If the seller turns the radio on, turn it off and listen to the vehicle, how does the engine sound? Does the suspension work on each corner and what about the brakes? Does a plume of smoke come out the exhaust when the vehicles starts or when you change gear and accelerate? Is the steering light or heavy? Does the engine heating gauge rise quickly? Are there any engine warning lights illuminated on the dashboard? Do all the lights work, dip, main beam, indicators, brake and inside? How much tread is on the tyres/tires, any cracks on the tyre wall or chunks of rubber missing? Do the windows go up and down? Are there two sets of keys? A vehicle which shows 80,000 miles on the clock could mean 180,000 or even 280,000! The seats and dashboard are often a good indicator of the actual use 'mileage' of a vehicle. If the vehicle is advertised as 4WD, sunroof or with AC, does it work? Some sunroofs are sealed shut, others leak! Does the hot and cold air heater work? Does the fuel gauge work? Do the windscreen wipers work, and the screen-wash jets? Are the blades on the windscreen wipers damaged?

A young British comedian said that he had driven 300,000 miles over the last few years on a comedy circuit around Britain. When buying a car, the difference between 56 or 54 mpg (miles per gallon) is fundamental and at 115p per litre there is a difference of fuel costs of just over £1,000 ($1,600). Your journey will be a lot less than 300,000 miles, but if it is 5,000 miles and the mpg difference between vehicles was 25 and 45 mpg, the difference in fuel cost is £465 ($744).[1]

What is the vehicle like under the bonnet/hood? Has oil or water sprayed out and covered the engine? If a head-gasket is on its way out, it could cost you a small fortune to repair, whilst a broken cam belt can seriously damage the engine. Is there oil on the floor where the vehicle resides? Most older vehicles drip a little oil, but you do not want a major issue, going from maximum to minimum every 100 miles is a major issue and costly on replacement oil. Check the levels of the radiator water, power steering and oil? If they are under the minimum mark, this can be an indicator that the vehicle has not been looked after. Is the battery a sealed unit or do you have to top up with distilled water? Topping up is an inconvenience.

Sellers are very good at hiding bodge jobs, the vehicle may be great for 100 miles, but not for 1,000, let alone 10,000! How does the chassis look, is there rust, cracks or weld marks etc.? What is it like inside the wheel arches? Have they rusted through and been touched up with scrunched up newspaper, a bit of fibreglass and paint! Does the seller actually own the vehicle (it's not stolen is it?), do they have the paperwork? Does the vehicle need a road safety certificate (MOT in the UK) to make it legal to drive? Remember, a vehicle may be advertised as 'one careful lady owner' but they won't tell you about her three boy-racer sons who were all on the insurance! Open up the boot/trunk, is there a spare wheel? How does the tyre/tire look, is it bald or flat? Does the vehicle come with any original maintenance tools, like a car jack? Roll back the carpet, is there rust or weld marks on or near the suspension mounts? Has thick paint (or black underguard) been added to cover up something?

Two friends bought a 4x4 in Kenya to start their journey in South Africa. They got the vehicle kitted out and it went well for a few weeks, until they had engine problems. A mechanic looked over the vehicle and it had a number of major issues, which to the untrained eye and ear, were not noticed at purchase. The trip was delayed by a number of weeks and in the end, the vehicle was repaired and then quickly sold on. Time and money was lost.

Buying a second-hand vehicle can be hit and miss at the best of times, but if you are buying it from abroad, then potential issues can be magnified. Remember to haggle for a vehicle and if you are not 100% satisfied or convinced, just walk away. It's better to wait an extra week in a city to get the right vehicle then to impulse purchase and make a mistake and get a banger or a lemon of a vehicle.

If you are buying some form of small motorhome, the chassis and engine etc. must be in good working order, like any other vehicle and make sure all the internal components of the 'home' work. Does the bench convert into a bed or is a piece missing? Does the stove and internal water supply work? Does the table pullout and other components that are designed to fold away, will they? What about the toilet, shower and the sink? Are they all functional and free-flowing or blocked up?

Your Own Vehicle

If you have your own vehicle (including a motorbike) you already have a feel for it and can often sense when something is not quite right as all vehicles give feedback, through the accelerator peddle, through the steering wheel, and sometimes through the exhaust pipe. If you are only driving around your own country, then parts should not be an issue. If you are driving abroad through developing countries then parts and spares can be more difficult to come across. However, local mechanics can work wonders and utilise as well as cannibalise other mechanical parts to get your vehicle back on the road, even if temporarily until you get to a major city.

In Tanzania, we met two men from South Africa, in their 4x4s who were driving up the East coast of Africa to Morocco in North Africa and into and around Europe, then back down the West Coast of Africa! A colossal adventure with huge fuel prices!

Your own Vehicle Considerations

- If you are taking your own vehicle, make sure it has a major service before you depart. All spark plugs and leads should be replaced and have an oil change and new oil filter. Brakes should also be checked and adjusted as necessary.
- Bring top-up oil for the engine, power steering and brakes.
- Do you need to replace all the tyres/tires, all the belts (fan and cam) just in case? Better to be safe than sorry.
- Pack your essential tools and spares, including the vehicle's maintenance manual, plus spare fuses and light bulbs. Additional fuel filters are recommended, as in some places fuel can be contaminated.
- Know your tyre/tire pressure and maintain it for fuel economy and safety. Take a foot pump with you or an air compressor that plugs into a vehicles' cigarette lighter.
- Do you need to buy jerry cans (spare fuel cans), a tent for the roof, and a winch? How extreme is your trip?
- Do you need SatNav or can you use your smartphone or a map? If using a digital device, do you need to download the relevant maps for the countries you are going to?
- Have you notified your insurance company and got the relevant paperwork to take your car abroad?
- Do you know what paperwork you need to take a vehicle from one country to the next? It is pretty straightforward in the European Union, but in some countries, at the border, you have to sign documentation stating that you will not sell the vehicle.

- Do you need an international driving license?
- If you will be driving in the European Union, do you have your European Continental Driving Kit? This includes a warning triangle, visibility vests/reflective waistcoats, bulb kits, plus other items. Do you need beam deflectors? So right-hand drive cars when driving on the right (and vice versa, for left-hand drive vehicles), do not blind oncoming traffic.
- Different countries have their own legal requirements for drivers, and in-case of breakdowns or accidents.

Protect your Vehicle from Theft

You want to protect your vehicle from being vandalised or stolen and the following are some tips.

- Before staying in accommodation, find out if they have a locked compound, garage or off-road parking. Is the area safe? Can you park outside your motel window? Can you park under a lamppost or under some light?
- Have a good alarm and immobiliser system installed. Can you buy a lock for the steering wheel, or from the clutch peddle to the steering wheel? It is a deterrent. Consider having an isolation switch fitted. This is a secret switch which when turned off, will not allow your car to start. It isolates the current to and from the ignition.
- Park the vehicle in gear, have the front wheels pointing into the kerb with the vehicles' steering lock on. This makes the vehicle more difficult to tow.
- Take some HD leads off, the vehicle cannot be driven correctly without them as the engine will not be firing on all cylinders. If your leads are the same length then mark them, or put a sticky label on them, which lead goes where.
- Do not leave valuables inside the vehicle, or cover any bags etc. with a blanket in the daytime, assuming they will not fit in the locked boot/trunk. Consider tinted windows for the rear of the vehicle, which also helps keep the heat out.
- Have lockable wheel nuts. Your steel wheels may be worth nothing, but the deep tread wide 4x4 tyres could be valuable.

When I went camping in the Black Mountains in Wales, I took off two (of four) HD leads to prevent my car from being driven away – stolen. The car was about two miles from where we camped and about 15 miles from the nearest town. The place was so isolated that the car was reported to the police as stolen and abandoned!

Chapter 35

Renting a Vehicle

Traffic regulations the world over are not the same, especially when it comes to who has the right of way. In parts of South-East Asia, it is common for vehicles to overtake on blind bends, whilst in India, and in other developing countries, it is the biggest vehicles that appear to have the right of way, as they intimidate smaller and slower vehicles, honking their horns and make them pull over, off the semi-paved roads and into the dust or onto grass verges! Some junctions in Vietnam were incredible, near bedlam, with hundreds of motorbikes and bicycles, cars and pedestrians, trying to cross in all and every opposite direction, with no traffic lights or person in authority to guide the traffic. It all appeared to work, just about, as each vehicle rolled past at a cautious pace, but there was much confusion, stopping, and occasional backing up of a motorbike.

Renting or Hiring a Car

If you are renting/hiring a car, it is often cheaper if you book in advance. You can even do this from your home country, if you know when you will arrive. For most companies you have to be 25 or older and there is a fee for each named driver. The bigger the car, the bigger the rental fee. Some rental companies have limited mileage which if you exceed, you have to pay x amount per mile extra. Collecting a car from different airports can incur different fees. It pays to compare how much the same type of car costs to be collected from different airports or cities in the same country. There are many comparison websites to help you in your search for the best deal.[1] Search online for special offers and promotional codes or a discount voucher. Have a look at the company's social media pages for special deals or offers.

With a group of friends we hired a car from the Czech Republic and drove around Europe for two weeks. We turned up at the rental company who did not have our category of car ready. They gave us an upgrade for the same cost as the smaller car which we booked and this upgrade worked out well. Before you drive off the forecourt, go round the car and mark any dents, scratches or the slightest of marks (on the inside and the outside) on your rental paper. Rental companies are notorious for taking your insurance excess for any minor marks (which may have occurred from the previous driver). Some rental companies work on a full tank of fuel to a full tank, or you have to fill up as soon as you leave the forecourt. On your return, fill up, so that you do not incur a financial penalty or try to leave the tank empty so that you have not spent money on fuel you have not used. Before you drive off the forecourt, make sure you know which gear is reverse, the correct fuel (is it a diesel?), where the petrol/gas cap is and how to open it. We hired a car in Cape Town, South Africa and parked on the opposite side of the street, not knowing that you have to park facing the direction of traffic. The local 'parking warden' (who collects money, and keeps an eye on cars, but who does not wear a uniform) told us we had to face the opposite way to be legally parked. I could not find reverse as it was not like my car, or any other I had owned or driven. Thankfully, a shop owner saw the predicament and showed me that I had to lift the gear knob and then reverse could be found. Other cars you push down, whilst still others slot into place as any other gear.

I got inside my hire car and found that the steering wheel was on the wrong side of the car. I pulled out of the airport thinking that I was driving on the correct side of the road until my passenger shouted at me. I turned left at the cross junction and kept on the right-hand side of the highway, unfortunately for me, both lanes of traffic were heading in my direction and the other vehicles were all tooting their horns and flashing their lights – I did a quick u-turn! Michael – America.

With a group of friends renting a car, decide before you depart, if you crash, whether or not the insurance excess will be spilt between all of you or just the driver at the time of the incident. Accidents happen, but also some people are foolhardy in other people's property and drive differently than if it was their own vehicle!

It has been widely reported in British newspapers how British citizens have rented cars in America, been caught speeding and have been issued with a speeding ticket. Many people do not pay the fine and fly home at the end of their holiday and think no more about it. However, when they have returned to America, or to the State they were convicted in, even after an absence of twenty years, some have been arrested at the airport and put in shackles!

In the late 1970s and into the 80s a man travelled through the Middle East and parts of Asia for his work. In India, as a passenger in the company's cab truck, the driver ran over a cow, which in Hindu culture is sacred. Immediately, the truck was pelted with stones which went in and out of the open windows! They drove on until they came across some police and explained what had happened. Some form of financial compensation was handed over and the men were free to carry on their work.

In South Africa, we twice hired a vehicle to visit sites off the tourist trail or out-of-the-way locations. Looking for an ancient monument, we pulled over and asked the locals for directions, they were polite, but not that helpful. When I told them we were tourists, they could not help us enough and gave precise directions and distances to where we wanted to go.

Charted Transport

Be very wary if other people jump aboard your chartered transport, a vehicle and its driver which you have hired for the day, or just to a destination. Sometimes, the driver brings his friends along for the ride (and you're paying for it), whilst at other times they are there to back him up or are dropped off along route. If you are female then you should never travel without being accompanied by another woman and should refuse to go anywhere if men begin to pile in the back of the pickup or car which you have hired. With chartered transport pay on arrival, not before you depart, though sometimes petrol/gas money may be needed to get you going. If so, you may (or may not) wish to give a percentage of the money before you drive off.

> I hired a pickup and its driver on the side of the road, to take me to an out-of-the-way location. After taking us to the middle of nowhere, the driver stopped and demanded additional money. Try to go with someone you trust. James – Malawi.

Renting a Motorbike or Scooter

If you are renting/hiring a motorbike or scooter, make sure you know how to ride it. Some hire companies work through places of accommodation, or the bike belongs to the owner who rents it out. Make sure you get a crash helmet and wear it. Some people hire out motorbikes or scooters without any safety gear or insurance. Many foreigners have been fined for not wearing a crash helmet when it is a legal requirement in many countries. In Phuket, Thailand, one policeman on a busy road was flagging down tourists who were not wearing a motorcycle helmet every five minutes or so and fining them. If you damage or crash your motorbike, you may be liable for its financial repair and for any other vehicle or person you hit!

> Back in 2003, for just $3 (£1.90) a day, we hired a 100cc scooter. I have a driving licence, but have no experience on two wheeled motorised forms of transport. The man at the hotel handed me the scooter, I got on it and test rode it around the courtyard. As I pulled the brake lever, my wrist pulled back on the throttle and I ended up driving up the hotel steps! It was embarrassing. Stuart – Cambodia.

Give the motorbike a once over, does it all look good to you? Do the brakes work, does it sound ok? Does the horn work and the lights? Does the throttle stick? Are you insured?

Remember that road regulations and highway maintenance may not be as good as your own country, so take extra caution when riding abroad.

Renting a Boat

In Cambodia, we hired a boat, a 'captain' (who was the local cafe owner who'd we arranged it through) and some equipment to go snorkelling off a reef on another island. We had two blow up car tyre/tire inner tubes and I really wish we had buoyancy aids. The swell was strong and a number of the times the waves crashed against the side of the boat and at other times we raced down the troughs and looked up at the peak of a wave, we thought we would be capsized.

One traveller was sat in front of the engine on a motorised canoe and lost his hearing for twenty-four hours, even though he was wearing a crash helmet. If you do not have ear plugs, then cotton wool is good for keeping noise out, or use rolled-up tissue paper! In May 2016, a speedboat in Thailand hit a large wave and capsized which led to the death of four tourists.

At many beach resorts or lakes you can hire kayaks, paddle boards, surfboards, peddleloes or paddleboats. For some of the larger items, you may have to show proof of identity, leave a deposit and possibly leave your passport with them. If you need a buoyancy aid make sure your hire a floatation jacket.

Chapter 36

Overland Bus and Researching an Organization

You may be joining a group of unknown travellers on a overland bus tour. They have different routes across different continents and countries and depart at different times of the year. Some tours go from London, England to Sydney, Australia or vice versa! You can travel from Ecuador to Brazil in South America, to central Asia or a variety of routes within Africa. Tour companies that cross continents often use a different bus for each leg of the journey. You can get to stay in hostels, hotels and even go camping under the stars. The cost can vary considerably and for some overland buses, you sleep and cook on the bus. Some overlanders offer 'budget' or 'comfort' trips where you pay extra for a private room for two of you (where available), instead of in a dormitory. Trips can range in duration from 14 to 85 days. Assisting in the chores of cooking, vehicle maintenance etc. is often part of the experience, as are your fellow travellers and the workers. If you are joining an overland bus tour, they will tell you the exact price of the travel and what it covers and just as importantly, what it does not cover. As with all things, it is always better to find out what is expected and what is not permitted before you sign on the dotted line and pay your deposit. Read the small print! What liability insurance does the company have? Make sure that the overland travel company is covered in case it folds, e.g. ATOL protected in the UK. This way you can reclaim your deposit or payments if the company goes bust.

Researching an Organization
Do thorough research before you decide to join any organization, whether you are a volunteer or a paying participant. Look at their website, especially the frequently asked questions page (FAQ), peruse their social media if you are serious about signing up for a period of time. Are you expected to financially contribute during the time you help them? If you are going as a volunteer, don't be surprised if you work alongside those who receive a wage. Do you need to ask for some literature, a brochure or a manual of rules? Do they have an open day where you can speak to representatives of the organization? Ask questions via email, social media or phone, have your questions written down. Do you know of anyone else who has been with them – what was their experience like? What age range do they cater for? Do they have lower or upper age limits? Do

they need any specialist skills or language requirements? What hours are you expected to work and for how many days in a week? What time do you start and finish work?

Will the organization or company look after you – what is their code of practice or conduct? Any organization, charity, non-governmental organization (NGO) or company will not downplay what is on offer, but they should show integrity in how they publish their opportunities and in what they offer. Inevitably, any organization or company will make mistakes, but ideally, they will learn from it, improve or correct certain features for future participants. At other times, there are circumstances beyond their control, such as natural disasters, wars and terrorist attacks, which can cause delays, close roads or airports. There is also equipment failure (breakdown of vehicles or the boiler) and all these events, alter the best of plans, which may delay departure from one place to another, close a door to certain areas of a country, or keep you from having a hot shower!

> We left the States to do practical work at an institution in Europe. Our two children cried all day long, as we scrubbed, painted and cleaned. Never again! Mr and Mrs — USA.

Accepted or Rejected

If you are applying to join an organization (or an overland travel group), please bear in mind that your application *may* be turned down. There is no automatic right of acceptance. Each charity or NGO has its own criteria and things that they look out for. You may be too young, too old, not in the best of health, not able enough or not have the correct skills. The same can apply for a visa, you may not be accepted for a visa, the right to enter a country.

> Before I signed up with an organization I was assured that many people of my own age would be there. When I arrived, everybody apart from myself was just out of high school and because of the age gap, it was difficult to connect. We had to ask permission every time we left the compound; the leaders were younger than me and we were not permitted to go out on our own. James – Africa.

Have the Same Vision and Aims

It is important that you share the same vision as the organization that you intend to work with – what is their vision, aims or mission statement? You (or they) may hold a particular religious, political or social view which can cause contentions. You may also disagree with their methods, policies, rules or constitution. There may be a number of different rules or regulations which may be considered strange or weird, but organizations and companies have them for a reason. It may be based on experience, governing constitution of the charity, the laws of the country, or the rules and condition of the NGOs permission to operate in a particular country or area.

Other issues may evolve around:

- What you can or cannot wear: revealing clothing or no trousers/pants for women.
- The time you begin and finish each day and the number of working hours or what day you may get off, if any.
- Your general appearance: not extreme to an outsider, hair length, piercings, fleshies or tattoos etc. In some countries you will blend in well, at other places it may cause alarm, offence or may not be culturally permitted.
- Headscarves for women: often in Islamic countries. In Iran and Saudi Arabia, women *have* to cover their head by law. In some towns in America, e.g. Florida City, Tennessee and Georgia City, you can be fined for wearing baggy trousers/saggy pants that expose the underwear covering your bottom, as it can be classified as 'indecently exposing yourself.'
- Things you need to bring or are not permitted to.
- Being accountable to the leadership.
- Excursions for days off may be optional. Some organizations allow their workers weekends off (or x amount of days per month) in which they may or may not be permitted to leave the area.
- There may be other rules that could apply to the charity, organization, NGO or overland travel bus that you are considering. Ask them and read the small print. Is there a rule book? Get hold of a copy.

Chapter 37

Humanitarian and Development Aid

The world of aid work, humanitarian agencies and non-government organizations (NGOs), alongside charities is broad in its spectrum with hundreds of opportunities across a multitude of destinations in a large variety of capacities. Humanitarian aid is helping people with their immediate needs. If you join a humanitarian organization you are going abroad as a helper to serve others and this must not be confused with an all-inclusive holiday/vacation. You may be going on an extended holiday and will use a week, a month or longer of your vacation time with the organization or NGO and then your holiday begins. For others, a change of routine and being in a different country is a holiday!

Most organizations are based in a single location. Some will move to a different area just once or twice within the year or the personnel move to different bases, centres or compounds. The latter approach will broaden the workers'/travellers' horizon, bring added experience and will reveal the different needs amongst those they are serving. The former helps people to concentrate all their efforts in one place, making it easier to see the fruit of one's labour. In the free enrolment in the college of life, we should all be students, ready and eager to learn from others.

The major types of humanitarian and development aid are: Education, working with children, building or feeding programmes, hydration (boreholes and making water wells), medical work, agricultural, mechanical maintenance and sport programmes.

Humanitarian aid is concerned with the interests and welfare of humans – helping those who are in immediate need. It is material or logistical assistance provided for humanitarian purposes, typically in response to a humanitarian crisis. The primary objective of humanitarian aid is to save lives, alleviate suffering and maintain human dignity.

Development aid, also known as development or technical assistance, international aid or foreign aid, can include: building programmes, education, agricultural techniques etc., and is a long-term solution. It addresses the underlying socio-economic factors (the study of the relationship between economic activity and social life), which may have led to a crisis or emergency. Development aid can be in the form of a cooperative or a lending bank, but these forms of aid or assistance continue over years or decades, giving small loans or "gifts" to those who wish to start up a small business to assist them or their community.

Civil wars, armed conflict, alongside poor government policies, often reveal the desperate straits of citizens when these events ravage a nation. Government finances are spent on armaments and it is the citizens that suffer; due to lack of agricultural implements, no seeds, bombed fields, unexploded devices, landmines and fear of the enemy that drives them into hiding, resulting in little to no harvest and great distress, turmoil and extreme desperation.

Humanitarian or development aid should involve giving someone a hand-up, rather than just a hand-out, though in times of famine and war, a hand-out is the only way. Lao Tzu said, "Give a man a fish and you feed him for a day, teach a man how to fish and you feed him for a lifetime." A hand-up could include: sheep, cattle, chickens, agricultural implements, seeds, or improved farming techniques, so that livestock can be raised, the land can be tilled effectively and families or even communities will become self-sustaining.

Major Types of Humanitarian and Development Aid

- Education – teaching English (or other subjects) at a school. Teaching English as a foreign language (TEFL).
- Working with children – orphans or those with disabilities.
- Building Programmes – homes, community centres and school projects.
- Feeding Programmes – feeding (and clothing) the poor and needy. Helping the malnourished, those whose harvests have failed or during a time of famine.
- Hydration – sinking boreholes and making water wells.
- Medical Work – health clinics, dentistry/oral hygienist, surgery and family advice etc. For trained doctors, physicians and nurses.
- Agricultural – improved farming techniques (training and equipment), better tools, seeds, poultry or cattle etc. which empowers citizens to become self-sustaining and can even grow into a local business employing people.
- Mechanical Maintenance – maintenance of vehicles, boats, ships and buildings etc.
- Sports Programmes – training, coaching and providing sports equipment to poor nations.
- Prison Ministry – visiting prisoners, helping to rehabilitate them and assisting their reintegration back into the community.
- Helping widows and orphans. In some cultures, it is the man's responsibility or the only person who is permitted to provide for his household and when he is absent, economic

problems and hardships can exist for the remainder of the family. Culture and pride are major obstacles to cross.

My parents wanted to go to the UK to help others. They are both in their late 50s, have many practical giftings and their English is ok. I emailed an acquaintance and asked him if he knew of any organization that wanted a 'handyman' and a 'general helper.' He referred me to a website, which listed numerous agencies and organizations, and three months later my parents found the right place for them. Els – Netherlands.

Working with Children

You could work with an orphanage in a developing country; many are run by Christian groups or charities. Many will expect you to pay a designated fee per day to help with your bed and board (meals), with extra on the top for the charity. One British owned orphanage in Kenya charges £15 ($24) per day. For this NGO, you need a British 'police check' before they will allow you near their children. A police check is to make sure you are not a convicted child abuser or on the sex register.

In Britain, ACRO Criminal Records Office issues Police Certificates. The website states: 'The International Child Protection Certificate (ICPC) is a criminal records check for UK nationals, or non-UK nationals who've previously lived in the UK, looking to work with children overseas. Many international schools and organizations around the world employ people from the UK as teachers, workers and volunteers. A police criminal records check is now available for UK nationals, and people who have resided in the UK, who are looking for work or are already employed overseas working with children.'[1]

In the 1990s I closed down my business and joined a humanitarian organization in Romania. When I went to Eastern Bloc Europe, my worldview changed and change does not always feel good. The first time I saw a "home" on a garbage dump made from junk – the family inside huddled together – my worldview began to change. Sometimes I recoil from the memories of children. Many street kids escaped the abuses they encountered by crawling into sewers near the factories. The children selected these rat and cockroach infested hellholes because the pipes from the factories helped to keep them warm in the winter.... I went to Romania to give children a fighting chance and to help establish an orphanage. My life has been deeply impacted by the broken and needy people I have encountered. Jim – America.

Chapter 38

Leading a Volunteer-Vacation

You may have the skills that fill a gap in a team or if a natural disaster occurs, you want to go and assist in immediate humanitarian aid, a volunteer-vacation. A group of friends or colleagues may band together for such a time as this, including specialist search and rescue teams, who receive leave to help others, especially during an earthquake, tornado strike, severe flood or other disasters. Many religious groups have regular trips abroad, volunteer-vacations to do good deeds and help other people (and to share their beliefs). These trips run by Christians are also known as short-term missions (STMs).[1]

Some teams build houses, churches, community centres, halls, help out with agriculture, farming, starting small businesses, working in health clinics and surgery (especially removing cataracts so people can see) and corrective surgery (face, feet and hands), as well as dental work. Other teams dig ditches for water pipes, drill a borehole for a community well or tackle other maintenance or first-starter projects. Some STM-ers work in a school, orphanage, child care, or teach young students how to use a sewing machine, make garments, carpentry, plumbing and other trades or sports.

> I was studying at a Bible College in the UK and during the Christmas holidays, I had the opportunity to go on a humanitarian mission to Eastern Europe. We travelled in an old school bus and went through at least six or seven countries and what an experience it was. Donald – Bulgaria.

Many Christian relief organizations will accept volunteers with skills who do not practice the Christian faith, when it is in the interest of those they serve. If you join such a organization, remember to keep an open-mind and not a closed heart. A short time of worship, Bible study and prayer is usually part of spiritual preparation for the practical work of helping others. (Once you are closer to God, you can be more closer to people in their time of need and distress). In such situations, it can be easy to seize up, fold one's arms and withdraw. Remember, you are going to have new experiences, embrace the opportunity, pull down your inner walls and go with the flow. You may be surprised at what happens to yourself, the change in your own life and that of the team.

Being a Leader

The person who leads a team on a trip abroad has more burdens, responsibilities, trials and problems than those who are part of the team, also see the following chapter. For a first time leader of an epic journey, it can be a daunting task. Heading up a team in one's own country is relatively easy, but being responsible abroad is quite another matter as the stakes get higher and problems can be more difficult to solve. In many different countries in Africa, I found out the mistake or fault may not have been mine, but the cost always was!

Some young adults are more mature than others. Some are quiet and shy, others are extroverts and some can be difficult. Many of us have had zeal without knowledge and we have all made mistakes in the past, so bear that in mind, before you decide to exclude or decline someone from joining the group.

If you are going with a group of friends then 'leader' may not be the right word, but a general consensus may be aimed at, whilst the casting vote, or the stronger personality makes the final call. The 'buck' has to stop somewhere and decisions have to be made.

Sometimes expectation and realisation is interlinked with the preparation or lack of it, long before you arrive at your destination. This is especially true in relation to working with a charity, NGO or humanitarian organization. This is also coupled with what they think you're going to do, what you have planned to do and whether or not this has been communicated clearly.

> I went on a short-term mission thinking that everyday I would be able to share the love of Jesus Christ. I wanted to let people know that Jesus Christ, the Son of God, died for them on a cross and after three days rose again! And by repenting and forsaking our sins [the bad things we do, say and think], whilst putting our trust and faith in Jesus Christ we may have eternal life. At times I realised I was preaching my culture, not the Bible. Africans celebrate their faith in Jesus Christ, hope for eternal life and forgiveness off sins in an exuberant way during worship. My culture was more reserved and austere and I had to learn from them! Angelina – Africa.

If you and a group of friends take two weeks or a month out to build a house, sink a borehole for a well or other charitable deed, does everybody know what each person is meant to do? What is their role in the group? As a leader, have you asked your host what they want you to do? Has this been passed on to your friends, the team, so that they know what they will be doing? Have you spoken to your host over the phone, by email or video conferencing to clarify all points? Do you and your host know the skills, talents and giftings that are available amongst the team? Does the host need money in advance for a deposit to book accommodation or larger amounts to buy in supplies ready for your arrival? Does the leader need to meet with the host face-to-face and discuss any number of issues and to see the available facilities? The host might be quite comfortable in his or her accommodation, but a Western team might not be used to roughing it.

Is the host clear on who is coming, exact numbers, general ages and how many of each sex, including any married couples? You should try to keep people of a similar age and same sex in each room/dormitory. At other times, friends band together in groups and they do the job for you, but beware of someone being left out!

If you are the leader who decides the team, then use your wisdom, common sense and discernment. Whether the trip should be open to selective ages (18-25, 20-30s etc.), to a limited number (4 to 12 people etc.) or a larger group (20 to 40 people). Remember that the larger the group the greater the logistics of plane seats, accommodation, transport, eating out, purchasing supplies in a small village for self-catering etc. Eating arrangements can be problematic for large groups, but generally not if you book in advance and do self-catering, even if only for breakfast and the evening meal. How many seats does the minibus or coach have? How many beds or rooms for camping mattresses/bed rolls does the hired hall or apartment have? Do not be a burden to your host.

You will need to know how much it will cost, or thereabouts and let each prospective team member know, the projected cost per person, or the actual amount.

There is often a set number of places for practical reasons. Whilst a large team can do more work than just a handful, they can be difficult to manage, especially if there are a few who are prone to rebel and do not desire to pull their own weight. If working on a building site, e.g. constructing a building or hospital, or boring a water hole, too many people will get in each other's way. There needs to be order and safety.

A leader should bring out the best in each member, and know or discover their qualities and strengths and utilise them. If your team consists of development aid where specialist skills are needed, *do not assume* the builder wants to build, the chef wants to cook, the bus driver wants to drive the hired mini-bus. The gravedigger may not want to dig ditches to lay water pipes, the teacher may not want to supervise the teenagers or work in the classroom and the accountant may not want to be the treasurer. Ask them.

Team Logistics
Within a large team, there needs to be someone in charge of the logistics which is the practical preparation of: transportation,

accommodation, how to feed the team, self-catering or eating out, purchasing supplies/materials for projects etc. This is often the team leader's responsibility, the host or shared responsibility, but some duties are delegated to responsible or veteran members of the team.

Sometimes the logistic's leader is largely stuck at base camp, especially if he/she is cooking for a large team, while the team goes off and does its work or religious ministry. From day-to-day, two members of the team may have to remain at base camp (on a rotational basis) to assist the logistics member or host member. Their work is no less important than the ones on the "front line" as each member has his or her duty to do. If a regiment was not fed and supplied then it would fail in its mission. Those at base camp may be cooking, doing the laundry, chauffeuring, buying supplies, confirming the meetings, obtaining permits, checking all details, liaise with local leaders and perform many other duties.

A leader of a group may consider flying to the host country from one year to eight months before the trip begins, though this may depend on the prospective number of team members, as there is a great difference in logistical planning between six or sixty team members! The reconnaissance mission helps build up the relationship between the host leader and the one who is planning the trip. They can see what resources are available, scout-out prospective accommodation, transport, cooking facilities or places to eat, see the land, shops and the general environment they will be working in etc. and take some photos or video footage as these make recruiting for humanitarian travels or a volunteer-vacation easier.

If you are involved in humanitarian work then be sure to pack what tools or equipment are needed. Distribute any tools or materials throughout the team and remind them to pack everything! Have all the team's passports with their visas arrived? Has every team member paid his or her money? Has the accommodation and plane's departure been confirmed? Is the mini-bus and a driver still available to take you to the airport? Beware of double bookings!

Problem People
- Members of your team who are uncommitted or half-hearted, and those who are unteachable.
- Those who come with ulterior motives – especially if the financial liability or responsibility is not theirs.
- Those who have come to see the sights and to shop till they drop or treat the trip *only* as a holiday/vacation.
- The isolationist who *only* wants to work alone.
- Those who think they are superior to others and look down on those they have been sent to help, assist and serve.

- Hygiene freaks, those who think they are allergic to anything and everything, and the hypochondriacs!
- Those who choose not to have contact with the locals.
- The moaners and complainers, about anything and everything. The 'If I had done this' personality, I would have done it this way, which would have been much better!

> I was in Europe with some other Americans doing NGO work. Around the breakfast table these people belittled the country and its people; declaring why it was all a mess. I was so embarrassed. Alex – Germany.

More Harm than Good

On any trip, an individual or an unprepared team can do more harm than good. Some negative and harmful traits, as well as oversights are:

- Little to no preparation – not understanding the culture, ignoring it or lack of resources etc.
- No vaccinations or personal medical supplies.
- Refusal to interact with the locals.
- Selfishness – do it my way.
- Arrogance and critical – I know best and am the best.
- Prideful – superior attitude, I have all the answers, I am better than everyone and you can't teach me anything!
- Flaunting your wealth – money, clothes, jewellery, gadgets and electrical or digital items.
- Acting like a cash-cow – giving money and gifts to anyone who asks with no regard to consequences.
- Stubborn – we will do it like this or not at all!
- Lack of communication – this is what we want to do, without asking the host or community what they want done.
- Leaving things undone – unfinished jobs, that which cannot be accomplished without further financial aid.
- Lack of foresight – if the water pump breaks, can the locals replace the parts? Do they have the money?

> I help feed orphan children in one of the most closed countries of the world. Even though we are a humanitarian organization, there are so many places that we are not permitted to visit. At an orphanage, one boy who looked five years old was actually nine. He was suffering from third degree malnutrition. Anonymous – North Korea.

Chapter 39

A Working-Vacation – Advice for Leaders

The leader of any team has the most demanding roles. He or she make the final decisions and have a whole host of other responsibilities to deal with, which includes keeping an eye on other members of the team, mediating between people, the logistics of travel; seeing that everything goes as smoothly as can be expected, as well as rallying the troops. The leader can also delegate duties to responsible members of the team. The leader should keep the team up-to-date. They have to deal with not only people and their successes, but their personalities and their problems, and to keep the group focused on its aims and goals. Also see the preceding chapter.

If you are going abroad to serve others, often as part of a team, working for or alongside a local group or organization then ask them what help *they* need – not what help *you think* they need! Ask them, "How can we best assist you?" It is vitally important to find out what they want you to do, or what they expect from you. You can email or chat via a webcam or Skype before your team departs. These people may be your host for several weeks, months or longer.

A leader may consider flying out two to three months before the start of the trip for a week or so to help oil the cogs of preparation and communication, and to purchase or order the needed materials, working alongside the host. To see what materials or resources are outstanding, to confirm any bookings or to inspect the transport, accommodation, (or newly laid foundations of a building which the team will build on), to double-check all items and discuss issues with the local host people or organization, so that all parties know what is expected from each other.

There is great difference in logistical planning between a team of eight or eighty working travellers! Some leaders fly out a week early, ahead of the team to finalise details and to double-check everything. Any tools or materials, which are not available, can then be purchased (weight and size permitting) by the team and flown out with the group.

Remember people's names but especially the host and the leader. Some names when heard for the first time can be difficult to pronounce, let alone remember. Ask the person to repeat it and say it out loud. Do this two or three times if need be, to get it lodged in your brain. In many cultures, titles and greetings are important. If you are unsure how to address someone, just ask them, "How do I address you?" Or "What is your name?" If they prefix it with a title e.g. Dr., Sir, Mayor, Rev. Pastor, Major etc. then that his how you address them.

Keep Receipts

If you are part of a group involved in humanitarian or religious work, the treasurer should keep a tight tab on the group's budget. He or she should carry a notebook to write down all the costs of the team which is wise. Where possible keep receipts, especially in regards to accommodation, transport, food, materials, tools, labour costs etc., as you may be accountable to others. Many cafes, restaurants, shops, food stalls and hardware stores or builders merchants may not issue receipts. Sometimes you just have to ask, or bring your own receipt stubbs and write on the amount and the item, and remember to calculate how much it costs in your home currency and write it on the receipt. There are always minor financial discrepancies at the end of the trip due to fluctuating exchange rates.

Report any breakages and don't let it be a surprise for your host, charity or NGO etc. after you have departed! If you break the tap/ faucet, tell someone, don't ignore it or the bathroom will soon be flooded!

Local Considerations

If you are to construct a home, build a community hall or sink a borehole for the community, find out who is providing the bricks, tools, pumps and all the other related materials and finances. Is planning permission or a permit needed? For a building, make sure the foundations have been laid before the team arrives, as they need time to settle and dry, unless you are staying long enough to be able to start work on other projects.

David Livermore, executive director of the Global Learning Center at Grand Rapids Theological Seminary noted, in 2005, in Monrovia, Liberia, tragedy occurred during the monsoon season, when a school building collapsed, killing two children. Visitors had built the school to their standards instead of Liberian standards. They relied on their own expertise whilst ignoring local authorities on the ground.

The host or community may not have the money to purchase the items needed and if you fly into the country expecting to buy a large quantity of bricks, hundreds of planks of wood or several tons of sand and cement straight from a Western style DIY depot, you and your team may be in for a surprise! The host will more often than not need the money forwarded onto them two to three months in advance (or when the leader flies out) so that the materials can be ordered and a deposit paid. The transportation, materials or equipment can take weeks or months to arrive and so forward planning is essential. If you are involved in construction, take into consideration the thoughts, designs, style and workmanship of the locals. Use a local architect if one is needed, what does your host say? Is planning permission or a permit needed for the new building? Techniques and methods in construction may also differ; you cannot demand and state, "This is how we do it at home," and proceed to change their set-up, style, method or architecture! How you do a thing at home may not be how it is done abroad, for better or for worse.

You should consider the scenario that in some places, local families could go hungry when foreigners are willing to do the work for free. Utilise the local expertise and work in partnership. Consider employing locals who specialise in certain trades to work alongside you for the duration of your working-vacation. A days wage for them, say £8 ($13) may be an hour's wage for you, or half an hour. Your host can inform you of the going rate. The locals may like to begin at dawn, take long lunches or have siestas. Consider all these factors, you should not go breaking local customs or culture.

In some cultures, friendships, relationships and the wider family are more important than tasks – the locals may turn up late, because they stopped to chat to a friend – they are not tied to time. The foreman meets you an hour later than you had planned, but makes no apology. You may find these situations a great inconvenience as well as frustrating, but as you are the foreigner in *their* culture, it is you who must give way. Go with the flow and embrace the experience! If the job is not completed, try not to see it as a failure because building lasting friendships and relationships with the locals is important. You could always come back next year or another team may complete the job.

Be gracious when inconveniences arise, be forgiving and understanding if the host, or other workers are not punctual, be patient when things are done differently than at home, and void of criticism and murmuring towards all.

As tiredness begins, human grace decreases, so don't stay up late and get out of bed too early. If you are dog-tired you may growl all day! You cannot burn the candle at both ends.

The Golden Rule of Silence
Silence is often hard, but golden. You may see an answer to a problem, but you may not have earned the respect to be heard! How

would you feel if a stranger came to your house or community and wanted to change things? On the other hand, you may perceive a problem, but to your host or the local community there is no problem. You are not on your working-vacation to change the world to your way of thinking, but are there to serve and to do your best.

Do not embarrass your host by your lack of concern for those who may have done all in their power to accommodate you and your team, to give you the best of what they have. This is especially true in regards to accommodation and food. Some people will give up their bed for you and sleep on the floor, or move their children into their room so that your small team can have some privacy. Would you do that for someone or for their team?

If you contact friends at home and things are not as good as you had hoped, then a good rule of thumb is to assume that someone from your host country is reading your email, text message, social media update, letter or fax, or is listening to your phone call! How would they feel if they could read what you have written or listen to your conversation? Do to others, as you would have them do unto you. Do not murmur or speak bad of others.

You may live in a free and democratic society where within limitations, you can say what you want to whoever, but this is not the case in many nations of the world. Do not endanger your host, your interpreter, the locals or the charity, organization or NGO you are working with. You will go home at the end of your travels, but they have to stay and there could be ramifications and consequences for your actions, which could be taken out on others! Some organizations etc. have lost their permits or license to operate or work within a country due to the actions and words of others.

Chapter 40

A Working Team

Within any group of people there will be differences and stronger characters will come to the fore. Within your team there should be the greatest of cooperation, but it is inevitable that problems will arise. Your fellow team members may have just as many problems as yourself and so conflict and tension can arise. There may be many underlying issues that affect individuals, as well as their gender, age, level of maturity and preconceived ideas.

Treat others how you would like to be treated; be kind, courteous, respectful, gracious and forgiving. Do not be a pain or a nuisance to your leader or to other members of the team. Have a laugh and a joke, enjoy yourself, but don't be a fool.

You may have just arrived at your destination or after a week think that you have made a major mistake and want to quit. Don't run away and go home or begin to murmur and complain! Never run away from the humanitarian organization, NGO or charity that you are part of or quit your trip because the going has got tough; you will regret it and what will your friends and family at home say?

If you have arrived at your final destination to begin your work. You will be allocated a room, or a bed in a room alongside other workers. There will probably be a team/group meeting. There may be introductions to members of the team who did not travel with you, alongside staff members who live on site. Listen to the leader and follow his or her instruction. Some ground rules will need to be stated and words of wisdom imparted, followed by a tour of the facilities or area.

Practical Duties and Chores

Many people are used to having everything done for them and it is easy to take things for granted. Meals appear on the table; dirty washing is thrown into a laundry basket and within a few days it reappears clean, and your bedroom is dusted and vacuumed regularly. If you are part of a team then each individual has to take responsibility for themselves and lookout for the overall welfare of the group. Within any team there are many different responsibilities and functions. If members of a sports team decided to do their own thing then the team would not function at its best.

If you are part of a NGO or charity; you may have to do some practical duties and chores, perhaps those you don't like. There may be a large rota placed in a prominent place so that each team member can see what their duties are and when. Larger groups are often split into group duties on a rotational basis, e.g. peeling the vegetables, washing up/cleaning the dishes, sweeping the yard, vacuuming the communal areas, doing the shopping at the local market, collecting and chopping firewood etc. Depending on age, a leader may be assigned with each group or a local worker from the NGO. You should not grumble or complain, but embrace the experience. You may learn a new skill.

Help others, it is also a good way of getting to know people. How many times have we left washing the dishes to another, yet we all ate at the meal table? Whilst others will try to justify their exemption from certain duties and being allergic to washing up liquid is a valid exemption, but that does not mean that they are exempt from laying the table, wiping up/drying the dishes and packing away or other important duties like peeling the potatoes or chopping vegetables!

Let us not be in the habit of making lame excuses to get out of practical chores, because we are only neglecting our duty and revealing to others our true character.

Defiance of rules can lead to open opposition, whether it is the rules of the nation or the rules of a charity, NGO or organization. Policies are frequently laid down in print because they have learnt from experience. It is possible not to break the letter of the law, but the spirit behind it. Don't be a rebel and look for loopholes! We must also be aware that we can listen but not hear, and look but not see. We can nod our head, but not understand; think we understand yet not comprehend. Often we have to read between the lines when we are communicating with others, and in another culture, that is even harder than at home, especially if you have to communicate in a second language.

> Community is the place where the person you least want to live with, always lives – Henri Nouwen.

What to Do
- Be punctual and prepared.
- Learn some local phrases.
- Honour people and walk in humility.
- Serve others, be kind and courteous.
- Be considerate of others, especially concerning bedtime, morning rising and midnight feasts.
- Look out for any insecure or lonely members of the team, befriend them, assist them and help boost their confidence.
- Be culturally, economically and politically sensitive.

- Think before you speak or act – try not to cause offence.
- If mercury in the thermometer begins to rise, drink plenty of fluids, cover up and consider knocking off early.
- Do something different as a team, go and visit a beauty spot.

'A fool vents all his feelings, but a wise man holds them back' (Proverbs 29:11, the Bible).

What not to Do
- Do not be selfish or lazy.
- Do not keep the team waiting.
- Do not overwork yourself or your team.
- Do not moan, murmur, criticise or grumble.
- Do not treat your host or leader like a maid or servant.
- Do not hog the shower or use all the hot water – there may be ten people outside queuing for the shower.
- Do not compare your host's: house, car, food, possessions, clothes etc., to yours.
- Do not flaunt your wealth or brag about your money and possessions.
- Do not speak negatively about your host, leader or other team members.
- Do not give your advice on the country's problems of which you know nothing about, unless your host or community has asked you, but not in public, just in case.
- Do not *demand* better food, accommodation or privacy.
- Do not be the group joker, attention seeker or boisterous.

Remember
- You have come to serve.
- Love is a universal language.
- Serve wholeheartedly, joyfully and wear a smile if culturally appropriate (it is not in Russia unless it is between friends).
- Be flexible, the best of plans often don't work out.
- Beware of cultural faux pas (a socially awkward or tactless act – a slip up).
- Misunderstandings will arise because of differences.
- Laugh at yourself, but be cautious of laughing at others.
- Don't dishonour your team mates, your host or the leader.
- You may share a room with six people, dozens of insects and some flies!

Life Changing Experience
As much as going on a working-vacation is about helping others, it is also a time for introspection as we see our true character and to

help us change ourselves with the opportunities that we encounter. It is also a time to evaluate our: life, priorities, worldview and more often than not to see how well-off we actually are compared to the majority of the developing world.

We are not invincible, we do not have all the answers and like our host or community, we have failings and difficulties in some areas of our lives. Let us not project an image of what we are not, but be open to learn and to receive help as well as give it when asked to.

> We were part of a large mixed team in a Muslim country and a group of us girls were invited by a bride to a three-day wedding feast! It was so exciting and we were the only foreigners there. Each day we would come back and report to the team about the day's events and on the last day of the feast we presented our presents to the bride and groom. We will never forget that trip. Keumhee – North Africa.

Travel Blessings and Gratitude

- Not being pick pocketed, or having anything stolen, lost or damaged.
- Locals who are happy to help and give directions and local knowledge. Many will go the extra mile.
- The team working together as one in an effective manner.
- Nobody is involved in an accident and the health of the team has been generally good.
- Flying into an airport and getting a visa for free, or for a small amount without any hassle.
- Not having security unpack your rucksack/backpack or suitcase at the airport, as a random security check.
- Everything going as planned or better than expected.
- Going home with good memories, a potential tan, a few kilograms lighter in weight, as well as a new skill, added life experience and travel tales.

Chapter 41

Can You Help Me – $ £ €

In developing countries, poverty is more apparent; more in your face and beggars and/or homeless people can be more numerous and prominent than in the West. Many do not know where their next meal will come from. On your travels, many people you meet will perceive you as the rich foreigner – and compared to them, you probably are. You will not solve the problems of world poverty, but you can make a difference in individual's lives, if you want to, though how and when is not always so straight forward.

Every guidebook to foreign destinations discourages the giving of independent gifts and money, as it encourages a culture of begging; it can cause problems for others and money can be used on substance abuse. They all suggest giving to charities who can distribute to those in need in the most effective manner. However, there may be some individuals who through no fault of their own are in dire circumstances, they look malnourished, are clothed in rags, and it is not always easy to turn a blind eye, or to walk by on the other side.

Regardless of where you are in the world, the how, what and when to give, always vexes the most compassionate and kindest of people. There are also professional beggars, con artists and addicts of various types, which complicates the issue of giving as you often cannot tell them apart. You will find these in your home country and abroad. You need to be wise and discerning. 'The righteous considers the cause of the poor, but the wicked does not understand such knowledge' (Proverbs 29:7, the Bible).

The policies of organizations, charities, tour companies and NGOs, concerning 'hand-outs' or gifts vary and may differ in different towns, districts or countries. Whatever rules they have, they have for a good reason and even governments and some local tourist information agencies have their own policies. They may be hard to follow or obey, but you should adhere to them, as the policy makers are able to see the bigger picture over a longer period of time.

Did you know? Giving money, food and clothing to children on the streets encourages them to remain on the streets. Your assistance can make a difference if given through established childcare facilities. – On a Billboard, by the Department of Social Welfare – Lusaka, Zambia.

The issue of Cape Town's street people is becoming increasingly problematic. As citizens, we feel helpless and empathetic, and thus donate what we can. In reality, this does not contribute to solving the bigger picture. Don't give to street people directly, here's why: Giving your donations of money, tips, food and clothing directly to street people who stand at traffic intersections or on the streets does not help the problem, it AGGRAVATES it. Instead of making a real difference, it condemns street people to a permanent life on the streets. It can also result in associated problems of drug and substance abuse and crime. – Leaflet by the City of Cape Town, South Africa.

Contact Details

In many places of the world people will ask for your telephone number, address, email, social media details. Some requests come from complete strangers, would you give your telephone number and address to a person you sat next to on the New York Metro, London Underground or the forthcoming Sydney Metro? I have asked people for directions and they have asked for my contact details! When I am travelling, often when I am asked, "Where do you live?" With a smile I state the country I am in as that is where I am living at that present time. If they ask me where I come from, then I tell them, England. If you worked with an NGO, or charity then there is a distinction between the people that you have worked alongside for weeks or months and the person you talked to for twenty minutes on the street. International phone calls can be expensive and your new friend may phone you and ask you to ring back! If you cannot afford to, then tell them or don't give your number out in the first place.

Sometimes, requests for items come after you have arrived home, having corresponded for a few months and can include things which they want you to buy and send them, a request for a letter of introduction or even an invite to your country with yourself as the host. A letter of invite can be used as part of a visa application process and you may be designating yourself as the guarantor of that person whilst he or she is within your country! The person concerned could be your responsibility. Remember, you will only receive requests at home if you have given out your contact details. Requests can easily be ignored by pressing 'delete,' putting the letter in the shredder, press unfriend or unfollow, or block them entirely.

Since the advent of widespread internet, I have never given out my home address. A name and address can be an asset to a scheming person, as one day you may find uninvited visitors, 'friends of a friend' on your doorstep, relating to the person you met whilst abroad. They have just arrived and have no place to stay, and little money! This is an extreme example, but not unknown!

The Rich Foreign Worker

You may be straight out of high school and taking a year out to travel the globe. In many developing countries, you can be perceived as incredibly well-off. You may spend $5 on a meal (or a bed in a youth hostel dormitory) but that could be 2 ½ days wage for a local! Some think that you are rich because you have flown to their country or are far from home, they only have to ask, after all, the worst you can say is no. You may be more financially secure than many people you meet, but many people will have their own land and home, which makes them wealthier than the average traveller who lives with their parents or who pays rent or has a mortgage on their home. Some people you meet on your travels are *only* out to get what they can from you, whilst others need genuine help.

Do not be offended if you get asked for money, if you were in their circumstances you would probably do the same. But before you begin to dispense the contents of your wallet or purse, you should find out the policy of the organization, charity or NGO you are working with, speak to your team leader.

One man asked me to pay his university fees; I felt quite grieved by his request as I never had the opportunity to go to university. I had to leave school and get a job. Jack – Africa.

Meeting and working with the locals brings new and unexpected challenges to bear and there are those in developing countries who will ask you for assistance – financially, practically or in other ways. There is a big difference between your host asking for assistance (or other people who have helped the team) and a relative stranger. Many organizations work with the same people or community and therefore long-term commitments and strong relationships are formed. If you joined an organization, charity or NGO then all non-verbal requests for assistance should be forwarded onto the organization. It may be a situation or an escalating problem that needs to be addressed because policies of mutual respect, honesty, trust and cooperation need to be adhered to. Not everybody who asks has a *need*, but a person may *want* some of your perceived wealth, whilst on the other hand, your little gift may go a long way to help a genuine person in need, whilst other requests are outlandish. One man asked for the price of a dowry for a wife! Another wanted a pair of designer trainers/sneakers, whilst another person, the latest mobile/cell phone! One person wanted English newspapers to be posted to him regularly, but the cost of Airmail postage/shipping is prohibitively high. Others want clothes, books, DVDs, CDs, pens, notepads…the list could go on and on.

There are some people who abuse the friendship of travellers and groups and resort to underhanded tactics to get what they want. Some will play one member of the team against another or individually try to solicit money from as many members as they can, or seek out the weaker members of the group. Some are even so brazen as to pick up items, which belong to travellers and walk away with them, or are subtle and admire an object whilst dropping so many hints that it becomes embarrassing. Not everybody who asks is in need – it can be just greed! On occasions, donations, gifts or items which have been given for a specific project or person, have been misappropriated or embezzled, and unfortunately it is a fact of life across the world.

I was travelling in the bus alongside this teenage lad. He had told me that he had gone on holiday to visit his uncle in another part of the country. After several hours, the bus ride ended and we were about to part company when he asked me for money for his next month school fees. I told him, "No," thinking to myself, if he can afford to travel half the country on public transport to enjoy a holiday, he can afford his fees. "That amount is nothing to you" he said. Again I responded "No," but thought to myself, you don't know me or the sacrifices I have made to go on this trip. John – Ethiopia.

For many travellers or NGO workers who have taken a year out, or those not long out of high school or college, they will not have the disposable income compared to someone who has worked for many years. Therefore, they may not be in a position to help and that's ok. However, local adults should not be asking teenagers for money. One local man repeatedly dropped hints about his need, a foreign worker responded, "I wish I was rich like you, you're married, have children and have your own home; I cannot afford to get married, start a family or move out and buy my own apartment."

Nearing the End of your Trip

Nearing the end of your trip, you may have some items of clothing or other possessions (books, penknife, umbrella, sleeping bag, etc.) that you brought with you which you no longer need and would be far better used or appreciated by the locals. As an independent traveller you can give an item to a fellow traveller, a worker at the youth hostel, or the waiter or waitress from the local cafe etc. If you are part of a team working in a community, be aware that problems arise when someone receives a gift and somebody else does not. It can cause friction and tension. There is also a danger that individuals will be friendly to future teams because of what they can get out of it and can lead to a culture of begging.

If you are part of a charity, you may wish to leave some money behind, instead of converting your spare cash back into your own currency (but leave some money for the airport!) or use this money to buy present(s) – something which an individual or a community needs. Does the organization or charity have a policy and/or what does your leader think? You may be in a position to hand over some of your own currency. £10 ($16) may *just* be a monthly phone top up for someone in the West, but it is eight days living expenses for those who live on £1.25 ($2) a day.

Empty Promises and Emotional Bonds

In the Western world there is an underlying culture of misleading politeness, which entails not telling the truth in the eyes of others. A common form is making promises and not fulfilling them, "I'll keep in touch," and you never write, email, phone or add them as a friend on social media! "I'll send you the book, photo, clothes, CD, DVD" etc. and you don't. It is a culture that has developed out of politeness and good intentions, but in different countries is taken as a promise; not just a loose saying. In the heat of the moment, the emotion of the trip or whilst saying our goodbyes we are prone to say the most normal, yet bizarre statements, "You must come and visit me sometime," "If you're in — look me up." If you don't want a person to visit you then don't make the offer because they may just turn up one day.

Don't make promises that you cannot keep or have no intention of keeping. The reply, "I'll think about it," in response to a request, can also be interpreted in other cultures as "yes," or that you will get back to them, whereas in the West it is often used as polite way to get someone to stop pestering you.

Working with the locals as part of a charity, organization or NGO can produce emotional bonds, ties of friendship and it can be emotionally traumatic for some people when they have to part. The same with fellow travellers whom you may have tied yourself up with. You may have mixed emotions, sad to leave but happy to go. You may feel sorry for those you leave behind, but they also may feel sorry for you, going back to the rat-race of a Western materialistic society.

As part of our six-week trip we drove across the border and stayed in an orphanage. I had been there a few times before and I knew most of the children's names. It was great to see them. Leaving was very hard for all concerned, the children hugged us and we all cried. Chris – Mexico.

Chapter 42

The End of the Journey

You should confirm your flight details three days or thereabouts before departure. The day before departure, settle all the bills (accommodation and other expenses), and confirm that you have transport or know how you will get to the airport. Pack your bag. If you have stayed with a host as part of a charity, organization or NGO, tidy up! Check-in online 24hrs before departure and you get to choose your seat on the flight home. On the day of departure, check your room and leave in plenty of time, as it is better to wait around for three hours at the airport than to miss the flight because the bus or the train was delayed. Remember, you have to be at the airport 2hrs before departure and at least one hour for an international ferry. Keep your plane ticket, passport and any valuables on you!

Your hand/carry-on luggage must be accessible at all times. If you need to phone home on arrival via a public call box, carry some change in your pocket or in your hand/carry-on luggage. If you are being met at the airport by your family or friend and your plane is delayed, try to phone up the driver or SMS/text to let them know that you will be late. If your plane arrives in at 4pm, it can take one hour to reclaim your bag, pass through Immigration and be at the pick-up point at arrivals. Airport parking is expensive and most drivers do not like to be kept waiting around unnecessarily.

One person went to Greece for his two-week holiday and whilst in the sun on one of the many Greek islands was offered a job, working on jet-skis. He flew home, handed in his notice, tied up his affairs in the UK and flew back out to the island. Within one month, he was back in the UK! He had flown to Greece, but the job had already been taken by someone else! Don't make any rash decisions!

Your travels may end when you arrive back at home and you could be greeted with all sorts of emotions, from jubilation to depression, loneliness, disorientation or reverse culture shock; and there will be many things that need to be done. There will be your bag to unpack, clothes to wash, friends and family wanting to know all about your trip. There will be a small mountain of correspondence to deal with, bank statements to check, junk mail to wade through, emails to check, social media updates and a whole host of other things.

Arriving back at 'home' can be daunting, especially the affluence, excess and waste of resources – this is most noticeable when you return from a developing country. You can feel ashamed at yourself for having a wardrobe/closet full of clothes, numerous pairs of shoes, the latest gadgets and three meals a day, whereas the people you walked past most days or worked alongside, may have been less fortunate than yourself, some of whom may have lived a day-to-day existence. Do not make any rash decisions like throwing the contents of your wardrobe/closet away, but ask yourself, "What can I learn from this?" "What can I do about it?" "Do I want to do something about it?"

Things to Do on Your Return

The following list is a general guide of things to do, largely dependent on what time of day or night you get back and your own particular routine.

1. Unpack your bag and put the washing machine on.
2. Have a hot shower or bath. You may really need it, or you will certainly appreciate it after your long journey home.
3. Have a powernap or sleep, especially if you have had a night flight, or you may just be generally tired.
4. Put washing out to dry or ask someone to do it for you.
5. Open your correspondence and throw away the junk mail. Leave checking your bank statements for when you are fresh and alert.
6. Let your friends and family know that you are home, just in case they don't know. Phone, email, SMS/text, WhatsApp or via social media, though your grandparents may appreciate a phone call if they are not a silver surfer (they are retired and do not use the internet).
7. Check your emails and social media.
8. Sort your digital photos out and save them.

You May Wish to Do

1. You may wish to write a summary of your trip – if not for yourself, for those who have financially supported you. Go through your journal for highlights and/or look through your sent emails whilst you were on your travels and use that as a framework. Or speak to people face to face or over the phone, whatever your preference.
2. Fulfil your obligations by sending items to those you have promised, e.g. book, DVD, photos etc. These items do not always arrive and don't expect an acknowledgment of thanks. Email or contact via social media and let them know you have posted/shipped the items. Sending items to some

countries is hit and miss. Economy/Surface Mail is cheaper than Airmail, though takes longer to arrive.

3. Get a job or continue with your studies, but try to have a few days rest on your return before resuming a routine. You may still be jetlagged or may even be unwell for a few days. It can take several weeks to readjust to normal life after travelling for many months.

4. If you think you may have caught something, see a doctor/physician and tell them where you have come back from. Malaria and other diseases or infections can appear months after your return, even up to two years!

Other Helpful Things

You may wish to add up the total cost of your trip. This is easier if you wrote a journal and kept your weekly and monthly accounts in the back, or if you joined an organization as you only have a few items to add. You may have received a wage for your humanitarian work! However, working out the cost of your trip and dividing it by the number of days you were there is an interesting sum and helps you budget for future travel. If you want to, you can evaluate and muse over your trip and make a note of different factors:

- Was my backpack/rucksack any good? Was it too big or too small? Were the side pockets the correct size, was it comfortable and what did I like or dislike about it?
- What I learnt.
- How could I have been more financially efficient?
- What things would I have done differently?
- Things to remember for the next time, what items would have been great to take and what to leave at home etc.
- The total cost of the trip.
- Where would I like to go in the future?

Thanks for taking the time to read this paperback (also available as an eBook). I hope you have learnt many things to make your travels economical, safe, exciting and memorable. If you have a spare minute, please give a shout out on social media and write a short review on your favourite review site. Thank you and enjoy your travels. ☺

For other books by Mathew Backholer, please visit:
www.ByFaithBooks.co.uk

Appendix A – Terrorist Attacks

- A shopping mall in Kenya was attacked by a gang of jihadists in September 2013. In April 2014, 269 schoolgirls were kidnapped in Nigeria. A jihadist gunman held customers hostage in a cafe in Sydney, Australia in December 2014. In 2014, they beheaded aid workers in Syria, whilst in Pakistan, the Taliban often kill health workers who immunise/vaccinate children against polio.

- In January 2015, jihadists shot satirists in Paris, France, at the Charlie Hebdo offices, as well as murdering shoppers in a Jewish supermarket. In April 2015, 28 Ethiopian Christians were martyred in Libya in two groups, one group of twelve men were beheaded and the other group of sixteen men were shot. In June 2015, 38 tourists were murdered on the beach and in a hotel in Sousse, Tunisia; whilst in the same month, a worker in France was beheaded and the jihadist tried to cause an explosion with a gas canister, whilst in Kuwait, a suicide bomber killed 27 and injured hundreds in a mosque. In April and December 2015, jihadists killed many citizens of Chad in a market. In October 2015, Two suicide bombers detonated themselves at a Peace Rally in Turkey. In November 2015, a team of jihadists attacked multiple places in Paris and killed 130 people whilst injuring nearly 300 others. In Mali, they attacked a hotel, killing dozens of people in November 2015.

- On 12 June 2016, 49 people were killed at a gay nightclub in Orlando, USA, and more than 50 were injured. The perpetrator claimed allegiance to ISIS (IS/ISIL), yet had frequented the gay club over many years as a patron! Even his wife stated he had "gay tendencies."

- On 28 June 2016, two explosions and gunfire at Istanbul's Atatürk Airport (Esenboğa International) led to the murder of at least 41 people and injured around 230. In just over one year, nearly 300 people have died in 17 bomb attacks and suicide bombings across Turkey, and more than one thousand have been injured. These have been carried out by a number of different groups.

- At the end of June 2016, the Movid Bar restaurant outside of Kuala Lumpur, Malaysia, received a terrorist attack which injured eight people. It was the first attack by so-called Islamic State in Malaysia.

- The 14 July 2016, saw the Bastille Day massacre in Nice, France. A 31-year old jihadist drove a lorry along a beach promenade for 2km (1.2 miles), killing at least 84 people, including many children. This was France's third Islamic terrorist attack in 18 months. President Holland said, "All of France is under threat from Islamic terrorists."

- On Friday, 15 July 2016, all 300,000 mosques across Bangladesh, had been asked to give a sermon against terrorism and extremism, written by the state-run Islamic Foundation. This was because of two deadly attacks in Bangladesh in recent weeks, including the Dhaka cafe siege that left 20 people dead, mostly foreigners.

- On 18 July 2016, a 17-year old Afghan refugee living with a family in Germany, went on the rampage in a train with an axe and a knife, injuring more than eighteen people.
- In July 2016, a terrorist group in Brazil swore allegiance to IS (ISIS/ISIL). This was the first group in South America to give its Islamic allegiance to this terrorist group, just weeks before the start of the 2016 Olympic Games in Rio, Brazil.
- In Thailand, beginning 12 August 2016, five provinces were hit by eleven bombs during terrorist attacks that lasted one day. The terrorist attacks were aimed at tourist destinations, killing four nationals and injuring 36 people, 10 of whom were tourists.

Appendix B – Writing Tips

- Think, why should an editor buy my article and why should someone read it. If you are writing about a famous destination, e.g. London or New York, what will make your piece different than the hundreds of already published articles about these popular travel locations. What is your special angle or slant? What can you write about the Pyramids of Giza or the Angkor Wat temples that I have not read before? What makes it unique? Narrow your story and enlarge your prospects.
- Tailor your work to suit your market. Submit the right type of article to the correct publication. A food magazine will have no interest in a great surfing location. A religious periodical will not want to publish a hedonistic travel article or about a trip to a nudist camp. However, a single destination could hold different articles for different publications. This is how most travel writers make ends meet.
- There is a difference between writing an article for a newspaper, a travel magazine and a website. They have different readerships and space in each publication. Writing for a travel guide is different yet again, with more facts and figures needed for some publications, whilst others have an overview of major cities and recommended places to visit.
- Be yourself and don't try to imitate other good travel writers. There are many tribute acts (e.g. Elvis, Cher) and bands (e.g. Beatles, Abba), but there is only one real thing, the original. This has to be you and your own particular style.
- Will the article be narrative or thematic? How many words should you write? Have an idea of the general length. Each word should count and the shorter the article the more concise you must be.
- You are not writing an advertising brochure. Accurately and honestly describe what you are writing about. Use your

observational skills and try to look at things from different perspectives. Get the facts and ask locals. Go off-the-beaten-track and discover the gems down a side street, over the next hill, at the bottom of a gorge, or ancient rock art inside a cave.

- Most travel articles are not journal based, i.e. not what you did every day, and may not necessarily be chronological. Some travel stories are personal and should stay that way, they are the exclusive property of the traveller and only to be shared with good friends and/or family.

- Have a theme and note any salient points. What is the most important event or theme? What are you trying to convey to the reader? Does the reader need to know this? Is the humorous bit funny to other people or only those in-the-know?

- Avoid clichés, e.g. snow-capped mountains or cacophony of sound. Stay clear of lazy language, e.g. the room was "nice," or the grass was green! Use similes and metaphors.

- Some travel articles and most guides to travel destinations, need additional details. Places to stay, good restaurants or cafes. Contact details of the owner, proprietor or tour company. The cost, times of travel by coach, distances etc. Double check your facts.

- Read and re-read your article. Is it too long or too short. Have I put too much of myself into the story or am I too distant? What words can be edited out? Do new words need to be added? Have I embellished the article (hope not) or is it true and accurate?

- Work with your editor, allow him or her to correct your article and follow his or her advice. If you have found a good editor, look after him/her and he/she will hopefully look after you.

- Accuracy is vital, integrity is essential and don't miss your deadlines! You need a notebook, pen, laptop or Tablet, a digital voice recorder to capture the sounds and for interviewing.

- Most travel writers scrape by and do not make a great living, but if you like to travel, the two can work well and be a means to an end.

Appendix C – Self-Publishing Tips

- You need to have a level of expertise to make self-publishing work for you. If you have to employ someone to design your cover, proofread your manuscript, format the book, reformat and resize your images etc., then the costs add up.

- If you go to a fulfilment self publishing company (an in-between company) for paperbacks, then you will pay them to do what you may be able to do yourself. They make money from your inability and the cost can run into thousands.

- A major point with publishing is, will my book be distributed? You can pay to get a book published and in to print, but will it sell worldwide or be an unknown book amongst the 17 million ISBNs issued in the UK? The USA and Australia etc. have their own ISBN issuing company. A book does not need an ISBN to sell, but without one, it will hinder sales and distribution. An ISBN is not needed for a kindle eBook and the sales on Amazon will not be hindered.

- If a self publishing company tries to sell you 100 or 1,000 books, ask yourself, how much will it cost me, can I sell that amount, where and to whom, and do I have the free space to store them for years or decades?
- Read the guidelines of each book provider (e.g. Kindle or CreateSpace). What are their specifications? Sign up with them and have an account. For a paperback 8.5x5.5 or 9x6 inches (portrait size) is a standard fiction and non-fiction size.
- Check your grammar, spelling and punctuation.
- Format your book correctly. With a paperback, mirror your margins and leave plenty of margin space and header and footer room (top and bottom of the book). Your first chapter must begin on the right-hand side of a page (an odd number, 3, 5, 7 etc.). The content's page on a physical book must be correct. To have the wrong page number or the incorrect chapter title is taboo in the publishing industry.
- If you are using images in an ebook, the file can become too big. Crop each image to the correct dimensions and recommended data size. Are you the copyright owner of every image or do you have permission to use the images?

Appendix D – Travel Photography

- As a "professional" photographer you will need a good DSLR camera and a tripod. You may be able to get away with a high quality digital camera, though not having interchangeable lenses can be problematic.
- Make sure you have enough battery power and memory cards to keep you going.
- Some publications will expect you to have a model-release form signed by the person in the image. If it relates to a building, garden or country house, you may need a property-release form signed by the owner or manager etc.
- Some museums and places of historical interest have signs which state no photography for commercial purposes. You have to get permission to be able to use the image. A local beauty spot on the Dorset Coast, the Lulworth Estate, UK, has similar signs, because it is a private estate, which includes a section of the 'Jurassic Coast,' Lulworth Cove and Durdle Door. It has been used in films, TV programmes, music videos, posters, postcards, fridge magnets etc.

Sources and Notes

Preface
1. I have had the privilege of visiting France nearly ten times, Tunisia five times, Netherlands four times, Germany and India three times, and Nepal, South Africa and America twice. I travelled to India three times on a multi-entry visa over the space of three months, flying in from the UK, crossing back into India from Nepal and flying back to India from Vietnam.
2. Due to Brexit, Britain voting to come out of the European Union in June 2016, there has been a dramatic drop in Pound Sterling against the American Dollar and the Euro. The pound against the dollar dropped 10% to a 31-year low within a few days to below $1.3 to £1 though rebounded shortly afterwards. The rate of $1.6 to £1 is an average figure based on the exchange rate over many years, and not just a dramatic swing due to market uncertainties.

Chapter 1
1. A short-term mission (STM) is where Christians go and help other people in need and share the Good News of Jesus Christ, at home or abroad. That Jesus Christ died for their sins and rose again, so that they may have eternal life for all who repent, forsake their sins (turn from their bad ways) and put their trust and faith in Jesus Christ as they live for Him. Read the New Testament (second section of the Bible) to find out more. Many STM groups team up with churches or Christian ministries abroad and work in partnership with them. See *How to Plan, Prepare and Successfully Complete Your Short-Term Mission* and *Short-Term Missions, A Christian Guide to STMs*, both by Mathew Backholer.
2. www.gov.uk/guidance/sanctions-embargoes-and-restrictions.

Chapter 3
1. Non-Muslims should avoid travelling to the Middle East at difficult times where Westerners can be a target, however, even Western Muslims can be a target. Western travellers should avoid Islamic countries during Ramadan, where there are forty days of not eating or drinking during daylight hours. Being hungry and dehydrated can make people more tense, aggravated and angry at seeming minor offences, whilst eating or drinking in public during Ramadan makes you stand out. Ramadan works on a lunar cycle and therefore is not a fixed date such as Christmas Day. In June 2016, in moderate Turkey, some locals who were not observing Ramadan, were inside a fashionable record shop, listening to Western music and drinking alcohol. They were threatened by a thug, and fled outside where a baying mob of twenty or so men were waiting for them. Some guidebooks also recommend that you stay away from mosques after Friday prayers. Tourist areas may be safer, but can no longer be called 'safe' as they were in times past. On 26 June 2015, 38 tourists, 30 of whom were British were murdered at a beach hotel at a popular family resort, seven miles from Sousse, Tunisia. On 18 March 2015, the Bardo National Museum in Tunis, Tunisia, was attacked by three jihadists, leading to the deaths of 22 people, including 20 tourists.

Chapter 6
1. http://gapadvice.org/gap-year/facts-figures/. Accessed 12 July 2016.

2. www.dailymail.co.uk/news/article-1191603/One-gap-year-travellers-experiencemedical-emergency-crime.html. Accessed 10 June 2009.

Chapter 7
1. According to the National Health Service (NHS), across Europe (excluding Russia), there are approximately 3,000 hospital admissions caused by Tick Borne Encephalitis (TBE) in Europe every year. Around one in every 100 cases of TBE is fatal. Accessed July 2016.
www.nhs.uk/Conditions/Tick-borne-encephalitis/Pages/Introduction.aspx.

Chapter 9
1. At the end of August 2016, India's Tourist Minister said that women visitors should not wear skirts or dresses, or walk alone at night amongst small towns or cities "for their own safety." The British government's travel advice is: 'Women should use caution when travelling in India. Reported cases of sexual assault against women and young girls are increasing; recent sexual attacks against female visitors in tourist areas and cities show that foreign women are also at risk. British women have been the victims of sexual assault in Goa, Delhi, Bangalore and Rajasthan and women travellers often receive unwanted attention in the form of verbal and physical harassment by individuals or groups of men. Serious sexual attacks involving Polish, German and Danish women travellers were reported in 2014. In January 2015, a Japanese woman was kidnapped and sexually assaulted close to Bodh Gaya and a Russian woman was seriously assaulted by an auto-rickshaw driver in the Vasant Kunj area of New Delhi. In July 2016 an Israeli national was sexually assaulted by a number of men while travelling in Manali. Women travellers should exercise caution when travelling in India even if travelling in a group. If you are a woman travelling in India you should respect local dress codes and customs and avoid isolated areas, including beaches, when alone at any time of day.'
www.gov.uk/foreign-travel-advice/india/safety-and-security. Accessed 29 August 2016.
2. 13 June 2016.
3. News outlets: 7 July 2016. By the end of July 2016, the law had passed.
4. After a tourist took a photo of a woman in a burkhini in a little bay at Sisco, on the island of Corsica, France, in August 2016, Muslim families objected and local youth came to the aid of the tourist. Within a short while a large brawl broke out as around forty French men and more local North Africans each came to defend their own. Five people were hospitalised as harpoons and hatchets had been used as weapons.

Chapter 12
1. After Brexit, Britian voted to leave the EU on 24 June 2016, uncertainty in the financial markets caused the pound to drop against the dollar to below $1.29 to £1 though rebounded within a few days. In September the rate dropped to $1.2.

Chapter 17
1. A number of comparison websites can be found on the second page of www.MissionsNow.co.uk under the 'Mission Related Links – World Travel' page. Links also to world facts and statistics, travel and health advice, maps, airline websites, world weather and money exchange etc.

Chapter 18
1. www.acro.police.uk/police_certificates.aspx. Accessed June 2016.

Chapter 20

1. Having travelled through France on a eight hour train journey we missed the ferry back to England by minutes. The security guard pointed us to a room, where we could sleep on the floor. There was also toilets and showers in an adjacent room for truck drivers. We missed our midnight train to Berlin, Germany, as the plane touched down too late, and so we slept inside the train station at Frankfurt – all went well until the cleaners came at 4am, when we were evicted and moved into a fast food outlet which opened at 5am. At London, Gatwick Airport, the flight left at 5am, so it was easier to travel to the airport the evening before, find a row of unoccupied seats in a darker corner, away from the tannoy and have a bit of shuteye.

Chapter 24

1. See *Short-Term Missions, A Christian Guide to STMs* by Mathew Backholer, pages 126-127.
2. Paul Backholer has written a number of books as well as TV documentaries which he has written and produced. For the ultimate travel book in the realms beyond this world, when the veil between earth and heaven becomes translucent, see the glories beyond and enter into: *Heaven, A Journey to Paradise and the Heavenly City* by Paul Backholer.

Chapter 26

1. A number of news sources, up to 15 August 2016.

Chapter 30

1. See *How to Plan, Prepare and Successfully Complete Your Short-Term Mission* by Mathew Backholer, page 186.

Chapter 33

1. www.moneysavingexpert.com/split-cheap-train-tickets/.

Chapter 34

1. http://www.fuel-economy.co.uk/calc.html. Accessed 11 July 2016.

Chapter 35

1. A number of comparison websites can be found on the second page of www.MissionsNow.co.uk, under the 'Mission Related Links' page.

Chapter 37

1. www.acro.police.uk/ICPC/. Accessed June 2016.

Chapter 38

1. For short-term missions (STMs), see footnote 1. under chapter 1.

www.ByFaith.co.uk
www.ByFaithBooks.co.uk
www.ByFaithDVDs.co.uk

ByFaith Media Books

Short-Term Missions (Christian Travel with a Purpose)
How to Plan, Prepare and Successfully Complete Your Short-Term Mission by Mathew Backholer. *For Churches, Independent STM Teams and Mission Organizations.* The books includes: mission statistics, quotes & more than 140 real-life STM testimonies.

Short-Term Missions, A Christian Guide to STMs by Mathew Backholer. *For Leaders, Pastors, Churches, Students, STM Teams and Mission Organizations – Survive and Thrive!* A full and concise guide to Short-Term Missions (STMs). What you need to know about planning a STM, or joining a STM team, and considering the options as part of the Great Commission, from the Good News to good works. This book is full of anecdotes and advice with informative timelines, and a biblical framework for STMs to help you engage in cross-cultural missions; with viable solutions to common mission issues to make your STM more effective to the glory of God.

Historical and Adventure
The Ark of the Covenant – Investigating the Ten Leading Claims by Paul Backholer. The mystery of the Bible's lost Ark of the Covenant has led to many myths, theories and claims. Join two explorers as they investigate the ten major theories concerning the location of antiquities greatest relic. Combining an on-site travel journal with 80+ exclusive colour photographs, take an adventure through Egypt, Ethiopia and beyond.

The Exodus Evidence In Pictures – The Bible's Exodus: The Hunt for Ancient Israel in Egypt, the Red Sea, the Exodus Route and Mount Sinai by Paul Backholer. Two brothers and explorers, Paul and Mathew Backholer search for archaeological data to validate the biblical account of Joseph, Moses and the Hebrew Exodus from ancient Egypt. With more than 100 full colour photos and graphics!

Britain, A Christian Country, A Nation Defined by Christianity and the Bible & the Social Changes that Challenge this Biblical Heritage by Paul Backholer. For more than 1,000 years Britain was defined by Christianity, with monarch's dedicating the country to God and national days of prayer. Discover this continuing legacy, how faith defined its nationhood and the challenges from the 1960s till today.

How Christianity Made the Modern World by Paul Backholer. Christianity is the greatest reforming force that the world has ever known, yet its legacy is seldom comprehended. But now, using personal observations from his research in over thirty-five nations, the author brings this legacy alive by revealing how Christianity helped create the path that led to Western liberty and laid the foundations of the modern world.

Celtic Christianity & the First Christian Kings in Britain: From St. Patrick and St. Columba, to King Ethelbert and King Alfred by Paul Backholer. Celtic Christians ignited a Celtic Golden Age of faith and light which spread into Europe. Discover this striking history and what we can learn from the heroes of Celtic Christianity.

Supernatural and Spiritual
Heaven, A Journey to Paradise and the Heavenly City by Paul Backholer. Join one person's exploration of paradise, guided by an angel and a glorified man, to witness the thrilling promise of eternity, and to provide answers to many questions about heaven. Anchored in the Word of God, the Bible, discover what heaven will be like!

Prophecy Now, Prophetic Words and Divine Revelations for You, the Church and the Nations by Michael Backholer. Visions, prophecies and words from the Holy Spirit to God's people.

Biography and Autobiography
Samuel, Son and Successor of Rees Howells: Director of the Bible College of Wales – A Biography by Richard Maton. The author invites us on a lifelong journey with Samuel, to unveil his ministry at the College, life of prayer and the support he received from numerous staff, students and visitors, as the history of BCW unfolds alongside the Vision to reach Every Creature with the Gospel. With 113 black and white photos in the paperback and hardback editions!

The Holy Spirit in a Man: Spiritual Warfare, Intercession, Faith, Healings and Miracles by R. B. Watchman. One man's compelling journey of faith and intercession – a gripping true-life story. Raised in a dysfunctional family and called for a Divine purpose, he ran from God, yet the world could not break nor tame him. Years later, he met with Christ in power through a dynamic encounter with the Holy Spirit and was changed forever. Sent out by God, he left employment to claim the ground for Christ, witnessing signs and wonders, spiritual warfare and deliverance. In a remarkable modern day story of miracles and faith, see how God can take a depressed, defeated individual, teach him faith and use him for His glory.

Revivals and Spiritual Awakenings

Revival Fires and Awakenings – Thirty-Six Visitations of the Holy Spirit: A Call to Holiness, Prayer and Intercession for the Nations by Mathew Backholer. With 36 fascinating accounts of revivals in nineteen countries from six continents, plus biblical teaching on revival, prayer and more. Also available as a hardback.

Understanding Revival and Addressing the Issues it Provokes by Mathew Backholer. Many who have prayed for revival have rejected it when it came because they misunderstood the workings of the Holy Spirit and only wanted God to bless the Church on their terms and not His. Let us intelligently cooperate with the Holy Spirit during times of revivals, heaven-sent spiritual awakenings and not reject His workings or be misled by the enemy.

Global Revival – Worldwide Outpourings, Forty-Three Visitations of the Holy Spirit: The Great Commission by Mathew Backholer. This book documents forty-three revivals from more than thirty countries on six continents. The author explores the Divine-human partnership of revival, explains how revivals are birthed, and reveals the fascinating links between pioneering missionaries and the revivals that they saw as they worked towards the Great Commission.

Revival Answers, True and False Revivals by Mathew Backholer. What is genuine revival and how can we tell the genuine from the false, the true from the spurious? Drawing from Scripture with examples across Church history, this book will sharpen your senses and take you on a journey of discovery. See the Holy Spirit at work!

Revival Fire – 150 Years of Revivals: Spiritual Awakenings and Moves of the Holy Spirit by Mathew Backholer. This book documents in detail, twelve revivals from ten countries on five continents. Through the use of detailed research, eye-witness accounts and interviews, *Revival Fire* present some of the most potent revivals that the world has seen in the past one hundred and fifty years. Learn from the past, be challenged for the present and be inspired for the future!

Christian Discipleship

Discipleship For Everyday Living – Christian Growth: Following Jesus Christ And Making Disciples of All Nations by Mathew Backholer. Engaging biblical teaching to aid believers in maturity, to help make strong disciples with solid biblical foundations who reflect the image of Jesus Christ. The book's fifty chapters are split into six sections: Firm Foundations, The Call of God, World Missions,

Evangelism and Teaching, Ministering in the Power of the Holy Spirit, and Ministry – Being Set Free and Delivered.

Extreme Faith, On Fire Christianity by Mathew Backholer. *Hearing from God and Moving in His Grace, Strength & Power – Living in Victory.* Discover the powerful biblical foundations for on-fire faith in Christ! God has given us powerful weapons to defeat the enemy, to take back the spiritual land in our lives and to walk in His glory through the power of the Holy Spirit. This book explores biblical truths and routines to shake your world!

Christian Teaching and Inspirational
Tares and Weeds in Your Church: Trouble & Deception in God's House, the End Time Overcomers by R. B. Watchman. Is there a battle taking place in your house, church or ministry, leading to division? Tares and weeds are counterfeit Christians used to sabotage Kingdom work; learn how to recognise them and neutralise them in the power of the Holy Spirit.

Holy Spirit Power: Knowing the Voice, Guidance and Person of the Holy Spirit by Paul Backholer. Power for Christian living; drawing from the powerful influences of many Christian leaders, including: Rees Howells, Evan Roberts, D. L. Moody, Duncan Campbell and other channels of God's Divine fire.

Jesus Today, Daily Devotional: 100 Days with Jesus Christ by Paul Backholer. Two minutes a day to encourage and inspire; 100 days of daily Christian Bible inspiration to draw you closer to God. Have you ever wished you could have sat at Jesus' feet and heard Him speak? Now you can. *Jesus Today* is a concise daily devotional defined by the teaching of Jesus and how His life can change yours. See the world from God's perspective and live abundantly in Christ!

Samuel Rees Howells: A Life of Intercession by Richard Maton is an in-depth look at the intercessions of Samuel Rees Howells alongside the faith principles that he learnt from his father, Rees Howells, and under the leading and guidance of the Holy Spirit. With 39 black and white photos in the paperback and hardback editions.

www.ByFaithBooks.co.uk

ByFaith Media DVDs

Christian Travel (Backpacking Style Short-Term Mission)
ByFaith – World Mission on 1 DVD is a Christian reality TV show that reveals the real experience of a backpacking style short-term mission in Asia, Europe and North Africa. Two brothers, Paul and Mathew Backholer shoot through fourteen nations, in an 85-minute real-life documentary. Filmed over three years, *ByFaith – World Mission* is the very best of ByFaith TV season one.

Historical and Adventure
Israel in Egypt – The Exodus Mystery on 1 DVD. A four year quest searching for Joseph, Moses and the Hebrew slaves in Egypt. Join Paul and Mathew as they hunt through ancient relics and explore the mystery of the biblical exodus, hunt for the Red Sea and climb Mt. Sinai. Discover the first reference to Israel outside of the Bible, uncover depictions of people with multicoloured coats, encounter the Egyptian records of slaves making bricks and find lost cities. 110 minutes. The very best of *ByFaith – In Search of the Exodus*.

ByFaith – Quest for the Ark of the Covenant on 1 DVD. Join two adventurers on their quest for the Ark, beginning at Mount Sinai where it was made, to Pharaoh Tutankhamun's tomb, where Egyptian treasures evoke the majesty of the Ark. The quest proceeds onto the trail of Pharaoh Shishak, who raided Jerusalem. The mission continues up the River Nile to find a lost temple, with clues to a mysterious civilization. Crossing through the Sahara Desert, the investigators enter the underground rock churches of Ethiopia, find a forgotten civilization and examine the enigma of the final resting place of the Ark itself. 100+ minutes.

Revivals and Spiritual Awakenings
Great Christian Revivals on 1 DVD is an inspirational and uplifting account of some of the greatest revivals in Church history. Filmed on location across Britain and drawing upon archive information, the stories of the Welsh Revival (1904-1905), the Hebridean Revival (1949-1952) and the Evangelical Revival (1739-1791) are brought to life in this moving 72-minute documentary. Using computer animation, historic photos and depictions, the events of the past are weaved into the present, to bring these heaven-sent revivals to life.

Notes

CPSIA information can be obtained
at www.ICGtesting.com
Printed in the USA
LVOW08s1959270217
525557LV00011B/1684/P